PRAXIS

ENGLISH LANGUAGE, LITERATURE, AND COMPOSITION 0041

By: Sharon Wynne, M.S.

XAMonline, INC.
Boston

To obtain permission(s) to use the material from this work for any purpose including workshops or seminars, please submit a written request to:

XAMonline, Inc.
25 First Street, Suite 106
Cambridge, MA 02141
Toll Free 1-800-509-4128
Email: info@xamonline.com
Web: www.xamonline.com
Fax: 1-617-583-5552

Library of Congress Cataloging-in-Publication Data

Wynne, Sharon A.
    PRAXIS English Language, Literature, and Composition 0041 / Sharon A. Wynne. 3rd ed
    ISBN 978-1-60787-045-6
    1. English Language, Literature, and Composition 0041
    2. Study Guides
    3. PRAXIS
    4. Teachers' Certification & Licensure
    5. Careers

Disclaimer:

The opinions expressed in this publication are the sole works of XAMonline and were created independently from the National Education Association, Educational Testing Service, or any State Department of Education, National Evaluation Systems or other testing affiliates.

Between the time of publication and printing, state specific standards as well as testing formats and Web site information may change and therefore would not be included in part or in whole within this product. Sample test questions are developed by XAMonline and reflect content similar to that on real tests; however, they are not former test questions. XAMonline assembles content that aligns with state standards but makes no claims nor guarantees teacher candidates a passing score. Numerical scores are determined by testing companies such as NES or ETS and then are compared with individual state standards. A passing score varies from state to state.

Printed in the United States of America   œ-1

PRAXIS English Language, Literature, and Composition 0041
ISBN: 978-1-60787-045-6

Table of Contents

DOMAIN III
COMPOSITION 141

SAMPLE TEST

ANSWER KEY

1. C	15. D	29. B	43. B	57. C	71. D	85. A	99. A	113. D
2. C	16. D	30. D	44. D	58. B	72. D	86. D	100. A	114. A
3. C	17. D	31. D	45. C	59. A	73. B	87. D	101. D	115. C
4. A	18. A	32. C	46. D	60. A	74. A	88. B	102. B	116. C
5. D	19. A	33. C	47. A	61. D	75. D	89. C	103. D	117. C
6. A	20. B	34. D	48. B	62. C	76. C	90. D	104. A	118. C
7. B	21. B	35. D	49. A	63. A	77. A	91. B	105. A	119. A
8. D	22. A	36. B	50. C	64. C	78. B	92. A	106. D	120. A
9. D	23. B	37. A	51. A	65. A	79. B	93. B	107. C	121. A
10. C	24. A	38. A	52. D	66. C	80. D	94. C	108. B	122. C
11. B	25. A	39. D	53. A	67. A	81. C	95. A	109. A	123. C
12. A	26. D	40. A	54. A	68. C	82. C	96. C	110. A	124. D
13. C	27. C	41. C	55. D	69. B	83. A	97. B	111. D	125. C
14. D	28. D	42. D	56. D	70. A	84. C	98. A	112. D	

RIGOR TABLE

Rigor level	Questions
Easy 25%	1, 9, 11, 12, 13, 14, 37, 45, 46, 71, 72, 78, 82, 85, 86, 87, 88, 89, 104, 105, 106, 107, 108, 109, 110
Average Rigor 50%	2, 3, 4, 10, 15, 16, 17, 18, 19, 20, 21, 22, 23, 24, 34, 35, 36, 38, 39, 40, 41, 51, 52, 55, 56, 57, 58, 59, 60, 61, 62, 67, 68, 69, 73, 74, 81, 83, 90, 91, 92, 93, 94, 95, 111, 112, 113, 114, 115, 116
Rigorous 50%	5, 6, 7, 8, 25, 26, 27, 28, 29, 30, 31, 32, 33, 42, 43, 44, 47, 48, 49, 50, 53, 54, 63, 64, 65, 66, 70, 75, 76, 77, 79, 80, 84, 96, 97, 98, 99, 100, 101, 102, 103, 117, 118, 119, 120, 121, 122, 123, 124, 125

PRAXIS

ENGLISH LANGUAGE, LITERATURE, AND COMPOSITION 0041

SECTION 1
ABOUT XAMONLINE

XAMonline—A Specialty Teacher Certification Company

Created in 1996, XAMonline was the first company to publish study guides for state-specific teacher certification examinations. Founder Sharon Wynne found it frustrating that materials were not available for teacher certification preparation and decided to create the first single, state-specific guide. XAMonline has grown into a company of over 1,800 contributors and writers and offers over 300 titles for the entire PRAXIS series and every state examination. No matter what state you plan on teaching in, XAMonline has a unique teacher certification study guide just for you.

XAMonline—Value and Innovation

We are committed to providing value and innovation. Our print-on-demand technology allows us to be the first in the market to reflect changes in test standards and user feedback as they occur. Our guides are written by experienced teachers who are experts in their fields. And our content reflects the highest standards of quality. Comprehensive practice tests with varied levels of rigor means that your study experience will closely match the actual in-test experience.

To date, XAMonline has helped nearly 600,000 teachers pass their certification or licensing exams. Our commitment to preparation exceeds simply providing the proper material for study—it extends to helping teachers **gain mastery** of the subject matter, giving them the **tools** to become the most effective classroom leaders possible, and ushering today's students toward a **successful future**.

SECTION 2
ABOUT THIS STUDY GUIDE

Purpose of This Guide

Is there a little voice inside of you saying, "Am I ready?" Our goal is to replace that little voice and remove all doubt with a new voice that says, "I AM READY. **Bring it on!**" by offering the highest quality of teacher certification study guides.

Organization of Content

You will see that while every test may start with overlapping general topics, each is very unique in the skills they wish to test. Only XAMonline presents custom content that analyzes deeper than a title, a subarea, or an objective. Only XAMonline presents content and sample test assessments along with **focus statements**, the deepest-level rationale and interpretation of the skills that are unique to the exam.

Title and field number of test

→Each exam has its own name and number. XAMonline's guides are written to give you the content you need to know for the specific exam you are taking. You can be confident when you buy our guide that it contains the information you need to study for the specific test you are taking.

Subareas

→These are the major content categories found on the exam. XAMonline's guides are written to cover all of the subareas found in the test frameworks developed for the exam.

Objectives

→These are standards that are unique to the exam and represent the main subcategories of the subareas/content categories. XAMonline's guides are written to address every specific objective required to pass the exam.

Focus statements

→These are examples and interpretations of the objectives. You find them in parenthesis directly following the objective. They provide detailed examples of the range, type, and level of content that appear on the test questions. **Only XAMonline's guides drill down to this level.**

How Do We Compare with Our Competitors?

XAMonline—drills down to the focus statement level.
CliffsNotes and REA—organized at the objective level
Kaplan—provides only links to content
MoMedia—content not specific to the state test

Each subarea is divided into manageable sections that cover the specific skill areas. Explanations are easy to understand and thorough. You'll find that every test answer contains a rejoinder so if you need a refresher or further review after taking the test, you'll know exactly to which section you must return.

How to Use This Book

Our informal polls show that most people begin studying up to eight weeks prior to the test date, so start early. Then ask yourself some questions: How much do you really know? Are you coming to the test straight from your teacher-education program or are you having to review subjects you haven't considered in ten years? Either way, take a **diagnostic or assessment test** first. Also, spend time on sample tests so that you become accustomed to the way the actual test will appear.

This guide comes with an online diagnostic test of 30 questions found online at *www.XAMonline.com*. It is a little boot camp to get you up for the task and reveal things about your compendium of knowledge in general. Although this guide is structured to follow the order of the test, you are not required to study in that order. By finding a time-management and study plan that fits your life you will be more effective. The results of your diagnostic or self-assessment test can be a guide for how to manage your time and point you toward an area that needs more attention.

After taking the diagnostic exam, fill out the **Personalized Study Plan** page at the beginning of each chapter. Review the competencies and skills covered in that chapter and check the boxes that apply to your study needs. If there are sections you already know you can skip, check the "skip it" box. Taking this step will give you a study plan for each chapter.

Week	Activity
8 weeks prior to test	Take a diagnostic test found at www.XAMonline.com
7 weeks prior to test	Build your Personalized Study Plan for each chapter. Check the "skip it" box for sections you feel you are already strong in. ✗ SKIP IT ☐
6-3 weeks prior to test	For each of these four weeks, choose a content area to study. You don't have to go in the order of the book. It may be that you start with the content that needs the most review. Alternately, you may want to ease yourself into plan by starting with the most familiar material.
2 weeks prior to test	Take the sample test, score it, and create a review plan for the final week before the test.
1 week prior to test	Following your plan (which will likely be aligned with the areas that need the most review) go back and study the sections that align with the questions you may have gotten wrong. Then go back and study the sections related to the questions you answered correctly. If need be, create flashcards and drill yourself on any area that makes you anxious.

SECTION 3
ABOUT THE PRAXIS EXAMS

What Is PRAXIS?

PRAXIS II tests measure the knowledge of specific content areas in K-12 education. The test is a way of insuring that educators are prepared to not only teach in a particular subject area, but also have the necessary teaching skills to be effective. The Educational Testing Service administers the test in most states and has worked with the states to develop the material so that it is appropriate for state standards.

PRAXIS Points

1. The PRAXIS Series comprises more than 140 different tests in over seventy different subject areas.

2. Over 90% of the PRAXIS tests measure subject area knowledge.

3. The purpose of the test is to measure whether the teacher candidate possesses a sufficient level of knowledge and skills to perform job duties effectively and responsibly.

4. Your state sets the acceptable passing score.

5. Any candidate, whether from a traditional teaching-preparation path or an alternative route, can seek to enter the teaching profession by taking a PRAXIS test.

6. PRAXIS tests are updated regularly to ensure current content.

Often **your own state's requirements** determine whether or not you should take any particular test. The most reliable source of information regarding this is either your state's Department of Education or the Educational Testing Service. Either resource should also have a complete list of testing centers and dates. Test dates vary by subject area and not all test dates necessarily include your particular test, so be sure to check carefully.

If you are in a teacher-education program, check with the Education Department or the Certification Officer for specific information for testing and testing timelines. The Certification Office should have most of the information you need.

If you choose an alternative route to certification you can either rely on our Web site at *www.XAMonline.com* or on the resources provided by an alternative certification program. Many states now have specific agencies devoted to alternative certification and there are some national organizations as well:

National Center for Education Information
http://www.ncei.com/Alt-Teacher-Cert.htm

National Associate for Alternative Certification
http://www.alt-teachercert.org/index.asp

Interpreting Test Results

Contrary to what you may have heard, the results of a PRAXIS test are not based on time. More accurately, you will be scored on the raw number of points you earn in relation to the raw number of points available. Each question is worth one raw point. It is likely to your benefit to complete as many questions in the time allotted, but it will not necessarily work to your advantage if you hurry through the test.

Follow the guidelines provided by ETS for interpreting your score. The web site offers a sample test score sheet and clearly explains how the scores are scaled and what to expect if you have an essay portion on your test.

Scores are usually available by phone within a month of the test date and scores will be sent to your chosen institution(s) within six weeks. Additionally, ETS now makes online, downloadable reports available for 45 days from the reporting date.

It is **critical** that you be aware of your own state's passing score. Your raw score may qualify you to teach in some states, but not all. ETS administers the test and assigns a score, but the states make their own interpretations and, in some cases, consider combined scores if you are testing in more than one area.

What's on the Test?

PRAXIS tests vary from subject to subject and sometimes even within subject area. For PRAXIS English Language, Literature, and Composition (0041), the test lasts for 2 hours and consists of approximately 120 multiple-choice questions. The breakdown of the questions is as follows:

Category	Approximate Number of Questions	Approximate Percentage of the test
I: Literature and Understanding Text	66	55%
II: Language and Linguistics	18	15%
III: Composition and Rhetoric	36	30%

This chart can be used to build a study plan. Fifty-five percent may seem like a lot of time to spend on Literature and Understanding Text, but when you consider that amounts to about 1 out of 2 multiple choice questions, it might change your perspective.

Question Types

You're probably thinking, enough already, I want to study! Indulge us a little longer while we explain that there is actually more than one type of multiple-choice question. You can thank us later after you realize how well prepared you are for your exam.

1. Complete the Statement. The name says it all. In this question type you'll be asked to choose the correct completion of a given statement. For example:

> **The Dolch Basic Sight Words consist of a relatively short list of words that children should be able to:**
>
> A. Sound out
>
> B. Know the meaning of
>
> C. Recognize on sight
>
> D. Use in a sentence

The correct answer is A. In order to check your answer, test out the statement by adding the choices to the end of it.

2. Which of the Following. One way to test your answer choice for this type of question is to replace the phrase "which of the following" with your selection. Use this example:

> **Which of the following words is one of the twelve most frequently used in children's reading texts:**
>
> A. There
>
> B. This
>
> C. The
>
> D. An

Don't look! Test your answer. _____ is one of the twelve most frequently used in children's reading texts. Did you guess C? Then you guessed correctly.

3. Roman Numeral Choices. This question type is used when there is more than one possible correct answer. For example:

> **Which of the following two arguments accurately supports the use of cooperative learning as an effective method of instruction?**
> I.   Cooperative learning groups facilitate healthy competition between individuals in the group.
> II. Cooperative learning groups allow academic achievers to carry or cover for academic underachievers.
> III. Cooperative learning groups make each student in the group accountable for the success of the group.
> IV. Cooperative learning groups make it possible for students to reward other group members for achieving.
>
> A. I and II
> B. II and III
> C. I and III
> D. III and IV

Notice that the question states there are **two** possible answers. It's best to read all the possibilities first before looking at the answer choices. In this case, the correct answer is D.

4. Negative Questions. This type of question contains words such as "not," "least," and "except." Each correct answer will be the statement that does **not** fit the situation described in the question. Such as:

> **Multicultural education is not**
> A. An idea or concept
> B. A "tack-on" to the school curriculum
> C. An educational reform movement
> D. A process

Think to yourself that the statement could be anything but the correct answer. This question form is more open to interpretation than other types, so read carefully and don't forget that you're answering a negative statement.

5. **Questions that Include Graphs, Tables, or Reading Passages.** As always, read the question carefully. It likely asks for a very specific answer and not a broad interpretation of the visual. Here is a simple (though not statistically accurate) example of a graph question:

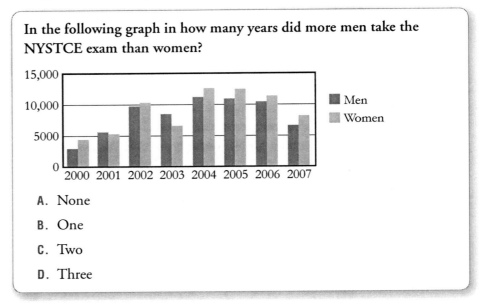

In the following graph in how many years did more men take the NYSTCE exam than women?

A. None

B. One

C. Two

D. Three

It may help you to simply circle the two years that answer the question. Make sure you've read the question thoroughly and once you've made your determination, double check your work. The correct answer is C.

SECTION 4
HELPFUL HINTS

Study Tips

1. **You are what you eat.** Certain foods aid the learning process by releasing natural memory enhancers called CCKs (cholecystokinin) composed of tryptophan, choline, and phenylalanine. All of these chemicals enhance the neurotransmitters associated with memory and certain foods release memory

enhancing chemicals. A light meal or snacks of one of the following foods fall into this category:

- Milk
- Rice
- Eggs
- Fish
- Nuts and seeds
- Oats
- Turkey

The better the connections, the more you comprehend!

2. **See the forest for the trees.** In other words, get the concept before you look at the details. One way to do this is to take notes as you read, paraphrasing or summarizing in your own words. Putting the concept in terms that are comfortable and familiar may increase retention.

3. **Question authority.** Ask why, why, why? Pull apart written material paragraph by paragraph and don't forget the captions under the illustrations. For example, if a heading reads *Stream Erosion* put it in the form of a question (Why do streams erode? What is stream erosion?) then find the answer within the material. If you train your mind to think in this manner you will learn more and prepare yourself for answering test questions.

4. **Play mind games.** Using your brain for reading or puzzles keeps it flexible. Even with a limited amount of time your brain can take in data (much like a computer) and store it for later use. In ten minutes you can: read two paragraphs (at least), quiz yourself with flash cards, or review notes. Even if you don't fully understand something on the first pass, your mind stores it for recall, which is why frequent reading or review increases chances of retention and comprehension.

5. **Place yourself in exile and set the mood.** Set aside a particular place and time to study that best suits your personal needs and biorhythms. If you're a night person, burn the midnight oil. If you're a morning person set yourself up with some coffee and get to it. Make your study time and place as free from distraction as possible and surround yourself with what you need, be it silence or music. Studies have shown that music can aid in concentration, absorption, and retrieval of information. Not all music, though. Classical music is said to work best

6. **Get pointed in the right direction.** Use arrows to point to important passages or pieces of information. It's easier to read than a page full of yellow highlights. Highlighting can be used sparingly, but add an arrow to the margin to call attention to it.

7. **Check your budget.** You should at least review all the content material before your test, but allocate the most amount of time to the areas that need the most refreshing. It sounds obvious, but it's easy to forget. You can use the study rubric above to balance your study budget.

The proctor will write the start time where it can be seen and then, later, provide the time remaining, typically fifteen minutes before the end of the test.

8. **The pen is mightier than the sword.** Learn to take great notes. A by-product of our modern culture is that we have grown accustomed to getting our information in short doses. We've subconsciously trained ourselves to assimilate information into neat little packages. Messy notes fragment the flow of information. Your notes can be much clearer with proper formatting. *The Cornell Method* is one such format. This method was popularized in *How to Study in College*, Ninth Edition, by Walter Pauk. You can benefit from the method without purchasing an additional book by simply looking up the method online. Below is a sample of how *The Cornell Method* can be adapted for use with this guide.

← 2½" → **Cue Column**	← 6" → **Note Taking Column**
	1. Record: During your reading, use the note-taking column to record important points.
	2. Questions: As soon as you finish a section, formulate questions based on the notes in the right-hand column. Writing questions helps to clarify meanings, reveal relationships, establish community, and strengthen memory. Also, the writing of questions sets the state for exam study later.
	3. Recite: Cover the note-taking column with a sheet of paper. Then, looking at the questions or cue-words in the question and cue column only, say aloud, in your own words, the answers to the questions, facts, or ideas indicated by the cue words.
	4. Reflect: Reflect on the material by asking yourself questions.
	5. Review: Spend at least ten minutes every week reviewing all your previous notes. Doing so helps you retain ideas and topics for the exam.
↑ 2" ↓	**Summary** After reading, use this space to summarize the notes from each page.

*Adapted from How to Study in College, Ninth Edition, by Walter Pauk, ©2008 Wadsworth

Testing Tips

1. **Get smart, play dumb.** Sometimes a question is just a question. No one is out to trick you, so don't assume that the test writer is looking for something other than what was asked. Stick to the question as written and don't overanalyze.

2. **Do a double take.** Read test questions and answer choices at least twice because it's easy to miss something, to transpose a word or some letters. If you have no idea what the correct answer is, skip it and come back later if there's time. If you're still clueless, it's okay to guess. Remember, you're scored on the number of questions you answer correctly and you're not penalized for wrong answers. The worst case scenario is that you miss a point from a good guess.

3. **Turn it on its ear.** The syntax of a question can often provide a clue, so make things interesting and turn the question into a statement to see if it changes the meaning or relates better (or worse) to the answer choices.

4. **Get out your magnifying glass.** Look for hidden clues in the questions because it's difficult to write a multiple-choice question without giving away part of the answer in the options presented. In most questions you can readily eliminate one or two potential answers, increasing your chances of answering correctly to 50/50, which will help out if you've skipped a question and gone back to it (see tip #2).

5. **Call it intuition.** Often your first instinct is correct. If you've been studying the content you've likely absorbed something and have subconsciously retained the knowledge. On questions you're not sure about trust your instincts because a first impression is usually correct.

6. **Graffiti.** Sometimes it's a good idea to mark your answers directly on the test booklet and go back to fill in the optical scan sheet later. You don't get extra points for perfectly blackened ovals. If you choose to manage your test this way, be sure not to mismark your answers when you transcribe to the scan sheet.

7. **Become a clock-watcher.** You have a set amount of time to answer the questions. Don't get bogged down laboring over a question you're not sure about when there are ten others you could answer more readily. If you choose to follow the advice of tip #6, be sure you leave time near the end to go back and fill in the scan sheet.

Do the Drill

No matter how prepared you feel it's sometimes a good idea to apply Murphy's Law. So the following tips might seem silly, mundane, or obvious, but we're including them anyway.

1. **Remember, you are what you eat, so bring a snack.** Choose from the list of energizing foods that appear earlier in the introduction.

2. **You're not too sexy for your test.** Wear comfortable clothes. You'll be distracted if your belt is too tight or if you're too cold or too hot.

3. **Lie to yourself.** Even if you think you're a prompt person, pretend you're not and leave plenty of time to get to the testing center. Map it out ahead of time and do a dry run if you have to. There's no need to add road rage to your list of anxieties.

4. **Bring sharp, number 2 pencils.** It may seem impossible to forget this need from your school days, but you might. And make sure the erasers are intact, too.

5. **No ticket, no test.** Bring your admission ticket as well as **two** forms of identification, including one with a picture and signature. You will not be admitted to the test without these things.

6. **You can't take it with you.** Leave any study aids, dictionaries, notebooks, computers, and the like at home. Certain tests **do** allow a scientific or four-function calculator, so check ahead of time to see if your test does.

7. **Prepare for the desert.** Any time spent on a bathroom break **cannot** be made up later, so use your judgment on the amount you eat or drink.

8. **Quiet, Please!** Keeping your own time is a good idea, but not with a timepiece that has a loud ticker. If you use a watch, take it off and place it nearby but not so that it distracts you. And **silence your cell phone**.

To the best of our ability, we have compiled the content you need to know in this book and in the accompanying online resources. The rest is up to you. You can use the study and testing tips or you can follow your own methods. Either way, you can be confident that there aren't any missing pieces of information and there shouldn't be any surprises in the content on the test.

If you have questions about test fees, registration, electronic testing, or other content verification issues please visit *www.ets.org*.

Good luck!

Sharon Wynne
Founder, XAMonline

D O M A I N   I
LITERATURE

PERSONALIZED STUDY PLAN

KNOWN MATERIAL/ SKIP IT

PAGE	COMPETENCY AND SKILL	
3	**1: Literature and Understanding Text**	☐
	1.1: Identifying major works and authors	☐
	1.2: Paraphrasing, comparing, and interpreting	☐
	1.3: Identifying figurative language and other literary elements	☐
	1.4: Understand how literary forms and genres may influence meaning	☐
	1.5: Situating authors and texts within historical, cultural, and critical contexts	☐
	1.6: Recognizing instructional approaches to teaching reading and textual interpretation	☐

COMPETENCY 1
LITERATURE AND UNDERSTANDING TEXT

SKILL Identifying major works and authors of American, British, World 1.1 (including non-Western), and young adult literature from various cultures, genres, and periods

American Literature

When compared to other countries, America has a relatively brief history and thus a comparatively smaller canon of literature. Nevertheless, its fiction and nonfiction have the depth and breadth to tell the story of its people. To study American literature is to study American history. Students will discover the importance of writing as a reflection of the historical, social, ethnic, political, and economic environment of the times.

American literature is defined by a number of clearly identifiable periods.

Native American works from various tribes

These works were originally part of a vast oral tradition that spanned most of continental America, dating as far back as before the fifteenth century.

Characteristics of Native American literature include:

- Reverence for and awe of nature
- The interconnectedness of the elements in the life cycle

Themes of Native American literature include:

- The hardiness of the native body and soul
- Remorse for the destruction of the native way of life
- The genocide of many tribes by the encroaching settlement and Manifest Destiny policies of the U.S. government

The Colonial period

Stylistically, early colonists' writings were neoclassical, emphasizing order, balance, clarity, and reason. Because the colonists had been schooled in England, their writing and speaking remained decidedly British, even as their thinking became entirely American.

Early American literature reveals the lives and experiences of the New England expatriates who left England to find religious freedom. William Bradford's excerpts from *The Mayflower Compact* relate vividly the hardships of crossing the Atlantic in a tiny vessel, the misery and suffering of the first winter, the approaches of the American Indians, the decimation of the colonists' ranks, and the establishment of the Bay Colony of Massachusetts.

Anne Bradstreet's poetry describes colonial New England life. From her journals, modern readers learn about the everyday life of the early settlers, the hardships of travel, and the responsibilities of different groups and individuals in the community. Early American literature also reveals the commercial and political adventures of the Cavaliers, who came to the New World with King George's blessing.

William Byrd's journal *A History of the Dividing Line*, concerning his trek into the Dismal Swamp separating the Carolinian territories from Virginia and Maryland, makes quite lively reading. A privileged insider to the English Royal Court, Byrd, like other Southern Cavaliers, was given grants to pursue business ventures.

The Revolutionary period

The Revolutionary period of American literature contains nonfiction genres: essay, pamphlet, speech, famous document, and epistle. There are many important writers and works of the Revolutionary Period.

Thomas Paine's pamphlet *Common Sense*, though written by a recently transplanted Englishman, spoke to the American patriots' common sense in dealing with issues in the cause of freedom.

Other contributions to Revolutionary literature are a collection of aphorisms from *Poor Richard's Almanac* and satires such as "Rules by Which a Great Empire May Be Reduced to a Small One" and "Dialogue Between Franklin and the Gout."

The Revolutionary period produced great orations such as Patrick Henry's "Speech to the Virginia House of Burgesses" (the "Give me liberty or give me death" speech) and George Washington's "Farewell to the Army of the Potomac." Less memorable are Washington's inaugural addresses, which often strike modern readers as lacking sufficient focus.

The *Declaration of Independence*, the brainchild predominantly of Thomas Jefferson (along with some prudent editing by Ben Franklin), is a prime example of neoclassical writing—balanced, well crafted, and focused.

Epistles include the exquisitely written, moving correspondence between John Adams and Abigail Adams. The poignancy of their separation—she in Boston, he in Philadelphia—is palpable and real.

> "If ever two were one, then surely we. If ever man were loved by wife, then thee."
>
> **Read more about Anne Bradstreet:**
>
> http://www.annebradstreet.com/Default.htm

> The *Revolutionary Period* of American literature contains nonfiction genres: essay, pamphlet, speech, famous document, and epistle.

The Romantic period

Early American folk tales and the emergence of a distinctly American style of writing constitute the next period, called the Romantic period.

Washington Irving's characters Ichabod Crane and Rip Van Winkle represent a uniquely American folklore devoid of English influences. The characters are indelibly marked by their environment and the superstitions of the New Englander. The early writings of James Fenimore Cooper, including his *Leatherstocking Tales*, provide readers a window into their uniquely American world through stirring accounts of drums along the Mohawk Trail, the French and Indian Wars, the futile British defense of Fort William Henry, and the brutalities of this period. Natty Bumppo, Chingachgook, Uncas, and Magua are unforgettable characters who reflect the American spirit in thought and action.

The poetry of the "Fireside Poets"—James Russell Lowell, Oliver Wendell Holmes, Henry Wadsworth Longfellow, and John Greenleaf Whittier—was recited by American families and read during the long New England winters. In "The Courtin'," Lowell used Yankee dialect to tell a story. Spellbinding epics by Longfellow (such as *Hiawatha, The Courtship of Miles Standish*, and *Evangeline*) told of adversity, sorrow, and ultimate happiness in a uniquely American fashion. The poem "Snowbound" by Whittier relates the story of a captive family isolated by a blizzard and stresses family closeness.

Nathaniel Hawthorne and Herman Melville are the preeminent early American novelists, writing on subjects definitely regional, specific, and American, yet sharing insights about human foibles, fears, loves, doubts, and triumphs.

Hawthorne's writings range from children's stories, such as *The Cricket on the Hearth* series, to adult fare that includes dark, brooding short stories such as "Dr. Heidegger's Experiment," "The Devil and Tom Walker," and "Rapuccini's Daughter." Hawthorne's masterpiece *The Scarlet Letter* criticizes the society of hypocritical Puritan New Englanders, who ostensibly left England to establish religious freedom but who became entrenched in judgmental finger-wagging. The Puritans in the novel ostracize Hester Prynne and condemn her child, Pearl, as a child of Satan. Great love, sacrifice, loyalty, suffering, and related epiphanies add universality to this tale. *The House of the Seven Gables* deals with kept secrets, loneliness, societal pariahs, and the triumph of love over horrible wrongs.

Herman Melville's great opus *Moby Dick* follows a crazed Captain Ahab on his Homeric odyssey to conquer the great white whale that has outwitted him and his whaling crews time and again. The whale has even taken Ahab's leg and, according to Ahab, wants all of him. Melville paints in painstaking detail and with insider knowledge the harsh life of a whaler out of New Bedford by way of Nantucket.

Nathaniel Hawthorne and Herman Melville are the preeminent early American novelists, writing on subjects definitely regional, specific, and American, yet sharing insights about human foibles, fears, loves, doubts, and triumphs.

Read about the life and works of Herman Melville:

http://www.melville.org/

For those readers who don't want to learn about every detail of the whaler's rigging, Melville offers up the succinct tale of *Billy Budd* and his Christ-like sacrifice to the black-and-white maritime laws on the high seas. In *Billy Budd*, an accident results in the death of one of the ship's officers, a slug of a fellow who had taken a dislike to the young, affable, shy Billy. Captain Vere must hang Billy for the death of Claggert but knows that his punishment is not just. However, an example must be given to the rest of the crew so that discipline can be maintained.

Edgar Allan Poe creates a distinctly American version of romanticism with his 16-syllable lines in "The Raven," the classical "To Helen," and his Gothic "Annabelle Lee." The horror short story can be said to originate from Poe's pen. "The Tell-Tale Heart," "The Cask of Amontillado," "The Fall of the House of Usher," and "The Masque of the Red Death" are exemplary short stories. In addition, the genre of detective story emerges with Poe's "Murders in the Rue Morgue."

American Romanticism has its own offshoot in the Transcendentalism of Ralph Waldo Emerson and Henry David Thoreau. Emerson wrote about transcending the complexities of life; Thoreau, who wanted to get to the marrow of life, immersed himself in nature at Walden Pond and wrote an inspiring autobiographical account of his sojourn, aptly titled *On Walden Pond*. Thoreau also wrote passionately regarding his objections to the interference of government in the life of the individual in "On the Duty of Civil Disobedience."

American Romanticism has its own offshoot in the Transcendentalism of Ralph Waldo Emerson and Henry David Thoreau.

Emerson's elegantly-crafted essays and war poetry still validate several important universal truths. Probably most remembered for his address to Thoreau's Harvard graduating class, "The American Scholar," Emerson defined the qualities of hard work and intellectual spirit required of Americans in their growing nation.

The transition between Romanticism and Realism

The Civil War period ushered in the poignant poetry of Walt Whitman and his homage to all who suffered from the ripple effects of war and presidential assassination. His "Come Up from the Fields, Father," about a Civil War soldier's death and his family's reaction, and "When Lilacs Last in the Courtyard Bloom'd," about the effects of Abraham Lincoln's death on the poet and the nation, should be required reading in any American literature course. Further, his *Leaves of Grass* gave America its first truly unique poetry form.

Find more sites about American literature:

http://www.wsu. edu/~campbelld/amlit/ sites.htm

Emily Dickinson, like Walt Whitman, left her literary fingerprints on a vast array of poems, all but three of which were never published in her lifetime. Her themes of introspection and attention to nature's details and wonders are, by any measurement, world-class works. Her posthumous recognition reveals the timeliness of her work. American writing had most certainly arrived!

Mark Twain also left giant footprints on the American literary landscape with his unique blend of tall tale and fable. "The Celebrated Jumping Frog of Calaveras County" and "The Man who Stole Hadleyburg" are epitomes of short story writing. With regard to the novel, Twain again rose above others by his bold, still-disputed, oft-banned *The Adventures of Huckleberry Finn*, which examines such taboo subjects as a white person's love of a slave, the issue of leaving children with abusive parents, and the outcomes of family feuds. Written partly in dialect and southern vernacular, *The Adventures of Huckleberry Finn* is touted by some as the greatest American novel.

The Realistic period

The late nineteenth century saw a reaction against the tendency of Romantic writers to look at the world through rose-colored glasses. Writers like Frank Norris (*The Pit*) and Upton Sinclair (*The Jungle*) used their novels to decry deplorable working conditions in slaughterhouses and wheat mills.

In *The Red Badge of Courage*, Stephen Crane wrote of the daily sufferings of the common soldier in the Civil War. Realistic writers wrote of common, ordinary people and events using realistic detail to reveal the harsh realities of life. They broached taboos by creating protagonists whose environments often destroyed them. In contrast, Romantic writers created protagonists whose indomitable wills helped them rise above adversity. Crane's *Maggie: A Girl of the Streets* deals with a young woman forced into prostitution to survive. In "The Occurrence at Owl Creek Bridge," Ambrose Bierce relates the unfortunate hanging of a Confederate soldier.

Short stories such as Bret Harte's "The Outcasts of Poker Flat" and Jack London's "To Build a Fire" deal with unfortunate people whose luck in life has run out. Many writers, subclassified as naturalists, believed that man was subject to a fate over which he had no control.

Contemporary American literature

Twentieth-century American writing can be divided into the following three genres: drama, fiction, and poetry.

American drama

The greatest and most prolific of American playwrights include the following:

- Eugene O'Neill, who wrote *Long Day's Journey into Night*, *Mourning Becomes Electra*, and *Desire Under the Elms*

- Arthur Miller, author of *The Crucible*, *All My Sons*, and *Death of a Salesman*

Read more about Upton Sinclair:

http://www.online-literature.com/upton_sinclair/

Realistic writers *wrote of common, ordinary people and events using realistic detail to reveal the harsh realities of life. They broached taboos by creating protagonists whose environments often destroyed them.*

Romantic writers *created protagonists whose indomitable wills helped them rise above adversity.*

- Tennessee Williams, author of *Cat on a Hot Tin Roof*, *The Glass Menagerie*, and *A Streetcar Named Desire*
- Edward Albee, who wrote *Who's Afraid of Virginia Woolf?*, *Three Tall Women*, and *A Delicate Balance*

American fiction

The renowned American novelists include the following authors, who wrote the works listed:

- Eudora Welty, *The Optimist's Daughter*
- John Updike, *Rabbit Run* and *Rabbit Redux*
- Sinclair Lewis, *Babbitt* and *Elmer Gantry*
- F. Scott Fitzgerald, *The Great Gatsby* and *Tender Is the Night*
- Ernest Hemingway, *A Farewell to Arms* and *For Whom the Bell Tolls*
- William Faulkner, *The Sound and the Fury* and *Absalom, Absalom!*
- Bernard Malamud, *The Fixer* and *The Natural*

American poetry

Review a timeline of British literature:
http://www.studyguide.org/ brit_lit_timeline.htm

The poetry of the twentieth century is multifaceted, as represented by Edna St. Vincent Millay, Marianne Moore, Richard Wilbur, Langston Hughes, Maya Angelou, and Rita Dove. One of the most well-loved twentieth-century American poets is Robert Frost. His New England motifs of snowy evenings, birches, apple picking, stone-wall mending, hired hands, and nature relate universal truths through exquisite diction, polysyllabic words, and rare allusions to either mythology or the Bible.

British Literature

Anglo-Saxon period

The Anglo-Saxon period spans six centuries but produced only a smattering of literature. The first British epic is *Beowulf*, anonymously written by Christian monks many years after the events in the narrative supposedly occurred. This Teutonic saga relates the triumph over monsters by the hero, Beowulf. A shorter poem titled "The Seafarer," along with some history and riddles, comprises the rest of the Anglo-Saxon canon.

Medieval period

The medieval period introduced Geoffrey Chaucer, the father of English literature, whose *Canterbury Tales* are written in the vernacular, or street language, of

England rather than in Latin. Thus the tales are said to be the first true work of British literature.

Next, Thomas Malory's *Le Morte d'Arthur* brought together extant tales from Europe concerning the legendary King Arthur, Merlin, Guinevere, and the Knights of the Round Table. This work is the generative work that gave rise to the many Arthurian legends that stir the chivalric imagination.

Renaissance and Elizabethan periods

The Renaissance period, synonymous with William Shakespeare, begins with the introduction of the Petrarchan or Italian sonnet into England. Sir Thomas Wyatt and Sir Philip Sydney wrote English versions of this form. Next, Sir Edmund Spenser invented a variation of the Italian sonnet form, aptly called the Spenserian sonnet. His masterpiece is the epic *The Faerie Queene*, honoring Queen Elizabeth I's reign. He also wrote books on the Red Cross Knight and St. George and the Dragon and wrote a series of Arthurian adventures. Spenser was dubbed the "poet's poet." He created a nine-line stanza—eight lines iambic pentameter and an extra-footed ninth line—called an *alexandrine*.

William Shakespeare, often called the Bard of Avon, wrote 154 sonnets, 39 plays, and two long narrative poems. The sonnets are justifiably called the greatest sonnet sequence in all of literature. Shakespeare dispensed with the octave/sestet format of the Italian sonnet and invented his three quatrains, one heroic couplet format.

Shakespeare's plays are divided into comedies, history plays, and tragedies. Great lines from these plays are more often quoted than those of any other author. The Big Four tragedies—*Hamlet, Macbeth, Othello,* and *King Lear*—are acknowledged to be the most brilliant examples of this genre.

Seventeenth century

John Milton's devout Puritanism was the wellspring of his creative genius, which marked the close of the remarkable productivity of the English Renaissance. His social commentary in such works as *Aereopagitica* and *Samson Agonistes*, along with his elegant sonnets, would be enough to solidify his stature as a great writer. But it is his masterpiece *Paradise Lost*, based in part on the Book of Genesis, that places Milton in the company of a handful of the most renowned writers of all time. Many feel that *Paradise Lost*, written in balanced, elegant neoclassic form, truly does justify the ways of God to man.

The greatest allegory about man's journey to the Celestial City (Heaven) is found in *The Pilgrim's Progress*, written at the end of the English Renaissance by John Bunyan. *The Pilgrim's Progress* describes virtues and vices personified. This work was for a long time second only to the Bible in numbers of copies printed and sold.

The Renaissance period of British literature is synonymous with William Shakespeare.

William Shakespeare, often called the Bard of Avon, wrote 154 sonnets, 39 plays, and two long narrative poems.

*John Milton's masterpiece **Paradise Lost**, based in part on the Book of Genesis, places him among a handful of the most renowned writers of all time.*

The Jacobean Age gave us the marvelously witty and cleverly constructed conceits of John Donne's metaphysical sonnets as well as his insightful meditations and his version of sermons or homilies. "Ask not for whom the bell tolls" and "No man is an island unto himself" are famous epigrams from Donne's *Meditations*. His most famous conceit is that which compares lovers to a footed compass, traveling seemingly separately but always leaning toward one another and conjoined, in "A Valediction: Forbidding Mourning."

Eighteenth century

The Restoration and Enlightenment periods of the eighteenth century reflected the political turmoil brought about by the regicide of Charles I, the Interregnum Puritan government of Oliver Cromwell, and the restoration of the monarchy to England by the coronation of Charles II, who had been given refuge by the French King Louis XIV. During this time Neoclassicism became the preferred writing style, especially for Alexander Pope. New genres, evidenced in works such as *The Diary of Samuel Pepys*, the novels of Daniel Defoe, the periodical essays and editorials of Joseph Addison and Richard Steele, and Alexander Pope's mock epic *The Rape of the Lock*, demonstrate the diversity of expression during this time.

Writers who followed were contemporaries of Dr. Samuel Johnson, the lexicographer of *The Dictionary of the English Language*. Fittingly, this Age of Johnson, which encompasses James Boswell's biography of Dr. Johnson, Robert Burns' Scottish dialect and regionalism in his evocative poetry, and the mystical pre-Romantic poetry of William Blake, ushered in the Romantic age and its revolution against neoclassicism.

Romantic period

Read more about the Romantic period:

http://www.wwnorton.com/college/english/nael/romantic/welcome.htm

The Romantic age encompasses what is known as the First Generation Romantics, William Wordsworth and Samuel Taylor Coleridge, who collaborated on *Lyrical Ballads,* which defines and exemplifies the tenets of the Romantic style of writing. The Second Generation includes George Gordon, Lord Byron; Percy Bysshe Shelley; and John Keats. These poets wrote sonnets, odes, epics, and narrative poems, most dealing with homage to nature.

Other famous works by Wordsworth include "Intimations on Immortality" and "The Prelude." Byron's satirical epic *Don Juan* and his autobiographical *Childe Harold's Pilgrimage* are irreverent, witty, self-deprecating, and cuttingly critical of other writers and critics.

Shelley's odes and sonnets are remarkable for their sensory imagery. Keats' sonnets, odes, and longer narrative poem *The Eve of St. Agnes* are remarkable for their introspection considering the tender age of the poet, who died when he was only twenty-five. In fact, all of the Second Generation writers died before their time. Wordsworth, who lived to be eighty, outlived them all, including Coleridge, his friend and collaborator.

Others who wrote during the Romantic age are the essayist Charles Lamb and the novelist Jane Austen. The Brontë sisters, Charlotte and Emily, wrote one novel each. Their two novels are noted as two of the finest ever written: *Jane Eyre* and *Wuthering Heights*. Mary Anne Evans, also known as George Eliot, wrote several important novels: her masterpiece *Middlemarch*, *Silas Marner*, *Adam Bede*, and *Mill on the Floss*.

Jane Austen, the Brontë sisters, and George Eliot are important writers from the Romantic Age.

Nineteenth century

The Victorian period is remarkable for the diversity and proliferation of work. Poets who are typified as Victorians include Alfred, Lord Tennyson, who wrote *Idylls of the King*, twelve narrative poems about the Arthurian legend; and Robert Browning, who wrote chilling, dramatic monologues such as "My Last Duchess" as well as long poetic narratives such as *The Pied Piper of Hamlin*. Browning's wife Elizabeth wrote two major works, the epic feminist poem *Aurora Leigh* and the deeply moving and provocative *Sonnets from the Portuguese*, in which she details her deep love for Robert and his startling, to her, reciprocation.

Read more about the Victorian era:

http://www.victorianweb. org/

Gerard Manley Hopkins, a Catholic priest, wrote poetry using sprung rhythm. A.E. Housman, Matthew Arnold, and the Pre-Raphaelites, especially the brother-and-sister duo Dante Gabriel Rosetti and Christina Rosetti, contributed much to the Victorian era poetic scene. The Pre-Raphaelites, a group of nineteenth-century English painters, poets, and critics, reacted against Victorian materialism and the neoclassical conventions of academic art by producing earnest, quasi-religious works. Medieval and early Renaissance painters up to the time of the Italian painter Raphael inspired the group.

During the Victorian Period, Robert Louis Stevenson, the great Scottish novelist, wrote his adventure/history lessons for young adults. Victorian prose ranges from the incomparable, keenly woven plot structures of Charles Dickens to the deeply moving Dorset/Wessex novels of Thomas Hardy, in which women are repressed and life is more struggle than euphoria. Rudyard Kipling wrote about colonialism in India in works such as *Kim* and *The Jungle Book*, which recreate exotic locales and dissect the Raj, the British colonial government during Queen Victoria's reign. Victorian drama is a product mainly of Oscar Wilde, whose satirical masterpiece *The Importance of Being Earnest* farcically details and lampoons Victorian social mores.

During the Victorian period, Robert Louis Stevenson, the great Scottish novelist, wrote his adventure/history lessons for young adults.

Twentieth century

The early twentieth century is represented mainly by the towering achievements of George Bernard Shaw's dramas: *St. Joan, Pygmalion, Man and Superman, Major Barbara,* and *Arms and the Man,* to name a few. Twentieth-century novelists are too numerous to list, but some of the greatest include Joseph Conrad, E. M. Forster, Virginia Woolf, James Joyce, Graham Greene, George Orwell, and D.H. Lawrence.

Twentieth-century poets of renown and merit include W. H. Auden, Robert Graves, T. S. Eliot, Edith Sitwell, Stephen Spender, Dylan Thomas, Philip Larkin, Ted Hughes, Sylvia Plath, and Hugh MacDiarmid. This list is by no means complete.

World Literature

North American literature

North American literature is divided among the United States, Canada, and Mexico. Canadian writers of note include feminist Margaret Atwood (*The Handmaid's Tale*); Alice Munro, a remarkable short story writer; and W. P. Kinsella, another short story writer whose two major subjects are North American Indians and baseball.

Mexican writers include the 1990 Nobel Prize winning poet Octavio Paz (*The Labyrinth of Solitude*) and feminist Rosario Castillanos (*The Nine Guardians*).

Central American/Caribbean literature

The Norton Anthology of World Literature:

http://www.wwnorton.com/college/english/nawol/

The Caribbean and Central America encompass a vast area and diverse cultures that reflect oppression and colonialism by England, Spain, Portugal, France, and the Netherlands. The Caribbean writers include Samuel Selvon of Trinidad and Armando Valladares of Cuba. Central American authors include dramatist Carlos Solorzano, from Guatemala, whose plays include *Dona Beatriz, The Hapless, The Magician,* and *The Hands of God.*

South American Literature

Chilean Gabriela Mistral was the first Latin American writer to win the Nobel Prize in Literature. She is best known for her collection of poetry, *Desolation and Feeling.*

Chile was also home to Pablo Neruda, who in 1971 won the Nobel Prize in Literature for his poetry. His twenty-nine volumes of poetry have been translated into more than 60 languages, attesting to his universal appeal. *Twenty Love Poems* and *Song of Despair* are justly famous. Isabel Allende is carrying on the Chilean literary standards with her acclaimed novel *House of Spirits.* Argentine Jorge Luis

Borges is considered by many literary critics to be the most important writer of his century from South America. His collection of short stories, *Ficciones*, brought him universal recognition. Also from Argentina, Silvina Ocampo, a collaborator with Borges on a collection of poetry, is famed for her poetry and short story collections, which include *The Fury* and *The Days of the Night*.

Horacio Quiroga represents Uruguay, and Brazil's Joao Guimaraes Rosa wrote the novel *The Devil to Pay*, considered by many to be first-rank world literature.

Continental European literature

Continental European literature expands the worlds of students and broadens their exposure to different cultures and values. This category as discussed below excludes British literature, which was covered previously.

Germany

German poet and playwright Friedrich von Schiller is best known for his history plays *William Tell* and *The Maid of Orleans*. He is a leading literary figure in Germany's Golden Age of Literature. Also from Germany, Rainer Maria Rilke, the great lyric poet, is one of the poets of the unconscious or stream of consciousness style. Other famous German authors include Herman Hesse (*Siddartha*), Gunter Grass (*The Tin Drum*), and the great German writer Johann Wolfgang von Goethe.

Scandinavia

Scandinavian literature includes the works of Hans Christian Andersen of Denmark, who advanced the fairy tale genre with such wistful tales as "The Little Mermaid" and "Thumbelina."

The social commentary of Henrik Ibsen of Norway startled the world through drama, exploring such issues as feminism (*The Doll's House* and *Hedda Gabler*) and the effects of sexually-transmitted diseases (*The Wild Duck* and *Ghosts*).

Sweden's Selma Lagerlof was the first woman to win the Nobel Prize in Literature. Her novels include *Gosta Berling's Saga* and the world-renowned *The Wonderful Adventures of Nils*, a children's work.

Russia

Russian literature is vast and monumental. Who has not heard of Fyodor Dostoyevsky's *Crime and Punishment* and *The Brothers Karamazov* or of Count Leo Tolstoy's *War and Peace*? These novels are examples of psychological realism. Dostoyevsky's influence on modern writers cannot be overstressed.

Tolstoy's *War and Peace* is a sweeping account of the invasion of Russia and Napoleon's taking of Moscow. This novel is called the national novel of Russia. Further advancing Tolstoy's greatness is his ability to create realistic and unforget-table female characters, especially Natasha in *War and Peace* and Anna in *Anna*

Read more about Henrik Ibsen:

http://www. theatredatabase.com/19th_ century/henrik_ibsen_001. html

Karenina. The Russian Alexander Pushkin is famous for great short stories; Anton Chekhov for drama (*Uncle Vanya*, *The Three Sisters*, *The Cherry Orchard*); and Yevgeny Yevtushenko for poetry (*Babi Yar*). Boris Pasternak won the Nobel Prize (*Dr. Zhivago*). Aleksandr Solzhenitsyn (*The Gulag Archipelago*) returned to Russia after years of expatriation in Vermont. Ilya Varshavsky, who creates fictional societies that are dystopias, or the opposite of utopias, represents the genre of science fiction.

France

France boasts a multifaceted canon of great literature that is universal in scope and that almost always champions some social cause. Examples include the poignant short stories of Guy de Maupassant; the fantastic poetry of Charles Baudelaire (*Fleurs du Mal*); the groundbreaking lyrical poetry of Rimbaud and Verlaine; and the existentialism of Jean-Paul Sartre (*No Exit*, *The Flies*, and *Nausea*), Andre Malraux (*The Fall*), and Albert Camus's (*The Stranger* and *The Plague*), the recipient of the 1957 Nobel Prize in Literature.

Drama in France is best represented by Rostand's *Cyrano de Bergerac* and the neoclassical dramas of Racine and Corneille. Feminist writers include Simone de Beauvoir and Sidonie-Gabrielle Colette, known for her short stories and novels. The great French novelists include André Gide, Honoré de Balzac (*Cousin Bette*), Stendel (*The Red and the Black*), and Alexandre Dumas (*The Three Musketeers* and *The Man in the Iron Mask*). Victor Hugo is the Charles Dickens of French literature, having penned the masterpieces *The Hunchback of Notre Dame* and *Les Misérables*. The stream of consciousness of Proust's *Remembrance of Things Past* and the Absurdist theatre of Samuel Beckett and Eugene Ionesco (*The Rhinoceros*) attest to the groundbreaking genius of the French writers.

Slavic nations

Austrian writer Franz Kafka (*The Metamorphosis, The Trial*, and *The Castle*) is considered by many to be the literary voice of the first half of the twentieth century. Poet Vaclav Havel represents the Czech Republic. Slovakia produced dramatist Karel Capek (*R.U.R.*), and Romania is represented by Elie Wiesel (*Night*), a Nobel Prize winner.

Spain

Spain's great writers include Miguel de Cervantes (*Don Quixote*) and Juan Ramon Jimenez. The anonymous national epic *El Cid* has been translated into many languages.

Italy

Italy's greatest writers include Virgil (*The Aeneid*), Giovanni Boccaccio (*The Decameron*), Dante Alighieri (*The Divine Comedy*), and the more contemporary Alberto Moravia.

Read more about Jean Paul Sartre:

http://www.users. muohio.edu/shermalw/ honors_2001_fall/ honors_papers_2001/ detwilerj_Sartre.htm

Ancient Greece

Greece will always be foremost in literary stature because of Homer's epics, *The Iliad* and *The Odyssey*. No one except Shakespeare is more often cited. The works of Plato and Aristotle in philosophy; of Aeschylus, Euripides, and Sophocles in tragedy; and of Aristophanes in comedy further solidify Greece's preeminence. Greece is the cradle not only of democracy but of literature as well.

African literature

African literary greats include South Africans Nadine Gordimer (winner of the Nobel Prize in Literature) and Peter Abrahams (author of *Tell Freedom: Memories of Africa*, an autobiography of life in Johannesburg). Chinua Achebe (*Things Fall Apart*) and the poet Wole Soyinka hail from Nigeria. Mark Mathabane wrote an autobiography titled *Kaffir Boy* about growing up in South Africa. Naguib Mahfouz of Egypt and Doris Lessing of Rhodesia—now Zimbabwe—write about race relations in their respective countries. Lessing won the 2007 Nobel Prize for literature. Because of her radical politics, Lessing was once banned from her homeland and the Union of South Africa. Also banned was Alan Paton, whose seemingly simple story *Cry, the Beloved Country* brought the plight of blacks and whites living under apartheid to the rest of the world.

> **Read more about postcolonial literature in English:**
>
> *http://www.english.emory.edu/Bahri/Intro.html*

Far East literature

The works of many modern Asian writers are now being translated for the Western reading public. India's Krishan Chandar has authored more than 300 stories. Rabindranath Tagore won the Nobel Prize in Literature in 1913 (*Song Offerings*). R. K. Narayan, India's most famous writer (*The Guide*), is interested in mythology and the legends of India. Santha Rama Rau's work *Gifts of Passage* is the true story of her life in a British school, where she tries to preserve her Indian culture and traditional home life.

Revered as Japan's most famous female author, Fumiko Hayashi (*Drifting Clouds*) by the time of her death had written more than 270 literary works.

In 1968, the Nobel Prize in Literature was awarded to Yasunari Kawabata (*The Sound of the Mountain, The Snow Country*). His *Palm-of-the-Hand Stories* take the essentials of haiku poetry and transform them into the short story genre.

Katai Tayama (*The Quilt*) is touted as the father of the Japanese confessional novel. His works, characterized as naturalism, are definitely not for the squeamish. The "slice of life" psychological writings of Ryunosuke Akutagawa gained him acclaim in the Western world. His short stories, especially "Rashamon" and "In a Grove," are greatly praised for style as well as content.

China, too, has given much to the literary world. Li Po, the T'ang dynasty poet from the Chinese Golden Age, shared his interest in folklore by preserving the folk songs and mythology of China. Po enables his readers to enter into the Chinese philosophy of Taoism and to understand feelings against expansionism during the T'ang dynastic rule. The T'ang dynasty, which was one of great diversity in the arts, saw Jiang Fang help create the Chinese version of a short story. His themes often express love between a man and a woman.

Ting Ling writes eloquently about modern feminist and political concerns under the pseudonym Chiang Ping-Chih. Her stories reflect her concerns about social injustice and her commitment to the women's movement.

Literature for Adolescents

Prior to twentieth-century research on childhood and adolescent development, books for adolescents were primarily didactic. They were designed to address history, manners, and morals.

Middle ages

As early as the eleventh century, Anselm, the Archbishop of Canterbury, wrote an encyclopedia designed to instill in children the beliefs and principles of conduct acceptable to adults in medieval society. Early monastic translations of the Bible and other religious writings were written in Latin for the edification of the upper classes.

Fifteenth-century hornbooks were designed to teach reading and religious lessons. William Claxton printed English versions of Aesop's *Fables*, Malory's *Le Morte d'Arthur,* and stories from Greek and Roman mythology. Though printed for adults, tales of the adventures of Odysseus and the Arthurian knights were also popular with literate adolescents.

Renaissance

The Renaissance saw the introduction of inexpensive chapbooks, small in size and 16 to 64 pages in length. Chapbooks were condensed versions of myths and fairy tales. Designed for the common people, chapbooks were grammatically imperfect but immensely popular because of their adventurous contents. Though most serious, educated adults frowned on the sometimes vulgar little books, they received praise from Richard Steele of *Tattler* fame for inspiring his grandson's interest in reading and in pursuing his other studies.

Meanwhile, the Puritans' three most popular reads were the Bible, John Foe's *Book of Martyrs*, and John Bunyan's *Pilgrim's Progress*. Though venerating religious martyrs and preaching the moral propriety that would lead to eternal happiness, the stories of the *Book of Martyrs* were often lurid in their descriptions of the fate

Chapbooks were condensed versions of myths and fairy tales. They were small in size and length and designed to be read by the common people.

The Puritans' three most popular reads were the Bible, John Foe's Book of Martyrs, and John Bunyan's Pilgrim's Progress.

of the damned. In contrast, *Pilgrim's Progress*, not written for children and difficult reading even for adults, was as attractive to adolescents for its adventurous plot as for its moral outcome. In Puritan America, the *New England Primer* set forth the prayers, catechisms, Bible verses, and illustrations meant to instruct children in the Puritan ethic. The seventeenth-century French used fables and fairy tales to entertain adults, but children found them enjoyable as well.

Seventeenth century

The late seventeenth century brought the first literature that specifically targeted the young. Pierre Peril's *Fairy Tales*, Jean de la Fontaine's retellings of famous fables, Mme. d'Aulnoy's novels based on old folktales, and Mme. de Beaumont's *Beauty and the Beast* were written to delight as well as instruct young people. In England, publisher John Newbury was the first to publish a literary line for children. This line included a translation of Perrault's *Tales of Mother Goose*; *A Little Pretty Pocket-Book*, "intended for instruction and amusement" but decidedly moralistic and bland in comparison to the previous century's chapbooks; and *The Renowned History of Little Goody Two Shoes*, allegedly written by Oliver Goldsmith for a juvenile audience.

Eighteenth century

Largely, eighteenth-century adolescents found their reading pleasure in adult books: Daniel Defoe's *Robinson Crusoe*, Jonathan Swift's *Gulliver's Travels*, and Johann Wyss's *Swiss Family Robinson*. More books were being written for children, and moral didacticism, though less religious, was nevertheless ever present.

The short stories of Maria Edgeworth, the four-volume *The History of Sandford and Merton* by Thomas Day, and Martha Farquharson's 26-volume *Elsie Dinsmore* series dealt with pious protagonists who learned restraint, repentance, and rehabilitation through sin and redemption.

Two bright spots in this period of didacticism were Jean Jacques Rousseau's *Emile* and *The Tales of Shakespeare*, Charles and Mary Lamb's simplified versions of Shakespeare's plays. Rousseau believed that a child's abilities were enhanced by a free, happy life, and the Lambs subscribed to the notion that children were entitled to entertaining literature written in language that was comprehensible to them.

Nineteenth century

Child and adolescent literature truly began its modern rise in nineteenth-century Europe. Hans Christian Andersen's *Fairy Tales* were fanciful adaptations of the somber tales of the Grimm brothers in the previous century. Andrew Lang's series of colorful fairy books contained the folklores of many nations and are still parts of the collections of many modern libraries. Clement Moore's "A Visit from St. Nicholas" is a cheery, non-threatening child's view of the night before Christmas. Lewis Carroll's books about Alice's adventures, Edward Lear's poems with caricatures, and Lucretia Nole's stories of the Philadelphia Peterkin family are full of fancy and contain not a smidgen of morality.

Other popular Victorian novels introduced the modern fantasy and science fiction genres; William Makepeace Thackeray's *The Rose and the Ring*, Charles Dickens' *The Magic Fishbone*, and Jules Verne's *Twenty Thousand Leagues Under the Sea* are examples. Adventures to exotic places became a popular topic; Rudyard Kipling's *Jungle Books*, Verne's *Around the World in Eighty Days*, and Robert Louis Stevenson's *Treasure Island* and *Kidnapped* were popular reads. In 1884, the first English translation of Johanna Spyri's *Heidi* appeared on the scene.

North America was also finding its voice for adolescent readers. American Louisa May Alcott's *Little Women* and Canadian L.M. Montgomery's *Anne of Green Gables* ushered in the modern age of realistic fiction. American youth were enjoying the adventures of Tom Sawyer and Huckleberry Finn. For the first time, children were able to read books about real people just like themselves.

Twentieth century

Childhood and adolescent literature of the twentieth century is extensive, diverse and, as in previous centuries, influenced by the adults who write, edit, and select books for youth consumption. In the first third of the twentieth century, suitable adolescent literature dealt with children from large families and good homes. These books projected an image of a peaceful, rural existence.

Though the characters and plots were more realistic, the stories maintained focus on topics that were considered emotionally and intellectually proper. Popular at this time were Laura Ingalls Wilder's *Little House on the Prairie* series and Carl Sandburg's biography *Abe Lincoln Grows Up*. English author J.R.R. Tolkein's fantasy *The Hobbit* prefaced modern adolescent readers' fascination with the works of Piers Antony, Madelaine L'Engle, and Anne McCaffery.

Suggested reading for fifth and sixth grades

The following classic and contemporary works combine the characteristics of multiple learning theories. Functioning at the concrete operations stage (Piaget), being of the "good person" orientation (Kohlberg), still highly dependent on external rewards (Bandura), and exhibiting all five needs from Maslow's hierarchy, most 11- to 12-year-olds should appreciate the following titles, grouped by

For more information, read Introductory Lecture on Children's & Adolescent Literature:

http://homepages. wmich.edu/~tarboxg/ Introductory_Lecture_on_ Children's_&_Adol_Lit. html

reading level. These titles are also cited for interest at that grade level and are not necessarily high-interest titles for older readers who read below grade level. Some high-interest titles for older readers will be cited later.

SUGGESTED TITLES FOR READING LEVELS 6.0 TO 6.9
Barrett, William. *Lilies of the Field*
Cormier, Robert. *Other Bells for Us to Ring*
Dahl, Roald. *Danny, Champion of the World; Charlie and the Chocolate Factory*
Lindgren, Astrid. *Pippi Longstocking*
Lindbergh, Anne. *Three Lives to Live*
Lowry, Lois. *Rabble Starkey*
Naylor, Phyllis. *The Year of the Gopher; Reluctantly Alice*
Peck, Robert Newton. *Arly*
Speare, Elizabeth. *The Witch of Blackbird Pond*
Sleator, William. *The Boy Who Reversed Himself*

Suggested reading for seventh and eighth grades

Most seventh- and eighth-grade students, according to learning theory, are still functioning cognitively, psychologically, and morally as sixth graders. As these are not inflexible standards, some twelve- and thirteen-year-olds are much more mature socially, intellectually, and physically than the younger children who share the same school. Seventh and eighth graders are becoming concerned with establishing individual and peer group identities, which often presents conflicts with authority and the rigidity of rules. Some students at this age are still tied firmly to the family and its expectations, while others identify more with those their own age or older.

Enrichment reading for this group must help them cope with life's rapid changes or provide escape and thus must be either realistic or fantastic, depending on the child's needs. Adventures and mysteries are still popular today. Preteens also become more interested in biographies of contemporary figures than in biographies of legendary figures of the past.

Check out these online resources for K–12 Teachers: Children's and Adolescent Literature:

http://www.indiana. edu/~reading/ieo/digests/ d149.html

SUGGESTED TITLES FOR READING LEVELS 7.0 TO 7.9
Armstrong, William. *Sounder*
Bagnold, Enid. *National Velvet*
Barrie, James. *Peter Pan*
London, Jack. *White Fang; Call of the Wild*
Lowry, Lois. *Taking Care of Terrific*
McCaffrey, Anne. *The Dragonsinger series*
Montgomery, L. M. *Anne of Green Gables and sequels*
Steinbeck, John. *The Pearl*
Tolkien, J. R. R. *The Hobbit*
Zindel, Paul. *The Pigman*

SUGGESTED TITLES FOR READING LEVELS 8.0 TO 8.9
Cormier, Robert. *I Am the Cheese*
McCullers, Carson. *The Member of the Wedding*
North, Sterling. *Rascal*
Twain, Mark. *The Adventures of Tom Sawyer*
Zindel, Paul. *My Darling, My Hamburger*

Suggested reading for ninth grade

Depending on the school environment, ninth graders may rank as the highest class in a middle school or the lowest in a high school. Much of their social development and thus their reading interests become motivated by peer associations. They are technically adolescents, operating at the early stages of formal operations in cognitive development. Their perceptions of their own identities are becoming well-defined, and they are fully aware of the ethics required by society. Ninth graders are more receptive to the challenges of classic literature but still enjoy popular teen novels.

SUGGESTED TITLES FOR READING LEVELS 9.0 TO 9.9
Brown, Dee. *Bury My Heart at Wounded Knee*
Defoe, Daniel. *Robinson Crusoe*
Dickens, Charles. *David Copperfield*
Greenberg, Joanne. *I Never Promised You a Rose Garden*
Kipling, Rudyard. *Captains Courageous*
Mathabane, Mark. *Kaffir Boy*
Nordhoff, Charles. *Mutiny on the Bounty*
Shelley, Mary. *Frankenstein*
Washington, Booker T. *Up from Slavery*

Suggested reading for tenth to twelfth grades

Most high school sophomores, juniors, and seniors can handle almost any type of literature, except for a few of the most difficult titles such as *Moby Dick* or *Vanity Fair*. However, since many high school students do not progress to the eleventh- or twelfth-grade reading level, they will still have their favorites among authors whose writings they can understand. Many will struggle with assigned novels but still read high-interest books for pleasure. A few high-interest titles are listed below without reading level designations, although most are level 6.0 to 7.9.

HIGH-INTEREST TITLES
Bauer, Joan. *Squashed*
Borland, Hal. *When the Legends Die*
Danzinger, Paula. *Remember Me to Harold Square*
Duncan, Lois. *Stranger with My Face*
Hamilton, Virginia. *The Planet of Junior Brown*
Hinton, S. E. *The Outsiders*
Paterson, Katherine. *The Great Gilly Hopkins*

Teaching challenges

Teachers of students at all levels must be familiar with the materials offered by the libraries in their own schools. Only then can they guide their students into appropriate selections for their social age and reading level.

Adolescent literature, because of the age range of its readers, is extremely diverse. Fiction for the middle group, usually ages ten to fifteen, deals with issues of coping with internal and external changes in their lives. Because children's writers in the twentieth century have produced increasingly realistic fiction, adolescents can now find problems dealt with honestly in novels.

Teachers of middle school students see the greatest change in interests and reading abilities. Fifth and sixth graders, included in elementary grades in many schools, are viewed as older children, while seventh and eighth graders are viewed as preadolescent.

Ninth graders, included sometimes as upper tier in middle school and sometimes as underlings in high school, definitely view themselves as teenagers. Their literature choices will often be governed more by interest than by ability—thus the wealth of high-interest, low-readability books that have flooded the market in recent years. Tenth through twelfth graders will still select high-interest books for pleasure reading but are also easily encouraged to stretch their literary muscles by reading classics.

> *Because of rapid social changes, topics that once did not interest young people until they reached their teens—suicide, gangs, and homosexuality—are now the subjects of books for younger readers.*

Because of rapid social changes, topics that once did not interest young people until they reached their teens—suicide, gangs, and homosexuality—are now the subjects of books for younger readers. The plethora of high-interest books reveals how desperately schools have failed to produce on-level readers and how the market has adapted to that need.

However, these high-interest books are now accessible to younger children whose reading levels are at or above normal. No matter how tastefully written, some content is inappropriate for younger readers. The problem becomes not so much one of steering these children toward books they can handle as one of encouraging them toward books whose content is appropriate to their level of cognitive and social development. A fifth-grader may be able to read and understand V.C. Andrews' book *Flowers in the Attic* but not possess the social or moral development to handle the deviant behavior of the characters. Because of the complex societal changes affecting adolescents, the teacher must be as well versed in learning theory and child development as in the subject matter of language and literature.

Sample Test Questions and Rationale

(Easy)

1. **The tendency to emphasize and value the qualities and peculiarities of life in a particular geographic area exemplifies:**

   A. Pragmatism

   B. Regionalism

   C. Pantheism

   D. Abstractionism

Answer: B

Rationale: Pragmatism is a philosophical doctrine according to which there is no absolute truth. All truths change their trueness as their practical utility increases or decreases. The main representative of this movement is William James, who in 1907 published *Pragmatism: A New Way for Some Old Ways of Thinking*. Pantheism is a philosophy according to which God is omnipresent in the world, everything is God, and God is everything. The great representative of this sensibility is Spinoza. Also, the works of writers such as Wordsworth, Shelly, and Emerson illustrate this doctrine. Abstract Expressionism is one of the most important movements in American art. It began in the 1940s with artists such as Willem de Kooning, Mark Rothko, and Arshile Gorky. The paintings are usually large and non-representational.

(Easy)

2. **Charles Dickens, Robert Browning, and Robert Louis Stevenson were:**

   A. Victorians

   B. Medievalists

   C. Elizabethans

   D. Absurdists

Answer: A

Rationale: The Victorian period is remarkable for the diversity and quality of its literature. Robert Browning wrote chilling monologues such as "My Last Duchess" and long poetic narratives such as *The Pied Piper of Hamlin*. Robert Louis Stevenson wrote his works partly for young adults, whose imaginations were quite taken by his *Treasure Island* and *The Case of Dr. Jekyll and Mr. Hyde*. Charles Dickens tells of the misery of the time and the complexities of Victorian society in novels such as *Oliver Twist* and *Great Expectations*.

Sample Test Questions and Rationale (cont.)

(Easy)

3. Among middle school students of low-to-average reading levels, which work would most likely stir reading interest?

   A. *Elmer Gantry*, Sinclair Lewis

   B. *Smiley's People*, John Le Carre

   C. *The Outsiders*, S.E. Hinton

   D. *And Then There Were None*, Agatha Christie

Answer: C

Rationale: The students can easily identify with the characters and the gangs in the book. S.E. Hinton has actually said about this book: "*The Outsiders* is definitely my best-selling book; but what I like most about it is how it has taught a lot of kids to enjoy reading." The other three novels have more mature subject matter, more complex characters, and higher reading levels. Lewis' novel satirizes hypocrisy in the character of a debauched evangelist. Le Carre's novel is the third part of a spy novel trilogy. Christie's mystery has a wide cast of characters who are murdered one by one.

(Easy)

4. What is considered the first work of English literature because it was written in the vernacular of the day?

   A. *Beowulf*

   B. *Le Morte d'Arthur*

   C. *The Faerie Queene*

   D. *Canterbury Tales*

Answer: D

Rationale: Chaucer wrote the *Canterbury Tales* in the street language of medieval England. *Beowulf* was written during the Anglo-Saxon period and is a Teutonic saga. *Le Morte d'Arthur*, by Thomas Malory, was written after Chaucer's work. Sir Edmund Spencer's *The Faerie Queene* was written during the Renaissance under the reign of Queen Elizabeth I.

(Average)

5. Considered one of the first feminist plays, this Ibsen drama ends with a door slamming, symbolizing the lead character's emancipation from traditional societal norms.

   A. *The Wild Duck*

   B. *Hedda Gabler*

   C. *Ghosts*

   D. *A Doll's House*

Answer: D

Rationale: Nora in *A Doll's House* leaves her husband and her children when she realizes her husband is not the man she thought he was. Hedda Gabler, another feminist icon, shoots herself. *The Wild Duck* deals with the conflict between idealism and family secrets. *Ghosts*, considered one of Ibsen's most controversial plays, deals with many social ills, some of which include alcoholism, incest, and religious hypocrisy.

Sample Test Questions and Rationale (cont.)

(Average)

6. Which of the following titles is known for its scathingly condemning tone?

   A. Boris Pasternak's *Dr Zhivago*

   B. Albert Camus' *The Stranger*

   C. Henry David Thoreau's "On the Duty of Civil Disobedience"

   D. Benjamin Franklin's "Rules by Which a Great Empire May Be Reduced to a Small One"

Answer: D

Rationale: In this work, Benjamin Franklin adopts a scathingly ironic tone to warn the British about the probable outcome in their colonies if they persist with their policies. These are discussed one by one in the text, and the absurdity of each is condemned.

(Average)

7. American colonial writers were primarily:

   A. Romanticists

   B. Naturalists

   C. Realists

   D. Neoclassicists

Answer: D

Rationale: The early colonists had been schooled in England, and even though their writing became quite American in content, their emphasis on clarity and balance in their language remained British. This literature reflects the lives of the early colonists, such as William Bradford's excerpts from "The Mayflower Compact," Anne Bradstreet's poetry, and William Byrd's journal *A History of the Dividing Line.*

(Average)

8. Arthur Miller wrote *The Crucible* as a parallel to what twentieth-century event?

   A. Senator McCarthy's House Un-American Activities Committee Hearing

   B. The Cold War

   C. The fall of the Berlin wall

   D. The Persian Gulf War

Answer: A

Rationale: The seventeenth century witch hunts in Salem, Mass., gave Miller a storyline that was very comparable to what was happening to persons suspected of communist beliefs in the 1950s.

Sample Test Questions and Rationale (cont.)

(Average)

9. **Which of the writers below is a renowned black memoirist?**

    A. Maya Angelou

    B. Sandra Cisneros

    C. Richard Wilbur

    D. Richard Wright

Answer: A

Rationale: Among her most famous work are *I Know Why the Caged Bird Sings* (1970), *And Still I Rise* (1978), and *All God's Children Need Traveling Shoes* (1986). Richard Wilbur is a poet and a translator of French dramatists Racine and Moliere, but he is not African American. Richard Wright is a very important African American author of novels such as *Native Son* and *Black Boy*; however, he is not a poet. Sandra Cisneros is a Latina author who is very important in developing Latina women's literature.

(Average)

10. **Which of the following is not a theme of Native American writing?**

    A. Emphasis on the hardiness of the human body and soul

    B. The strength of multicultural assimilation

    C. Contrition for the genocide of native peoples

    D. Remorse for the destruction of the Native American way of life

Answer: B

Rationale: Native American literature was first a vast body of oral traditions dating from as early as before the fifteenth century. The characteristics of Native American literature include reverence for and awe of nature and the interconnectedness of the elements in the life cycle. The themes often reflect the hardiness of body and soul, remorse for the destruction of the Native American way of life, and the genocide of many tribes by the encroaching settlements of European Americans. These themes are still present in today's contemporary Native American literature, such as in the works of Duane Niatum, Gunn Allen, Louise Erdrich, and N. Scott Momaday.

(Average)

11. **The writing of Russian naturalists is:**

    A. Optimistic

    B. Pessimistic

    C. Satirical

    D. Whimsical

Answer: B

Rationale: Although the Russian naturalist movement, which originated with the critic Vissarion Belinsky, was particularly strong in the 1840s, it can be said that the works of Dostoevsky, Tolstoy, Chekov, Turgenev, and Pushkin owe much to it. These authors' works are among the best in international literature, yet are shrouded in stark pessimism. Tolstoy's *Anna Karenina* or Dostoevsky's *Crime and Punishment* are good examples of this dark outlook.

Sample Test Questions and Rationale (cont.)

(Average)

12. Most children's literature written prior to the development of popular literature was intended to be didactic. Which of the following would not be considered didactic?

    A. "A Visit from St. Nicholas" by Clement Moore

    B. *McGuffy's Reader*

    C. Any version of Cinderella

    D. Parables from the Bible

Answer: A

Rationale: "A Visit from St. Nicholas" is a cheery, non-threatening child's view of "The Night before Christmas." *Didactic* means intended to teach some lesson.

(Average)

13. Written at the sixth-grade reading level, most of S. E. Hinton's novels (for instance, *The Outsiders*) have the greatest reader appeal with:

    A. Sixth graders

    B. Ninth graders

    C. Twelfth graders

    D. Adults

Answer: B

Rationale: Adolescents are concerned with their changing bodies, their relationships with each other and with adults, and their place in society. Reading *The Outsiders* makes them confront problems that they are only now beginning to experience as teenagers, such as gangs and social identity. The book is universal in its appeal to adolescents.

(Average)

14. Children's literature became established in the:

    A. Seventeenth century

    B. Eighteenth century

    C. Nineteenth century

    D. Twentieth century

Answer: A

Rationale: In the seventeenth century, Jean de La Fontaine's fables, Pierre Perreault's tales, Mme d'Aulnoye's novels based on old folktales, and Mme de Beaumont's *Beauty and the Beast* all created a children's literature genre. In England, Perreault was translated, and a work allegedly written by Oliver Smith, *The Renowned History of Little Goody Two Shoes,* also helped to establish children's literature in England.

Sample Test Questions and Rationale (cont.)

(Rigorous)

15. After watching a movie of a train derailment, a child exclaims, "Wow, look how many cars fell off the tracks. There's junk everywhere. The engineer must have really been asleep." Using the facts that the child is impressed by the wreckage and assigns blame to the engineer, a follower of Piaget's theories would estimate the child to be about:

A. Ten years old

B. Twelve years old

C. Fourteen years old

D. Sixteen years old

Answer: A

Rationale: According to Piaget's theory, children seven to eleven years old begin to apply logic to concrete things and experiences. They can combine performance and reasoning to solve problems. They have internalized moral values and are willing to confront rules and adult authority.

(Rigorous)

16. The most significant drawback to applying learning theory research to classroom practice is that:

A. Today's students do not acquire reading skills with the same alacrity as they did when greater emphasis was placed on reading classical literature.

B. Development rates are complicated by geographical and cultural factors. In analyzing literature and in looking for ways to bring a work to life for an audience, the use of comparable themes and ideas from other pieces of literature and from one's own life experiences, including from reading the daily newspaper, is very important and useful.

C. Homogeneous grouping has contributed to faster development of some age groups.

D. Social and environmental conditions have contributed to a more escalated maturity level than research done twenty of more years ago would seem to indicate.

Answer: D

Rationale: Because of rapid social changes, topics that were not interesting to young readers are now topics of books for even younger readers. Many books deal with difficult topics, and the teacher's challenge is to steer students toward books they are ready for and to try to keep them away from books whose content, although well written, is not yet appropriate for the students' level of cognitive and social development. There is sometimes a fine line between responsible teaching and censorship.

Sample Test Questions and Rationale (cont.)

(Rigorous)

17. Which of the following is the best definition of existentialism?

   A. The philosophical doctrine that matter is the only reality and that everything in the world, including thought, will, and feeling, can be explained in terms of matter

   B. A philosophy that views things as they should be or as one would wish them to be

   C. A philosophical and literary movement, variously religious and atheistic, stemming from Kierkegaard and represented by Sartre

   D. The belief that all events are determined by fate and are hence inevitable

Answer: C

Rationale: Even though there are other very important thinkers in the movement known as Existentialism, such as Camus and Merleau-Ponty, Sartre remains the main figure in this movement.

(Rigorous)

18. The following lines from Robert Browning's poem "My Last Duchess" come from an example of what form of dramatic literature?

That's my last Duchess painted on the wall,
Looking as if she were alive. I call
That piece a wonder now: Frà Pandolf's hands
Worked busily a day and there she stands.
Will 't please you sit and look at her?

   A. Tragedy

   B. Comic opera

   C. Dramatis personae

   D. Dramatic monologue

Answer: D

Rationale: A dramatic monologue is a speech given by a character or narrator that reveals characteristics of the character or narrator. This form was first made popular by Robert Browning, a Victorian poet. Tragedy is a form of literature in which the protagonist is overwhelmed by opposing forces. Comic opera is a form of sung music based on a light or happy plot. Dramatis personae is the Latin phrase for the cast of a play.

(Rigorous)

19. "Every one must pass through Vanity Fair to get to the Celestial City" is an allusion from a:

   A. Chinese folk tale

   B. Norse saga

   C. British allegory

   D. German fairy tale

Answer: B

Rationale: This is a reference to John Bunyan's *Pilgrim's Progress* from *This World to That Which Is to Come* (Part I, 1678; Part II, 1684), in which the hero, Christian, flees the City of Destruction and must undergo different trials and tests to get to the Celestial City.

Sample Test Questions and Rationale (cont.)

(Rigorous)

20. **Which author did not write satire?**

    A. Joseph Addison

    B. Richard Steele

    C. Alexander Pope

    D. John Bunyan

Answer: D

Rationale: John Bunyan was a religious writer known for his autobiography *Grace Abounding to the Chief of Sinners,* as well as other books, all religious in their inspiration. Such titles include *The Holy City, or the New Jerusalem* (1665), *A Confession of My Faith, and a Reason of My Practice* (1672), and *The Holy War* (1682).

(Rigorous)

21. **What were two major characteristics of the first American literature?**

    A. Vengefulness and arrogance

    B. Bellicosity and derision

    C. Oral delivery and reverence for the land

    D. Maudlin and self-pitying egocentricism

Answer: D

Rationale: This characteristic can be seen in Captain John Smith's work as well as in William Bradford's and Michael Wigglesworth's works.

(Rigorous)

22. **Hoping to take advantage of the popularity of the Harry Potter series, a teacher develops a unit on mythology comparing the story and characters of Greek and Roman myths with the story and characters of the Harry Potter books. Which of these is a commonality that would link classical literature to popular fiction?**

    A. The characters are gods in human form with human-like characteristics

    B. The settings are realistic places in the world where the characters interact as humans would

    C. The themes center on the universal truths of love and hate and fear

    D. The heroes in the stories are young males and only they can overcome the opposing forces

Answer: C

Rationale: Although the gods in Greek and Roman myths take human form, they are immortal, as gods must be. The characters in the Harry Potter books may be wizards, but they are not immortal. Although the settings in these stories have familiar associations, their worlds are vastly different from those inhabited by mortals and Muggles. While male heroes may dominate the action, the females (Hera, Dianna, Hermione) are powerful as well.

Sample Test Questions and Rationale (cont.)

(Rigorous)

23. **In the following poem, what literary movement is reflected?**

    "My Heart Leaps Up" by William Wordsworth
    My heart leaps up when I behold
       A rainbow in the sky:
    So was it when my life began;
       So is it now I am a man;
    So be it when I shall grow old,
       Or let me die!
    The Child is father of the Man;
    And I could wish my days to be
    Bound each to each by natural
       piety

    A. Neoclassicism

    B. Victorian literature

    C. Romanticism

    D. Naturalism

Answer: C

Rationale: The Romantic period of the nineteenth century is known for its emphasis on feelings, emotions, and passions. William Wordsworth and William Blake were two notable poets from this period. In the neoclassicism of the previous period, the literature echoed the classical ideals of proportion, common sense, and reason over raw emotion and imagination, and the purpose was more didactic than celebratory. The Victorian period of the late nineteenth century exerted more restraint on emotions and feelings. In naturalistic writing, authors depict the world more harshly and more objectively.

SKILL 1.2 Paraphrasing, comparing inferentially) various type: *poetry, essays, drama, and grap*

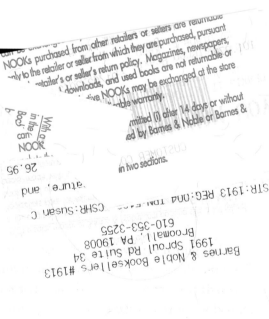

The purpose of any given text is communication to occur, there h text) and a receiver (the audience be internally well-suited to conve receptive capacities of the audienc

Current learning theory establishe: some learn better through auditory learn kinesthetically. With this learι accessible to students with different generally understood than a text pres audio clips, and video clips incorporat outcomes for the most students possible.

...documents enhance the

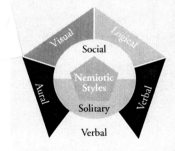

Learning Styles

Learn more about learning styles at:

http://www.learning-styles-online.com/overview/

Aside from considerations of learning style, a text that is presented in a medium that suits the cultural or experiential background of its audience will be better received than one presented without consideration of such characteristics.

Obviously, a text has a better chance of conveying its message if it is presented in an engaging manner. For instance, if a story is read in a monotone, the outcome is surely less positive than if the same story is read with prosody. Furthermore, today's students are used to more media stimulation than the adults who typically teach them. Without sufficient stimulation, students may have difficulty maintaining attention.

Still another way in which medium of text presentation can affect a reader's experience involves whether the text provides opportunities for students to participate in brain-friendly processing routines. Such routines include opportunities for various types of role playing, for discussion of ethical dilemmas (one person talks, the other listens and then paraphrases), and for dramatization of scenes or issues within the text.

Interpreting Text

To **INTERPRET** means essentially to read with understanding and appreciation. It is not as daunting as it is made out to be. Simple techniques for interpreting literature follow.

INFERENCING is a process whereby the reader makes a reasonable judgment based on the information given. You can develop and enhance this key skill by reading an expository book aloud. Next, demonstrate for the students the following reading habits: looking for clues, using clues to figure out what the author means/intends, and incorporating prior knowledge about the topic.

Identifying main ideas in an expository text is easier when the reader has an explicit strategy for identifying important information. Students can make this strategy part of their everyday reading style. Have students "walk" through the following exercises during guided reading sessions.

1. Identify the main topic of the passage. It will be what most of the passage is about.

2. Be on the lookout for a sentence within the expository passage that summarizes the key information in the paragraph.

3. Read the rest of the passage in light of this information, and also note which information in the paragraph is less important. The important information can be used to formulate the author's main idea. You can use some of the author's own language in stating the main idea.

> **INTERPRET:** to read a piece of literature with understanding and appreciation

> **INFERENCING:** a process whereby the reader makes a reasonable judgment based on the information given

MONITORING means self-clarifying. As they read, students often realize that what they are reading is not making sense. They then need a plan for making sense out of the excerpt—a "stop and think" strategy. If they conclude that the material is not making sense, they can reread the text, read ahead in the text, look up unknown words, or ask for help.

> **MONITORING:** self-clarifying, or being aware of whether the material one is reading makes sense

Some readers will try these approaches without ever being explicitly taught to use them in school by a teacher. However, in most cases, these strategies need to be explicitly modeled and practiced under the guidance of the teacher.

SUMMARIZING asks the reader to pull into a cohesive whole the essential bits of information within a longer passage or excerpt of text. Readers can be taught to summarize informational or expository text by following these guidelines:

> **SUMMARIZING:** asks the reader to pull into a cohesive whole the essential bits of information within a longer passage or excerpt of text

1. First, look at the topic sentence of the paragraph or the text and ignore the trivia

2. Next, search for information that has been mentioned more than once and make sure it is included only once in the summary

3. Find related ideas or items and group them under a unifying heading

4. Search for and identify a main idea sentence

5. Finally, write the summary

Generating questions is a way to motivate and enhance readers' comprehension because they become actively involved. The following guidelines will help generate meaningful questions that will trigger constructive reading of expository texts.

1. First, readers should preview the text by reading the titles and subheadings and looking at any illustrations and pictures. Then they should read the first paragraph. The initial preview should yield an impressive batch of specific questions.

2. Next, readers should ask themselves a "think" question. After they write down the question, they should read to find important information to answer their "think" question. Ask that they write down the answer they found and copy the sentence or sentences where they found the answer. Also have them consider whether, in light of further reading through the text, their original question was a good one.

Determining the author's context entails examining the author's feelings, beliefs, past experiences, goals, needs, and physical environment as suggested by the prose. Readers' experiences will be enriched if they can appreciate and understand how these elements may have affected the writing.

Understanding symbols can help to unearth a meaning the author might have intended but not expressed or even never intended at all. Often referred to as a sign, a SYMBOL designates something that stands for something else. In most cases, a symbol stands for something that has a deeper meaning than its literal denotation. Symbols can have personal, cultural, or universal associations.

SYMBOL: designates something that stands for something else. In most cases, a symbol stands for something that has a deeper meaning than its literal denotation

---

Sample Test Questions and Rationale

(Average)

1. Sometimes readers are asked to demonstrate their understanding of a text. This might include all of the following except:

   A. Role playing

   B. Paraphrasing

   C. Storyboarding a part of the story with dialogue bubbles

   D. Reading the story aloud

   Answer: D

   Rationale: Reading the text aloud may help readers understand the text, but it won't demonstrate their understanding of it. By role playing, paraphrasing, or storyboarding, readers will convey their understanding of the purpose and main ideas of the text.

(Average)

2. Which of the following reading strategies calls for higher-order cognitive skills?

   A. Making predictions

   B. Summarizing

   C. Monitoring

   D. Making inferences

   Answer: D

   Rationale: Making inferences involves using other reading skills such as making predictions, skimming, scanning, summarizing, and then coming to conclusions or making inferences that are not directly stated in the text.

SKILL Identifying and interpreting figurative language and other literary
1.3 elements *(e.g., metaphor, simile, voice, point of view, tone, style, setting,*
diction, mood, allusions, irony, clichés, analogy, hyperbole, personification,
alliteration, and foreshadowing)

Figurative Language

Figurative language allows for the statement of truths that more literal language cannot provide. Skillfully used, a figure of speech will help the reader see more clearly and focus upon particulars. Figures of speech add many dimensions of richness to our reading and understanding; they also allow many opportunities for worthwhile analysis.

Poets use figures of speech to sharpen the effect and meaning of their poems and to help readers see things in ways they have never seen them before. Marianne Moore observed that a fir tree has "an emerald turkey-foot at the top." Her poem makes us aware of something we probably had never noticed before. The sudden recognition of the likeness yields pleasure in the reading.

In analyzing a poem on the basis of its figures of speech, ask the following questions:

- What does the figure of speech do for the poem?
- Does it underscore meaning?
- Does it intensify understanding?
- Does it increase the intensity of our response?

Essential terminology and literary devices germane to literary analysis are included in the following table.

Note that in alliteration, the words only have to be close to one another. Alliteration that attempts to connect too many words is little more than a tongue twister.

TERMS USED IN LITERARY ANALYSIS	
Alliteration	Alliteration occurs when the initial sounds of a word (beginning with either a consonant or a vowel) are repeated in close succession. Examples include "Athena and Apollo," "Nate never knows," and "people who pen poetry." The function of alliteration, like rhyme, might be to accentuate the beauty of language in a given context, or to unite words or concepts through a kind of repetition. Alliteration, like rhyme, can follow specific patterns. Sometimes the consonants aren't always the initial ones, but they are generally the stressed syllables. Alliteration is less common than rhyme, but because it is less common, it can call our attention to a word or line in a poem that might not have the same emphasis otherwise. In its simplest form, alliteration reinforces one or two consonant sounds. An example is from Shakespeare's Sonnet #12: *When I do count the clock that tells the time* Some poets have used more complex patterns of alliteration by creating consonants both at the beginnings of words and at the beginnings of stressed syllables within words. An example is from Shelley's "Stanzas Written in Dejection Near Naples": *The City's voice itself is soft like Solitude's*
Antithesis	Balanced writing about conflicting ideas, usually expressed in sentence form. Some examples are "expanding from the center," "shedding old habits," and "searching but never finding."
Aphorism	A focused, succinct expression about life from a sagacious viewpoint. Writings by Ben Franklin, Sir Francis Bacon, and Alexander Pope contain many aphorisms. "Whatever is begun in anger ends in shame" is an aphorism by Benjamin Franklin.

Table continued on next page

Apostrophe	Literary device of addressing an absent or dead person, an abstract idea, or an inanimate object. Sonneteers such as Sir Thomas Wyatt, John Keats, and William Wordsworth have addressed the moon, the stars, and the dead Milton.
	For example, in William Shakespeare's *Julius Caesar*, Mark Antony addresses the corpse of Caesar in the speech that begins:
	O, pardon me, thou bleeding piece of earth / That I am meek and gentle with these butchers! / Thou art the ruins of the noblest man / That ever lived in the tide of times. / Woe to the hand that shed this costly blood!
Assonance	If alliteration occurs at the beginning of a word and rhyme at the end, assonance takes the middle territory. Assonance occurs when the vowel sound within a word matches the same sound in a nearby word, but the surrounding consonant sounds are different. "Tune" and "June" are rhymes; "tune" and "food" are assonant. The function of assonance is frequently the same as end rhyme or alliteration; all serve to give a sense of continuity or fluidity to the verse. Assonance can be especially effective when rhyme is absent: It gives the poet more flexibility, and it is not typically used as part of a predetermined pattern. Like alliteration, it does not so much determine the structure or form of a poem but rather is more ornamental.
Bathos	A ludicrous attempt to portray pathos—that is, to evoke pity, sympathy, or sorrow. Bathos may result from inappropriately dignifying the commonplace, using elevated language to describe something trivial, or from greatly exaggerated pathos.
Blank Verse	Poetry written in iambic pentameter but unrhymed. Works by Shakespeare and Milton are epitomes of blank verse. Milton's *Paradise Lost* states:
	Illumine, what is low raise and support, / That to the highth of this great argument / I may assert Eternal Providence / And justify the ways of God to men.
Caesura	A pause, usually signaled by punctuation, in a line of poetry. The earliest usage occurs in *Beowulf*, the first English epic dating from the Anglo-Saxon era.
	"To err is human, // to forgive, divine." (Pope)

For more information, consult Glossary of Poetry Terms:

http://www.infoplease.com/ spot/pmglossary1.html

Table continued on next page

Climax	A number of phrases or sentences are arranged in ascending order of rhetorical forcefulness. Here is an example from Melville's *Moby Dick*: *All that most maddens and torments; all that stirs up the lees of things; all truth with malice in it; all that cracks the sinews and cakes the brain; all the subtle demonisms of life and thought; all evil, to crazy Ahab, were visibly personified and made practically assailable in Moby Dick.*
Conceit	A comparison, usually in verse, between seemingly disparate objects or concepts. John Donne's metaphysical poetry contains many clever conceits. For instance, Donne's "The Flea" (1633) compares a flea bite to the act of love; and in "A Valediction: Forbidding Mourning" (1633) separated lovers are likened to the legs of a compass, the leg drawing the circle eventually returning home to "the fixed foot."
Connotation	The ripple effect surrounding the implications and associations of a given word, distinct from the denotative or literal meaning. For example, the word rest in *Hamlet's* "Good night, sweet prince, and flights of angels sing thee to thy rest" refers to a burial.
Consonance	The repeated use of similar consonant sounds, most often in poetry. "Sally sat sifting seashells by the seashore" is a familiar example.
Couplet	Two rhyming lines of poetry. Shakespeare's sonnets end in heroic couplets written in iambic pentameter. Pope is also a master of the couplet. His *Rape of the Lock* is written entirely in heroic couplets.
Denotation	What a word literally means, as opposed to its connotative meaning.
Diction	The right word in the right place for the right purpose. The hallmark of a great writer is precise, unusual, and memorable diction.
Epiphany	The moment when something is realized and comprehension sets in. James Joyce used this device in his short story collection *The Dubliners*.
Euphemism	The substitution of an agreeable or inoffensive term for one that might offend or suggest something unpleasant. Many euphemisms are used to refer to death, such as "passed away," "crossed over," or nowadays "passed."
Exposition	Fill-in or background information about characters meant to clarify and add to the narrative; the initial plot element that precedes the buildup of conflict.
Free Verse	Poetry that does not have any predictable meter or patterning. Margaret Atwood, e. e. cummings, and Ted Hughes write in this form.
Hyperbole	Exaggeration for a specific effect. An example from Shakespeare's *The Merchant of Venice*: *Why, if two gods should play some heavenly match* *And on the wager lay two earthly women,* *And Portia one, there must be something else* *Pawned with the other, for the poor rude world* *Hath not her fellow.*

Table continued on next page

Iambic Pentameter	The two elements in a set five-foot line of poetry. An iamb is two syllables, unaccented and accented, per foot or measure. Pentameter means five feet of these iambs per line or ten syllables.
Imagery	Imagery can be described as a word or sequence of words that refers to any sensory experience—that is, anything that can be seen, tasted, smelled, heard, or felt on the skin or fingers. While prose writers may also use these images, they are most distinctive of poetry. The poet intends to make an experience available to the reader. In order to do that, the poet must appeal to one of the senses. The most often used sense, of course, is the visual sense. The poet will deliberately paint a scene in such a way that the reader can "see" it. However, the purpose is not simply to stir the visceral feeling but also to stir the emotions. A good example is "The Piercing Chill" by Taniguchi Buson (1715–1783): *The piercing chill I feel:* *My dead wife's comb, in our bedroom,* *Under my heel . . .* In only a few short words, the reader can feel many things: the shock that might come from touching the corpse, a literal sense of death, the contrast between the woman's death and the memories the poet has of her when she was alive. Imagery might be defined as speaking of the abstract in concrete terms—a powerful device in the hands of a skillful poet.
Inversion	An atypical sentence meant to create a given effect or interest. Francis Bacon and Milton's work use inversion successfully. Emily Dickinson was fond of arranging words outside of their familiar order. For example, in "Chartless," she writes "Yet know I how the heather looks" and "Yet certain am I of the spot." Instead of saying "Yet I know" and "Yet I am certain", she reverses the usual order and shifts the emphasis to the more important words.
Irony	An unexpected disparity between what is written or stated and what is really meant or implied by the author. Verbal, dramatic, and situational are the three literary ironies. *Verbal irony* is when an author says one thing and means something else. *Dramatic irony* is when an audience perceives something that a character in the literature does not know. *Irony of situation* is a discrepancy between the expected result and actual results. Shakespeare's plays contain numerous and highly effective uses of irony. O. Henry's short stories have ironic endings. In poetry, irony is often used as a sophisticated or resigned awareness of contrast between what is and what ought to be and expresses a controlled pathos without sentimentality. An early example is the Greek comic character Eiron, a clever underdog who by his wit repeatedly triumphs over the boastful character Alazon.
Kenning	Another way to describe a person, place, or thing so as to avoid prosaic repetition. The earliest examples can be found in Anglo-Saxon literature such as *Beowulf* and "The Seafarer." In "The Seafarer," instead of writing "King Hrothgar," the anonymous monk wrote "great Ring-Giver" or "Father of his people." A lake becomes "the swans' way," and the ocean or sea becomes "the great whale's way." In ancient Greek literature, this device was called an *epithet*.

Table continued on next page

Malapropism	A verbal blunder in which one word is replaced by another similar in sound but different in meaning. This term derives from Sheridan's character Mrs. Malaprop in *The Rivals* (1775). Thinking of the geography of contiguous countries, Mrs. Malaprop spoke of the "geometry" of "contagious countries." Meaning "the pinnacle of perfection," she describes someone as the "pineapple of perfection."
Metaphor	Indirect comparison between two things. It is the use of a word or phrase denoting one kind of object or action in place of another to suggest a comparison between them. While poets use metaphors extensively, they are also integral to everyday speech. For example, chairs are said to have "legs" and "arms" although we know that in reality only humans and other animals have these appendages.
Metaphysical Poetry	Verse characterized by ingenious wit, unparalleled imagery, and clever conceits. One of the greatest metaphysical poets is John Donne. Henry Vaughan and other seventeenth century British poets contributed to the metaphysical poetry movement, as in "The World": *"I saw eternity the other night, / like a great being of pure and endless light."*
Metonymy	Use of an object or idea closely identified with another object or idea to represent the second. "Hit the books" means "go study." "Washington, D.C." means "the U.S. government," and "the White House" means "the U.S. president."
Motif	A key, oft-repeated phrase, name, or idea in a literary work. Dorset/Wessex in Hardy's novels and the moors and the harsh weather in the Bronte sisters' novels model effective use of motifs. Shakespeare's *Romeo and Juliet* represents the motif of ill-fated young lovers.
Ottava Rima	A specific eight-line stanza of poetry whose rhyme scheme is abababcc. Lord Byron's mock epic *Don Juan* is written in ottava rima.
Onomatopoeia	The naming of a thing or action by a vocal imitation of the sound associated with it, such as "buzz" or "hiss." A good example comes from "The Brook" by Tennyson: *I chatter over stony ways,* *In little sharps and trebles,* *I bubble into eddying bays,* *I babble on the pebbles.*

Table continued on next page

Share this Web site with your students— NewsHour Extra: Poetry:

http://www.pbs.org/ newshour/extra/poetry/#

Oxymoron	A contradiction in terms deliberately employed for effect. An oxymoron is usually seen in a qualifying adjective whose meaning is contrary to that of the noun it modifies, such as "wise folly." Other examples include "jumbo shrimp," "unkindly kind," or singer John Mellencamp's line "It hurts so good."
Paradox	A seemingly untrue statement that when examined more closely proves to be true. John Donne's sonnet "Death Be Not Proud" postulates that death shall die and humans will triumph over death, an idea at first thought not true but ultimately explained and proven in this sonnet.
Parallelism	The arrangement of ideas in phrases, sentences, and paragraphs that balance one element with another of equal importance and similar wording. An example is seen in Francis Bacon's *Of Studies*: "Reading maketh a full man, conference a ready man, and writing an exact man." The psalms in the King James Version of the Bible contain many examples of parallelism.
Personification	Human characteristics are attributed to an inanimate object, an abstract quality, or an animal. For example, John Bunyan named characters Death, Knowledge, Giant Despair, Sloth, and Piety in his work *Pilgrim's Progress*. The metaphor of an arm of a chair is a form of personification. Carl Sandburg, in his poem "Fog," writes, *"The fog comes / on little cat feet. // It sits looking / over harbor and city / on silent haunches / and then moves on."*
Quatrain	A poetic stanza composed of four lines. A Shakespearean or Elizabethan sonnet is made up of three quatrains and ends with a heroic couplet.
Scansion	The two-part analysis of a poetic line: Count the number of syllables per line and determine where the accents fall; then divide the line into metric feet. Name the meter by the type and number of feet. Much is written about scanning poetry. Try not to inundate your students with this jargon; rather, allow them to feel the power of the poets' words, ideas, and images instead.
Slant Rhyme	Occurs when the final consonant sounds are the same but the vowels are different. Slant rhyme occurs frequently in Irish, Welsh, and Icelandic verse. Examples include "green and gone," "that and hit," "ill and shell."

Table continued on next page

Simile	Direct comparison between two things using "like," "as," or "such as." For example: "My love is like a red, red rose."
Soliloquy	A highlighted speech, in drama, usually delivered by a major character, expounding on the author's philosophy or expressing universal truths. A soliloquy is given by the character alone on the stage, as in Hamlet's famous "To be or not to be" soliloquy.
Spenserian Stanza	Invented by Sir Edmund Spenser for use in *The Faerie Queene*, his epic poem honoring Queen Elizabeth I. Each stanza consists of nine lines, eight in iambic parameter. The ninth line, called an alexandrine, has two extra syllables or one additional foot.
Sprung Rhythm	Invented and used extensively by the poet Gerard Manley Hopkins. Sprung rhythm consists of variable meter, which combines stressed and unstressed syllables fashioned by the author. See "Pied Beauty" or "God's Grandeur."
Stream of Consciousness	A style of writing that reflects the mental processes of the characters, expressing at times jumbled memories, feelings, and dreams. James Joyce, Virginia Woolf, and William Faulkner use stream of consciousness in their writings.
Symbolism	A symbol is an object or action that can be observed with the senses in addition to its suggesting many other things. The lion is a symbol of courage; the cross is a symbol of Christianity; the color green is a symbol of envy. These symbols can almost be defined as metaphors because society agrees on their meaning. Symbols used in literature are usually of a different sort. They tend to be private and personal; their significance is only evident in the context of the work wherein they are used. A good example of a symbol in poetry is the "mending wall" in Frost's poem of the same name._ A symbol can have more than one meaning, and the meaning may be as personal as the memories and experiences of the particular reader. In analyzing a poem or a story, students should identify the symbols and their possible meanings._ Looking for symbols is often challenging, however, the following suggestions may be useful: • Pick out all references to concrete objects such as newspapers, black cats, or other nouns. Note any that the poet emphasizes by describing them in detail, repeating them, or placing them at the very beginning or ending of a poem. • Ask yourself, what is the poem about? Paraphrase the poem and determine whether its meaning depends on certain concrete objects. Then ponder what the concrete object symbolizes in the particular poem. • Look for a character with the name of a prophet who only utters prophecies or a trio of women who resemble the Three Fates. A symbol may be a part of a person's body, such as the eye of the murder victim in Poe's story "The Tell-Tale Heart," or a look, a voice, or a mannerism._ Some things a symbol is *not*: an abstraction such as truth, death, or love; in narrative, a well-developed character who is not at all mysterious; the second term in a metaphor. In Emily Dickinson's "The Lightning Is a Yellow Fork," the symbol is the lightning, not the fork.

Table continued on next page

Synecdoche	A synecdoche is a figure of speech in which the word for part of something is used to mean the whole; for example, "sail" for "boat," or vice versa.
Terza Rima	A series of poetic stanzas that use the recurrent rhyme scheme of aba, bcb, cdc, ded, and so forth. The second-generation Romantic poets—Keats, Byron, Shelley, and to a lesser degree Yeats—used this Italian verse form, especially in their odes. Dante used terza rima in *The Divine Comedy*.
Tone	The discernible attitude inherent in an author's work regarding the subject, readership, or characters. Jonathan Swift or Pope's tone is satirical. James Boswell's tone toward Samuel Johnson is admiring.
Wit	Writing characterized by genius, keenness, and sagacity as expressed through clever use of language. Alexander Pope and the Augustans wrote about and were said to possess wit.

Literary Elements

The elements of fiction vary in importance and development from story to story. Some stories are mainly plot-driven, while others are character studies. Some stories are so tightly constructed that all elements work together to develop the theme and entertain the reader. Although readers can certainly enjoy a story without an in-depth understanding of its literary elements, understanding these elements can help readers develop a deeper appreciation for an author's talent and writing skill.

Read about tone and style:

http://www.delmar.edu/ engl/wrtctr/handouts/ ToneStyle.pdf

Plot

PLOT is sometimes called action, or the sequence of the events. If the plot does not *move*, the story quickly dies. Therefore, the successful writer of stories uses a wide variety of active verbs in creative and unusual ways. If a reader is kept interested by the movement of the story, the experience of reading it will be pleasurable. The reader will probably want to read more of this author's work. Careful, unique, and unusual choices of active verbs will bring about that effect.

PLOT: the action or the sequence of events in a story

William Faulkner is a good example of a successful writer whose stories are lively and memorable because of his use of unusual active verbs. In analyzing the development of plot, analytical readers will look at the verbs. However, the development of believable conflicts is also vital. If there is no conflict, there is no story. In critical thinking readers should ask: What devices does a writer use to develop the conflicts, and are they real and believable?

Character

Character is portrayed in many ways: description of physical characteristics, dialogue, interior monologue, the attitudes of other characters toward the character in question, and so on.

If the description of a character's appearance is a visual one, then the reader must be able to *see* the character. What is the shape of the character's nose? What color are his or her eyes? How tall or how short is this character? Is he or she thin or chubby? How does the character move? How does the character walk? Writers choose terms that will create a picture for the reader. It's not enough to say that the character's eyes are blue, for example. What kind of blue? Often the color of eyes is compared to something else to enhance the readers' ability to visualize the character.

A good test of characterization is the level of emotional involvement of the reader in the character. If the reader is to become involved, the description must provide an actual experience—seeing, smelling, hearing, tasting, or feeling. In the following example, Isaac Asimov deftly describes a character both directly and indirectly.

> *Undersecretary Albert Minnim was a small, compact man, ruddy of skin, and graying, with the angles of his body smoothed down and softened. He exuded an air of cleanliness and smelled faintly of tonic. It all spoke of the good things of life that came with the liberal rations obtained by those high in Administration.*
>
> —Isaac Asimov, *The Robot Series: The Naked Sun*

Dialogue will also reflect characteristics. Is it clipped? Is it highly dialectal? Does a character rely on colloquialisms (*y'all, bling*)? The ability to portray the speech of a character can make or break a story.

The kind of person the character is in the mind of the reader is dependent on impressions created by description and dialogue. How do other characters feel about this character as revealed by their treatment of him or her, their discussions of him or her with each other, or their overt descriptions of the character? For example, the line "John, of course, can't be trusted with another person's possessions" reveals another character's impression of John. In analyzing a story, it's useful to discuss the devices used to produce character.

A good portrayal of a character includes:

• Description of physical characteristics
• Speech patterns/dialogue
• Interior monologue
• Other characters' opinions of the character in question

Setting

Setting may be visual, temporal, psychological, or social. In Edgar Allan Poe's description of the house in "The Fall of the House of Usher," as the protagonist/narrator approaches the house, the air of dread and gloom that pervades the story is caught in the setting and sets the stage for the story. A setting may also be symbolic, as it is in Poe's story, where the house is a symbol of the family that lives in it. As the house disintegrates, so does the family.

The language used in all of aspects of a story—plot, character, and setting—creates the MOOD of a story. Poe's first sentence in "The Fall of the House of Usher" establishes the mood of the story:

> During the whole of a dull, dark, and soundless day in the autumn of the year, when the clouds hung oppressively low in the heavens, I had been passing alone, on horseback, through a singularly dreary tract of country; and at length found myself, as the shades of the evening drew on, within view of the melancholy House of Usher.

MOOD: the "feeling" of a story evoked by the language used to describe plot, character, and setting

Why did the author write this story? This question will lead to the THEME—the underlying main idea. Whether a story is escapist or interpretive, it will have a controlling idea that is integral to its development. This idea is more than a topic (love, anger, guilt, jealousy); it is the author's view of the topic.

THEME: the underlying main idea of a story

Sometimes the title of a story will help reveal the theme. For example, in "The Tell-Tale Heart," Poe tells us a story about guilt and the effect it has on one's conscience. The title foreshadows the outcome and helps the reader understand the theme.

Sample Test Questions and Rationale

(Easy)

1. **Which definition best defines** *diction*?

    A. The specific word choices used by an author to create a particular mood or feeling in the reader

    B. Writing that explains something thoroughly

    C. The background, or exposition, for a short story or drama

    D. Word choices that help teach a truth or moral

    Answer: A

    Rationale: Diction refers to an author's choice of words, expressions, and style to convey his or her meaning.

(Average)

2. **In the following quotation, Marc Antony addresses the dead body of Caesar as though it were still a living being.**

    O, pardon me, thou
    Bleeding piece of earth
    That I am meek and gentle
    with
    These butchers.
        –Marc Antony from *Julius Caesar*

    This passage employs:

    A. Apostrophe

    B. Allusion

    C. Antithesis

    D. Anachronism

    Answer: A

    Rationale: This rhetorical figure addresses personified things, absent people, or gods. An allusion, on the other hand, is a quick reference to a character or event known to the public. An antithesis is a contrast between two opposing viewpoints, ideas, or characters. An anachronism is the placing of an object or person out of the time period of the text. The best-known example is the clock in Shakespeare's *Julius Caesar*.

(Average)

3. **The literary device of personification is used in which example below?**

    A. "Beg me no beggary by soul or parents, whining dog!"

    B. "Happiness sped through the halls, cajoling as it went."

    C. "O wind thy horn, thou proud fellow."

    D. "And that one talent which is death to hide."

    Answer: B

    Rationale: Happiness, an abstract concept, is described as if it were a person with the words "sped" and "cajoling."

Sample Test Questions and Rationale (cont.)

(Average)

4. **An extended metaphor comparing two very dissimilar things (one lofty, one lowly) is a definition of a(n):**

   A. Antithesis

   B. Aphorism

   C. Apostrophe

   D. Conceit

Answer: D

Rationale: A conceit is an unusually far-fetched metaphor in which an object, person, or situation is presented in a parallel and simpler analogue between two apparently very different things or feelings—one very sophisticated and one very ordinary—usually taken either from nature or a well-known, everyday concept, familiar to both reader and author alike. The conceit was first developed by Petrarch and spread to England in the sixteenth century.

(Average)

5. **Which of the following is a characteristic of blank verse?**

   A. Meter in iambic pentameter

   B. Clearly specified rhyme scheme

   C. Lack of figurative language

   D. Unspecified rhythm

Answer: A

Rationale: An iamb is a metrical unit of verse having one unstressed syllable followed by one stressed syllable. This is the most commonly used metrical verse in English and American poetry. Iambic pentameter is a ten-syllable verse made up of five of these metrical units, either rhymed as in sonnets, or unrhymed as in blank verse.

(Average)

6. **Which is the best definition of free verse, or *vers libre*?**

   A. Poetry that consists of an unaccented syllable followed by an unaccented sound

   B. Short lyrical poetry written to entertain but with an instructive purpose

   C. Poetry that does not have a uniform pattern of rhythm

   D. A poem that tells the story and has a plot

Answer: C

Rationale: Free verse has lines of irregular length (but it does not run on like prose).

Sample Test Questions and Rationale (cont.)

(Rigorous)

7. **Which term best describes the form of the following poetic excerpt?**

> And more to lulle him in his
> slumber soft,
> A trickling streake from high rock
> tumbling downe,
> And ever-drizzling raine upon
> the loft.
> Mixt with a murmuring winde,
> much like a swowne
> No other noyse, nor peoples
> troubles cryes.
> As still we wont t'annoy the
> walle'd towne,
> Might there be heard: but
> careless Quiet lyes,
> Wrapt in eternall silence farre
> from enemyes.

A. Ballad

B. Elegy

C. Spenserian stanza

D. Ottava rima

Answer: D

Rationale: The ottava rima is a specific eight-line stanza whose rhyme scheme is abababcc. A ballad is a narrative poem. An elegy is a form of lyric poetry typically used to mourn someone who has died. A form of the English sonnet created by Edmond Spenser combines the English form and the Italian. The Spenserian sonnet follows the English quatrain and couplet pattern but resembles the Italian in its rhyme scheme, which is linked: abab bcbc cdcd ee.

(Rigorous)

8. **In the phrase "The Cabinet conferred with the President,"** *Cabinet* **is an example of a(n):**

A. Metonym

B. Synecdoche

C. Metaphor

D. Allusion

Answer: B

Rationale: In a synecdoche, a whole is referred to by naming a part of it. Also, a synecdoche can stand for the whole of which it is a part; for example, the *Cabinet* stands for the *government*. Metonymy is the substitution of a word for a related word. For example, "hit the books" means "to study." A metaphor is a comparison such as "a cat burglar." An allusion is a reference to someone or something in history. To say that "she met her Waterloo and was fired" alludes to Napoleon's defeat at Waterloo.

Sample Test Questions and Rationale (cont.)

(Rigorous)

9. What syntactic device is most evident in the following excerpt from Abraham Lincoln's "Gettysburg Address"?

It is rather for us to be here dedicated to the great task remaining before us—that from these honored dead we take increased devotion to that cause for which they gave the last full measure of devotion—that we here highly resolve that these dead shall not have died in vain— that this nation, under God, shall have a new birth of freedom—and that govern- ment of the people, by the people, for the people, shall not perish from the earth.

A. Affective connotation

B. Informative denotation

C. Allusion

D. Parallelism

Answer: D

Rationale: Parallelism is the rep- etition of grammatical structure. In speeches such as this, as well as the speeches of Martin Luther King, Jr., parallel structure cre- ates a rhythm and a balance of related ideas. Lincoln's repetition of clauses beginning with "that" ties four examples back "to the great task." Connotation is the emotional attachment of words; denotation is the literal meaning of words. Allusion is a reference to a historic event, person, or place

---

SKILL 1.4 Understand how patterns, structures, and characteristics of literary forms and genres may influence the meaning and effect of work

Literary forms

Definitions of selected genres

The major literary genres include allegory, ballad, drama, epic, epistle, essay, fable, novel, poem, romance, and short story.

Check out more than 180 items—allegories, fables, parables, and teaching tales:

http://www.insight-books. com/ALLF

LITERARY GENRES	
Allegory	A story in verse or prose with characters representing virtues and vices. There are two meanings, symbolic and literal. John Bunyan's *The Pilgrim's Progress* is the most renowned of this genre.
Drama	A play—comedy, modern, or tragedy—typically in five acts. Traditionalists and neoclassicists adhere to Aristotle's unities of time, place, and action. Plot development is advanced through dialogue. Literary devices include asides, soliloquies, and the chorus, which represents public opinion. Many agree that the greatest of all dramatists/playwrights is William Shakespeare. Other dramaturges include Henrik Ibsen, Tennessee Williams, Arthur Miller, George Bernard Shaw, Tom Stoppard, Jean Racine, Moliére (Jean Baptiste de Poquelin), Sophocles, Aeschylus, Euripides, and Aristophanes.
Epic	A long poem, usually of book length, reflecting values inherent in the generative society. Epic devices include an invocation to a muse for inspiration, a purpose for writing, a universal setting, a protagonist and an antagonist who possess supernatural strength and acumen, and interventions of God or the gods. Understandably, there are very few epics: Homer's *Iliad* and *Odyssey*, Virgil's *Aeneid*, John Milton's *Paradise Lost*, Edmund Spenser's *The Faerie Queene*, Elizabeth Barrett Browning's *Aurora Leigh*, and Alexander Pope's mock-epic, *The Rape of the Lock*.
Epistle	A letter that was not necessarily intended for public distribution but that, because of the fame of the sender and/or recipient, became public domain. Paul wrote epistles that were later placed in the Bible.
Essay	Typically a limited-length prose work focusing on a topic and propounding a definite point of view and authoritative tone. Great essayists include Thomas Carlyle, Charles Lamb, Thomas DeQuincy, Ralph Waldo Emerson, and Michel de Montaigne, who is credited with defining this genre.
Fable	A terse tale offering up a moral or exemplum. Geoffrey Chaucer's "The Nun's Priest's Tale" is a fine example of a *bête fabliau* or beast fable in which animals speak and act characteristically human, illustrating human foibles.
Legend	A traditional narrative or collection of related narratives, popularly regarded as historically factual but actually a mixture of fact and fiction.

Table continued on next page

Myth	A story that is more or less universally shared within a culture to explain its history and traditions.
Novel	The longest form of fictional prose containing a variety of characterizations, settings, local color, and regionalism. Most novels have complex plots, expanded description, and attention to detail. Some of the great novelists include Jane Austen, Charlotte Brontë, Emily Brontë, Mark Twain, Leo Tolstoy, Victor Hugo, Thomas Hardy, Charles Dickens, Nathaniel Hawthorne, E.M. Forster, and Gustave Flaubert.
Poem	A verse whose only requirement is rhythm. Subgenres include fixed types of literature such as the sonnet, elegy, ode, pastoral, and villanelle. Unfixed types of literature include blank verse and dramatic monologue.
Romance	A highly imaginative tale set in a fantastical realm dealing with the conflicts between heroes and villains and/or monsters. "The Knight's Tale" from Chaucer's *Canterbury Tales*, *Sir Gawain and the Green Knight* and John Keats' "The Eve of St. Agnes" are prime representatives.
Short Story	Typically a terse narrative with less developmental background about characters. A short story may include description, the author's point of view, and tone. Edgar Allen Poe emphasized that a successful short story should create one focused impact. Some great short story writers are Ernest Hemingway, William Faulkner, Mark Twain, James Joyce, Shirley Jackson, Flannery O'Connor, Guy de Maupasssant, Saki (H.H. Munro), Edgar Allen Poe, and Alexander Pushkin.

Types of drama

Since the days of the Greeks, drama has undergone many permutations. Definitions that were once rigid have softened as theater has become a more accurate picture of the lives it depicts.

Tragedy

The classic definition, dating back to Aristotle, is that a tragedy is a work of drama, written in either prose or poetry, telling the story of a brave, noble hero who, because of some tragic character flaw (*hamartia*), brings ruin upon himself or herself. It is characterized by serious, poetic language that evokes pity and fear.

In modern times, dramatists have tried to update drama's image by drawing its main characters from the middle class and showing their nobility through their

Read more about Greek tragedy:

http://depthome.brooklyn. cuny.edu/classics/dunkle/ studyguide/tragedy.htm

nature instead of their societal standing. Sophocles' *Oedipus Rex* is the classic example of tragedy, while works of Henrik Ibsen and Arthur Miller epitomize modern tragedy.

Comedy

The comedic form of dramatic literature is meant to amuse and often ends happily. It uses techniques such as satire or parody, and can take many forms, from farce to burlesque. Examples include Dante Alighieri's *The Divine Comedy,* Noel Coward's play *Private Lives,* some of Geoffrey Chaucer's *Canterbury Tales,* and some of William Shakespeare's plays, such as *A Midsummer Night's Dream.*

Comic drama

As the name suggests, comic drama is a combination of serious and light elements. It originated in the Middle Ages under the auspices of the Catholic Church, which tried to reach the common people via mystery and morality plays. The modern equivalent would be television's "dramedies," which present a serious plot with comic elements.

Melodrama

Melodrama is a form of extreme drama that has a somewhat formulaic structure. The hero saves the day from the dastardly villain and wins the heart of the wholesome heroine. The word is a combination of *melody* and *drama,* because music was used to heighten the emotions. Although the term is sometimes used as a critical pejorative, it is a true art form with stereotyped characters and plot manipulations. Oftentimes, various operas are melodramatic, so it should be no surprise that soap operas are considered part of this genre.

Farce

Farce is an extreme form of comedy marked by physical humor, unlikely situations, and stereotyped characters. It is often considered a form of low comedy and is represented in movies by the Three Stooges, Charlie Chaplin, Harold Lloyd, and Buster Keaton. Today's students might easily recognize farce in movies such as *Dumb and Dumber, There's Something About Mary,* and *Talladega Nights.*

Dramatic monologue

A dramatic monologue is a speech given by an actor as if talking to himself or herself, but actually intended for the audience. It reveals key aspects of the character's psyche and sheds insight on the situation at hand. The audience takes the part of the silent listener, passing judgment and giving sympathy at the same time. This form was used predominantly by Victorian poet Robert Browning.

Tempo

Tempo refers to pace. Dialogue must be connected to motivation and detail. The director is concerned with pace and seeks a variation of tempo. If the overall pace is too slow, then the action becomes dull and dragging. If the overall pace is too fast, then the audience will not be able to understand what is going on.

Dramatic arc

Good drama is built on conflict of some kind—an opposition of forces or desires that must be resolved by the end of the story. The conflict can be internal, involving emotional and psychological pressures, or it can be external, drawing the characters into tumultuous events. These themes are presented to the audience in a narrative arc that looks roughly like this:

Narrative Arc

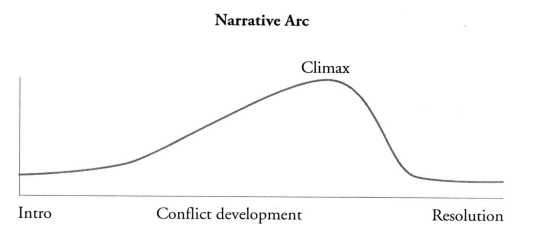

Although any performance may have a series of rising and falling levels of intensity, in general the opening should set in motion the events that will generate an emotional high toward the middle or end of the story. Then, regardless of whether the ending is happy, sad, bittersweet, or despairing, the resolution eases the audience down from those heights and establishes some sense of closure.

Types of poetry

Narrative Poetry

The greatest difficulty in analyzing narrative poetry is that it partakes of many genres. It can have all the features of poetry—meter, rhyme, verses, and stanzas—but it also can have all the features of prose—not only fictional prose, but also nonfictional. It can have a protagonist, characters, conflicts, action, plot, climax, theme, and tone. It can also be a persuasive discourse and have a thesis (real or derived) and supporting points. The arrangement of an analysis will depend to a great extent on the peculiarities of the poem itself.

In drama that follows a narrative arc, reaching the climax too soon undermines the dramatic impact of the remaining portion of the performance, whereas reaching it too late rushes the ending and creates a jarringly abrupt end to events.

Narrative poetry has been very much a part of the output of modern American writers, totally apart from attempts to write epics. Many of Emily Dickinson's poems are narrative in form and retain the features that we look for in the finest of American poetry. The first two verses of "A Narrow Fellow in the Grass" illustrate the use of narrative in a poem:

> *A narrow fellow in the grass*
> *Occasionally rides;*
> *You may have met him—did you not?*
> *His notice sudden is.*
> *The grass divides as with a comb,*
> *A spotted shaft is seen;*
> *And then it closes at your feet*
> *And opens further on. . . .*

This is certainly narrative in nature and has many of the aspects of prose narrative. At the same time, it is a poem with rhyme, meter, verses, and stanzas and can be analyzed as such.

Epic poetry

In an epic, the conflicts take place in the social sphere rather than the personal sphere. An epic has a historical basis or one that is accepted as historical. The conflict is between opposing nations or races and involves diverging views of civilization that are the foundation of the conflict. Often an epic poem will involve the pitting of a group that conceives of itself as a higher civilization against a "lower" civilization and, more often than not, divine will determines that the "higher" civilization wins, exerting its force over the lower, barbarous, and profane enemy.

Examples are the conflict of Greece with Troy, the fates of Rome with the Carthaginian and the Italian, the Crusaders with the Saracen, or even of Milton's Omnipotent versus Satan. In analyzing these works, the protagonist and antagonist need to be clearly identified, the conflicts clearly established, and the climax and final outcome (that presumably sets the world right) clearly shown.

At the same time, the form of the epic as a poem must be considered. What meter, rhyme scheme, verse form, and stanza form has the author chosen to tell the story? Is the form consistent? If it varies, where does it vary and what does the variation do for the poem/story? What about figures of speech? Does the author use alliteration or onomatopoeia?

The epic is a major literary form historically, although it began to fall out of favor by the end of the seventeenth century. At that time the short story and the novel

Narrative poetry contains elements of poetry as well as prose elements such as characters, conflicts, plot, and theme.

Learn more about narrative poetry:

http://www.poetry-portal. com/styles9.html

began to take over the genre. There have been notable efforts to produce an American epic, but these efforts always seem to slide into prose. Even so, some would say that *Moby Dick* is an American epic.

Lyric poetry

The Greek poets used to sing their poetry and accompany their songs by playing a lyre. Thus a musical quality characterizes the many types of lyric poetry.

Epic poetry has a historical basis and involves conflict between opposing nations, races, or civilizations.

Sonnet

The SONNET is a fixed-verse form of Italian origin that consists of fourteen lines that are typically five-foot iambics that rhyme according to a prescribed scheme. Popular since its creation in the thirteenth century in Sicily, the sonnet spread at first to Tuscany, where Petrarch adopted it. The Petrarchan sonnet generally has a two-part theme. The first eight lines, called the octave, state a problem, ask a question, or express an emotional tension. The last six lines, called the sestet, resolve the problem, answer the question, or relieve the tension. The rhyme scheme of the octave is abbaabba; that of the sestet varies.

SONNET: a poetry form of Italian origin consisting of fourteen lines of five-foot iambics that rhyme according to a prescribed scheme

Sir Thomas Wyatt and Henry Howard, Earl of Surrey, introduced this form in England in the sixteenth century. The sonnet played an important role in the development of Elizabethan lyric poetry. A distinctive English sonnet developed that was composed of three quatrains, each with an independent rhyme scheme, ending with a rhymed couplet.

A form of the English sonnet created by Edmund Spenser combines the English form and the Italian. The Spenserian sonnet follows the English quatrain-and-couplet pattern but resembles the Italian sonnet in its rhyme scheme, which is linked: abab bcbc cdcd ee. Many poets wrote sonnet sequences wherein several sonnets were linked together, usually to tell a story. One of the greatest of all sonnet sequences was written by Shakespeare. The sonnets are addressed to a young man and a "dark lady," and the love story is overshadowed by the underlying reflections on time and art, growth and decay, and fame and fortune.

The sonnet continued to develop, more in topic than in form. When John Donne, in the seventeenth century, used the sonnet form for religious themes and personal reflections ("When I consider how my light is spent"), there were no longer any boundaries on the themes a sonnet could take.

The sonnet has been used in a wide range of themes, from more frivolous concerns to statements about time and death. William Wordsworth, John Keats, and Elizabeth Barrett Browning used the Petrarchan form of the sonnet. A well-known example is Wordsworth's "The World Is Too Much With Us." Rainer Maria Rilke's *Die Sonette an Orpheus* (1922) is a well-known twentieth-century sonnet.

ANALYSIS OF A SONNET
Does it fit a traditional pattern, or does it break from tradition? If so, why did the poet choose to make that break?
Does the form reflect the purpose of the poem?
What is the poem's theme? What is its purpose?
Is the poem narrative? If so, what story does it tell and is there an underlying meaning?
Is the sonnet form appropriate for the subject matter?

Ballad

> **BALLAD:** a story told or sung, usually in verse and accompanied by music

A **BALLAD** is a story told or sung, usually in verse and accompanied by music. Literary devices found in ballads include the refrain, or repeated section, and incremental repetition, or anaphora, for effect. The earliest forms were anonymous folk ballads; later forms include Coleridge's Romantic masterpiece "The Rime of the Ancient Mariner."

Limerick

The **LIMERICK** probably originated in County Limerick, Ireland, in the eighteenth century. It is a form of short, humorous verse, often nonsensical, and often ribald. Its five lines rhyme aabbaa with three feet in all lines except the third and fourth, which have only two. Rarely presented as serious poetry, this form is popular because almost anyone can write it.

In the nineteenth century, Edward Lear popularized the limerick in *A Book of Nonsense*. Here's an example:

> *There was an Old Man with a beard,*
> *Who said, "It is just as I feared!*
> *Two Owls and a Hen,*
> *Four Larks and a Wren,*
> *Have all built their nests in my beard!"*

Analysis of a limerick should focus on its form. Does it conform to a traditional pattern or does it break from the tradition? If so, what impact does that have on the meaning? Is the poem serious or frivolous? Is it funny? Is there a serious meaning underlying the frivolity?

Cinquain

> **CINQUAIN:** a poem with a five-line stanza containing two syllables in the first and last lines and four, six, and eight in the middle three lines

A **CINQUAIN** is a poem with a five-line stanza. Adelaide Crapsey (1878–1914) called a five-line verse form a cinquain and invented a particular meter for it. Similar to the haiku, there are two syllables in the first and last lines and four, six, and eight in the middle three lines. The cinquain has a mostly iambic cadence. Crapsey's poem "November Night" is an example:

> Listen...
> With faint dry sound
> Like steps of passing ghosts,
> the leaves, frost-crisp'd, break from the trees
> And fall.

Haiku

HAIKU is a very popular unrhymed form that is limited to seventeen syllables arranged in three lines of five, seven, and five syllables. This verse form originated in Japan in the seventeenth century. It is accepted in Japan as serious poetry and is Japan's most popular form. Originally, a haiku dealt with the season, the time of day, and the landscape. As the haiku has come into more common use, the subject matter has become less restricted. The haiku form often is used in classrooms to introduce students to the writing of poetry.

Here's an example by Japanese poet Kobaayashi Issa, translated by American poet Robert Haas:

> New Year's morning—
> everything is in blossom!
> I feel about average.

Analysis of a cinquain or a haiku poem should focus on form first. Does the haiku poem conform to the seventeen-syllable requirement, and are the syllables arranged in a five-seven-five pattern? For a cinquain, does it have only five lines? Does the poem distill the words so as much meaning as possible can be conveyed? Does it treat a serious subject? Is the theme discernable?

Short forms such as these may seem simple to dash off; however, they are not effective unless the words are chosen and pared so that the intended meaning is conveyed. The impact should be forceful, and thus the short form often takes more effort, skill, and creativity than longer forms. Students should consider all of this in their analyses.

Mythology and oral tradition

LITERARY ALLUSIONS (references to famous literary characters) are drawn from classical mythology, national folklore, and religious writings. The work from which the allusion is drawn should be so familiar to the reader that he or she can

HAIKU: an unrhymed poetic form that is limited to seventeen syllables arranged in lines of five, seven, and five syllables

LITERARY ALLUSION: a reference to a famous literary character from a work that is easily recognizable by the reader

easily recognize the connection between the subject of the allusion and the person, place, or event in the reading.

Children and adolescents who have knowledge of proverbs, fables, myths, epics, and the Bible can understand these allusions and thereby appreciate literature to a greater degree than those who do not recognize them.

Biblical stories provide many literary allusions. Parables—moralistic fables with human characters—include the stories of the Good Samaritan and the Prodigal Son. The Bible also describes the treachery of Cain and the betrayal of Christ by Judas Iscariot, two events that are often alluded to in literature.

Classical mythology

Much of the mythology in world literature is a product of ancient Greece and Rome, largely because Greek and Roman myths have been liberally translated. Some Norse myths are also well known.

Children are generally fond of myths because in these stories, ancient people sought explanations for what happened in their lives in a manner familiar to children. These stories provide insight into the order and ethics of life. In them, ancient heroes overcome the terrors of the unknown, and explanations are given for thunder and lightning, the changing seasons, the origin and function of magical creatures of the forests and seas, and frightening natural phenomena. There is often a childlike directness in the emotions of supernatural beings. Many good translations of myths exist, but Edith Hamilton's *Mythology* is the definitive choice for adolescents.

Fairy tales

FAIRY TALES are lively fictional stories involving children or animals that come in contact with super beings via magic. Fairy tales provide happy solutions to human dilemmas. The fairy tales of many nations are peopled by trolls, elves, dwarfs, and pixies, child-sized beings capable of fantastic accomplishments.

Among the most famous fairy tales are "Beauty and the Beast," "Cinderella," "Hansel and Gretel," "Snow White and the Seven Dwarfs," "Rumplestiltskin," and "Tom Thumb." In each tale, the protagonist survives prejudice, imprisonment, ridicule, and even death to receive justice in a cruel world.

Older readers encounter a kind of fairy tale world in Shakespeare's *The Tempest* and *A Midsummer Night's Dream*, two tales that use pixies and fairies as characters. Adolescent readers today are as fascinated by the fantasy realms in the works of Piers Anthony and Anne McCaffrey. Interest in the supernatural is evident in the popularity of science fiction, a genre in which current knowledge is used to predict the possible course of the future.

FAIRY TALES: lively fictional stories involving children or animals that come in contact with super beings via magic

Check out Sur La Lune Fairy Tales and Folklore:

http://www.surlalunefairytales.com/introduction/index.html

Angels (or sometimes fairy godmothers) play a role in some fairy tales. Milton, in *Paradise Lost* and *Paradise Regained*, also used symbolic angels and devils.

Fables and folktales

Fables and folktales were originally transmitted orally to the common populace to provide models of exemplary behavior or show deeds worthy of recognition and homage.

In FABLES, animals talk, feel, and behave like human beings. Fables always have a moral, and the animals depict specific people or groups indirectly. For example, in Aesop's *Fables,* the lion represents the King and the wolf represents the cruel, often unfeeling nobility. In *The Lion and the Mouse,* the moral is that "little friends may prove to be great friends." In *The Lion's Share,* the lesson is that "might makes right." British folktales (*How Robin Became an Outlaw* and *St. George Slaying of the Dragon*) investigate the interplay between power and justice.

> **FABLE:** a story in which animals talk, feel, and behave like human beings and that contains a moral

American folktales

American folktales are divided into two categories: tall tales and legends.

TALL TALES, also called imaginary tales, are humorous tales based on fictional characters developed through blatant exaggeration.

- John Henry is a two-fisted steel driver who beats out a steam drill in a competition.

- Rip Van Winkle sleeps for twenty years in the Catskill Mountains and upon awakening cannot understand why no one recognizes him.

- Paul Bunyan, a giant lumberjack, owns a great blue ox named Babe and has extraordinary physical strength. He is said to have plowed the Mississippi River, while the impression of Babe's hoof prints created the Great Lakes.

> **TALL TALE:** a humorous tale based on fictional characters developed through blatant exaggeration

LEGENDS, also called real tales, are based on real persons who accomplished the feats that are attributed to them, even if the accomplishments are slightly exaggerated.

- For more than forty years, Johnny Appleseed (John Chapman) roamed Ohio and Indiana planting apple seeds.

- Daniel Boone—scout, adventurer, and pioneer—blazed the Wilderness Trail and made Kentucky safe for settlers.

- Paul Revere, a colonial patriot, rode through the New England countryside warning of the approach of British troops.

- George Washington cut down a cherry tree, a fact he could not deny. Or did he?

> **LEGEND:** a tale based on a real person whose feats or accomplishments are exaggerated in the story

Sample Test Questions and Rationale

(Easy)

1. A traditional, anonymous story, ostensibly having a historical basis, usually explaining some phenomenon of nature or aspect of creation, defines a/an:

   A. Proverb

   B. Idyll

   C. Myth

   D. Epic

   Answer: C

   Rationale: A myth is usually traditional and anonymous and explains natural and supernatural phenomena. Myths are usually about creation, divinity, the significance of life and death, and natural phenomena. A proverb is a saying or adage. An idyll is a short, pastoral poem. In its simplest form, an epic is a narrative poem.

(Easy)

2. Which of the following is not a characteristic of a fable?

   A. Animals that feel and talk like humans

   B. Happy solutions to human dilemmas

   C. Teaches a moral or standard for behavior

   D. Illustrates specific people or groups without directly naming them

   Answer: D

   Rationale: A fable is a short tale with animals, humans, gods, or even inanimate objects as characters. Fables often conclude with a moral, delivered in the form of an epigram (a short, witty, and ingenious statement in verse). Fables are among the oldest forms of writing in human history; a fable appears in Egyptian papyri of c 1500 BC. The most famous fables are those of Aesop, a Greek slave living in about 600 BC. In India, the *Pantchatantra* appeared in the third century. The most famous modern fables are those of seventeenth century French poet Jean de La Fontaine.

(Rigorous)

3. Which poem is typified as a villanelle?

   A. "Do not go gentle into that good night"

   B. "Dover Beach"

   C. *Sir Gawain and the Green Knight*

   D. *Pilgrim's Progress*

   Answer: A

   Rationale: This poem by Dylan Thomas typifies the villanelle because it was written as such. A villanelle is a form that was invented in France in the sixteenth century and used mostly for pastoral songs. It has an uneven number of tercets (usually five) rhyming aba, with a final quatrain rhyming abaa. This poem is the most famous villanelle written in English. "Dover Beach" by Matthew Arnold is not a villanelle, while *Sir Gawain and the Green Knight* was written in alliterative verse by an unknown author usually referred to as The Pearl Poet around 1370. *Pilgrim's Progress* is a prose allegory by John Bunyan.

Sample Test Questions and Rationale (cont.)

(Rigorous)

4. In classic tragedy, a protagonist's defeat is brought about by a tragic flaw, which is called:

 A. Hubris

 B. Hamartia

 C. Catarsis

 D. The skene

Answer: B

Rationale: Hubris is excessive pride, a type of tragic flaw. Catarsis is an emotional purging felt by the character. *Skene* is the Greek word for *scene*. All of these terms come from Greek drama.

(Rigorous)

5. Which sonnet form describes the following?

My galley chargèd with forgetfulness,
Through sharp seas, in winter night doth pass
'Tween rock and rock; and eke mine enemy, alas,
That is my lord steereth with, cruelness;
And every oar a thought with readiness,
As though that death were light in such a case.
An endless wind doth tear the sail apace
Or forc'ed sighs and trusty fearfulness.
A rain of tears, a cloud of dark disdain,
Hath done the wearied cords great hinderance;
Wreathed with error and eke with ignorance.
The stars be hid that led me to this pain;
Drowned is reason that should me consort,
And I remain despairing of the poet.

 A. Petrarchan or Italian sonnet

 B. Shakespearian or Elizabethan sonnet

 C. Romantic sonnet

 D. Spenserian sonnet

Answer: A

Rationale: The Petrarchan sonnet, also known as the Italian sonnet, is named after the Italian poet Petrarch (1304–74). It is divided into an octave rhyming abbaabba and a sestet normally rhyming cdecde.

Sample Test Questions and Rationale (cont.)

(Rigorous)

6. **What is the salient literary feature of this excerpt from an epic?**

> Hither the heroes and the nymphs resort,
> To taste awhile the pleasures of a court;
> In various talk th'instructive hours they pass'd,
> Who gave the ball, or paid the visit last;
> One speaks the glory of the British queen,
> And another describes a charming Indian screen;
> A third interprets motion, looks, and eyes;
> At every word a reputation dies.

A. Sprung rhythm

B. Onomatopoeia

C. Heroic couplets

D. Motif

Answer: C

Rationale: A couplet is a pair of rhyming verse lines, usually of the same length. It is one of the most widely used verse forms in European poetry. Chaucer established the use of couplets in English, notably in the *Canterbury Tales,* using rhymed iambic pentameters (a metrical unit of verse having one unstressed syllable followed by one stressed syllable) later known as heroic couplets. Other authors who used heroic couplets include Ben Jonson, Dryden, and especially Alexander Pope, who became the master of them.

SKILL 1.5 Situating authors and texts within historical, cultural, and critical contexts to aid in interpretation

One way of interpreting literature is to examine the various contexts in which it was written.

Historical and Cultural Context

LOCAL COLOR: the presentation of the peculiarities of a particular locality and its inhabitants

Local color

LOCAL COLOR is defined as the presentation of the peculiarities of a particular locality and its inhabitants. Local color was introduced primarily after the Civil War, although there were certainly precursors, such as Washington Irving and his depiction of life in the Catskill Mountains of New York. However, the local colorist movement is generally considered to have begun in 1865, when humor began to permeate the writing of those who were focusing on a particular region of the country.

Samuel L. Clemens (Mark Twain) is best known for his humorous works about the Southwest, such as "The Notorious Jumping Frog of Calaveras County." The country had just emerged from its "long night of the soul," a time when death, despair, and disaster had preoccupied the nation for almost five years. It's no wonder that artists sought to relieve the grief and pain and lift spirits, nor is it surprising that their efforts brought such a strong response. Mark Twain is generally considered to be not only one of America's funniest writers but also one who also wrote great and enduring fiction.

Other examples of local colorists inlcude:

- George Washington Cable

- Joel Chandler Harris

- Bret Hart

- Sarah Orne Jewett

- Harriet Beecher Stowe

Slavery

The most well known of the early writers who used fiction to make a political statement about slavery is Harriet Beecher Stowe, author of *Uncle Tom's Cabin*. *Uncle Tom's Cabin* was Stowe's first novel. It was published first as a serial in 1851, and then as a book in 1852. This antislavery book infuriated many Southerners. However, Stowe herself had been angered by the 1850 Fugitive Slave Law that made it legal to indict those who assisted runaway slaves. The law took away the rights not only of the runaways but also of free slaves. Stowe intended to generate a protest of the law and of slavery in general. *Uncle Tom's Cabin* was the first effort to depict the lives of slaves from their standpoint.

The novel is about three Kentucky slaves, Tom, Eliza, and George. Eliza and George are married to each other but have different masters. They successfully escape with their little boy, but Tom does not escape. Although he has a wife and children, he is sold, ending up finally with the monstrous Simon Legree, on whose property he eventually dies.

Stowe cleverly used depictions of motherhood and Christianity to stir her readers. When President Lincoln met her, he told her it was her book that started the Civil War.

Many writers used the printed word to protest slavery:

- Frederick Douglass

- William Lloyd Garrison

Read more about regional realism:

http://www.learner. org/amerpass/unit08/ usingvideo.html

- Benjamin Lay, a Quaker

- Jonathan Edwards, a Connecticut theologian

- Susan B. Anthony

Immigration

Immigration has been a popular topic in literature from the time of the Louisiana Purchase in 1804. The recent work *Undaunted Courage* by Stephen E. Ambrose is ostensibly the autobiography of Meriwether Lewis but is actually a recounting of the Lewis and Clark expedition. Presented as a scientific expedition by President Jefferson, the expedition was actually intended to provide maps and information for the expansion of the American West. A well-known novel depicting the settling of the West by immigrants from other countries is *Giants in the Earth* by Ole Edvart Rolvaag, himself a descendant of immigrants.

During the twentieth century, immigration increased rapidly and the American population swelled. Literature documented the resultant changes in the American culture. For example, John Steinbeck's *Cannery Row* and *Tortilla Flats* glorify the lives of Mexican migrants in California. Amy Tan's *The Joy Luck Club* deals with the problems faced by Chinese immigrants.

Leon Uris's *Exodus* explores the social history that led to the founding of the modern state of Israel. It was published in 1958, only a short time after the Holocaust. It deals with the attempts of concentration camp survivors to get to the land that had become the new Israel. In many ways, it is the quintessential work on immigration causes and effects.

Civil rights

Many of the abolitionists were also early crusaders for civil rights. However, the 1960s Civil Rights movement focused attention on the plight of the people who had been "freed" by the Civil War. The movement brought about long-overdue changes in the opportunities and rights of African Americans.

David Halberstam, who was a reporter in Nashville at the time of the sit-ins by eight young black college students that initiated the Civil Rights movement, wrote *The Children*, published in 1998 by Random House, for the purpose of reminding Americans of their courage, suffering, and achievements. Congressman John Lewis, Fifth District, Georgia, was one of those eight young men. Lewis has gone on to a life of public service. Halberstam records that when older black ministers tried to persuade these young people not to pursue their protest, John Lewis responded: "If not us, then who? If not now, then when?"

Some examples of protest literature include:

- James Baldwin, *Blues for Mister Charlie*
- Martin Luther King, *Where Do We Go from Here?*
- Langston Hughes, *Fight for Freedom: The Story of the NAACP*
- Eldridge Cleaver, *Soul on Ice*
- Malcolm X, *The Autobiography of Malcolm X*
- Stokely Carmichael and Charles V. Hamilton, *Black Power*
- Leroi Jones, *Home*

Vietnam

An America that was already divided over the Civil Rights movement faced even greater divisions over the war in Vietnam. Those who were in favor of the war and who opposed withdrawal saw it as the major front in the war against communism. Those who opposed the war and who favored withdrawal of the troops believed that it would not serve to defeat communism and was a quagmire.

Though set in the last years of World War II, *Catch-22* by Joseph Heller was a popular antiwar novel that became a successful movie of the time.

Authors Take Sides on Vietnam, edited by Cecil Woolf and John Bagguley, is a collection of essays by 168 well-known authors throughout the world. *Where is Vietnam?*, edited by Walter Lowenfels, consists of ninety-two poems about the war.

While writers were publishing works for and against the war, musicians let their sentiments be known through their music. Bob Dylan was an example of the musicians of the time. His music represented the hippie aesthetic, characterized by brilliant, swirling colors and hallucinogenic imagery—a style that came to be called *psychedelic*. Some other bands that originated during this time and became well known for their psychedelic music, primarily about the Vietnam War in the early years, are the Grateful Dead, Jefferson Airplane, Big Brother, and Sly and the Family Stone. In England, the antiwar movement attracted the Beatles and the Rolling Stones.

Periods of Literature

Another way to examine literature is by understanding its four major time periods: Neoclassicism, Romanticism, Realism, and Naturalism. Certain authors—among them Chaucer, Shakespeare, and Donne—although writing during a particular literary period, are considered to have a style all their own.

Neoclassicism

Patterned after the great writings of classical Greece and Rome, NEOCLASSIC LITERATURE is characterized by a balanced, graceful, well-crafted, refined, and elevated style. Major proponents of this style are poet laureates John Dryden and Alexander Pope. The eras in which they wrote are called the Ages of Dryden and Pope. In neoclassical writing, the self is not exalted. Focus is on the group rather than the individual.

NEOCLASSIC LITERATURE: characterized by a balanced, graceful, well-crafted, refined, and elevated style

Romanticism

ROMANTIC LITERATURE emphasizes the individual. Emotions and feelings are validated, and nature acts as an inspiration for creativity. Romantics hearken back to medieval, chivalric themes and ambiance. They also emphasize supernatural, Gothic themes and settings, which are characterized by gloom and darkness. Imagination is stressed. New types of romantic literature include detective and horror stories and autobiographical introspection (for example, the works of William Wordsworth).

ROMANTIC LITERATURE: emphasizes the individual; emotions and feelings are validated, and nature acts as an inspiration for creativity

There are two Romantic generations in British Literature. The First Generation includes the works of William Wordsworth and Samuel Taylor Coleridge, whose collaboration *Lyrical Ballads* defines romanticism and its exponents. Wordsworth maintained that the scenes and events of everyday life and the speech of ordinary people were the raw material from which poetry could and should be made. Romanticism spread to the United States, where Ralph Waldo Emerson and Henry David Thoreau adopted it in their transcendental romanticism, which emphasized reasoning. Further extensions of this style are found in Edgar Allan Poe's Gothic writings.

The First Generation Romantics believed that scenes and events from everyday life were the raw material from which poetry could and should be made.

The Second Generation Romantics include the ill-fated Englishmen Lord Byron, John Keats, and Percy Bysshe Shelley. Byron and Shelley, whom for some epitomize the romantic poet (in their personal lives as well as in their work), wrote resoundingly in protest against social and political wrongs and in defense of the struggles for liberty in Italy and Greece. The Second Generation romantics stressed personal introspection and a love of beauty and nature as requisites for inspiration.

The Second Generation Romantics stressed personal introspection and a love of beauty and nature, and protested social and political wrongs.

Realism

Unlike classical and neoclassical writing, which often deal with aristocracies and nobility or the gods, REALISTIC WRITING deals with the common man and his socioeconomic problems in a non-sentimental way. Muckraking, social injustice, domestic abuse, and inner city conflicts are examples of topics explored by writers of realism. Realistic writers include Thomas Hardy, George Bernard Shaw, and Henrik Ibsen.

REALISTIC WRITING: deals with the common man and his socioeconomic problems in a nonsentimental way

Naturalism

NATURALISM is realism pushed to its limit—writing that exposes the underbelly of society, usually the lower-class struggles. Naturalism deals with the world of penury, injustice, abuse, ghetto survival, hungry children, single parenting, and substance abuse. Émile Zola was inspired by his readings in history and medicine and attempted to apply methods of scientific observation to the depiction of pathological human character, notably in his series of novels devoted to several generations of one French family.

> **NATURALISM:** exposes the underbelly of society and deals with injustice, abuse, and survival

Sample Test Questions and Rationale

(Average)

1. **In preparing a unit on twentieth-century immigration, you prepare a list of books for students to read. Which book would not be appropriate for this topic?**

   A. The Things They Carried by Tim O'Brien

   B. *Exodus* by Leon Uris

   C. *The Joy Luck Club* by Amy Tan

   D. *Tortilla Flats* by John Steinbeck

Answer: A

Rationale: O'Brien's book centers on American soldiers serving in Vietnam. Uris' book details the founding of Israel after World War II. Tan's novel contrasts her family's life in China and in the United States. Steinbeck's novel illustrates the plight of Mexican migrant workers.

Sample Test Questions and Rationale (cont.)

(Average)

2. In exploring the relationship of literature to modern life, which of these activities would not enable students to explore comparable themes?

   A. After studying various world events, such as the Palestinian-Israeli conflict, students write an updated version of *Romeo and Juliet* using modern characters and settings

   B. Before studying *Romeo and Juliet,* students watch *West Side Story*

   C. Students research the major themes of *Romeo and Juliet* by studying news stories and finding modern counterparts for the story

   D. Students compare the romantic themes of *Romeo and Juliet* and *The Taming of the Shrew*

Answer: D

Rationale: By comparing the two plays by Shakespeare, students will be focusing on the culture of the period in which the plays were written. In Answer A, students should be able to recognize modern parallels with current culture clashes. By comparing *Romeo and Juliet* to the 1950s update of *West Side Story*, students can study how themes are similar in two completely different historical periods. In Answer C, students can study local, national, and international news for comparable stories and themes.

(Rigorous)

3. Mr. Phillips is creating a unit to study *To Kill a Mockingbird* and wants to familiarize his high school freshmen with the attitudes and issues of the historical period. Which activity would familiarize students with the attitudes and issues of the Depression-era South?

   A. Create a detailed timeline of fifteen to twenty social, cultural, and political events that focus on race relations in the 1930s

   B. Research and report on the life of author Harper Lee. Compare her background with the events in the book

   C. Watch the movie version and note language and dress

   D. Write a research report on the stock market crash of 1929 and its effects

Answer: A

Rationale: By identifying the social, cultural, and political events of the 1930s, students will better understand the attitudes and values of America during the time of the novel. While researching the author's life could add depth to students' understanding of the novel, it is unnecessary to the appreciation of the novel itself. The movie version is an accurate depiction of the novel's setting but it focuses on the events in the novel, not the external factors that fostered the conflict. The stock market crash and the subsequent Great Depression would be important to note on the timeline, but students would be distracted from themes of the book by narrowing their focus to only these two events.

Sample Test Questions and Rationale (cont.)

(Rigorous)

4. Which choice below best defines *naturalism*?

   A. A belief that the writer or artist should apply scientific objectivity in his or her observation and treatment of life without imposing value judgments

   B. The doctrine that teaches that the existing world is the best to be hoped for

   C. The doctrine that teaches that God is not a personality, but that all laws, forces, and manifestations of the universe are God-related

   D. A philosophical doctrine that professes that the truth of all knowledge must always be in question

Answer: A

Rationale: Naturalism is a movement that was started by French writers Jules and Edmond de Goncourt with their novel *Germinie Lacerteux* (1865), but its real leader is Émile Zola, who wanted to bring "a slice of life" to his readers. His saga *Les Rougon Macquart* consists of twenty-two novels depicting various aspects of social life. Other authors representative of this movement include George Moore and George Gissing in England, but the most important naturalist novel written in English is Theodore Dreiser's *Sister Carrie*.

SKILL 1.6 Recognizing and identifying various instructional approaches to and elements of teaching reading and textual interpretation *(e.g., cueing systems, activating prior knowledge, constructing meaning through context, and meta-cognitive strategies)*

Techniques to Improve Reading Skills

Students can use various techniques to improve their reading and comprehension skills. Descriptions of these techniques follow.

Prior knowledge

PRIOR KNOWLEDGE can be defined as all of one's prior experiences, learning, and development. Prior knowledge is what one brings to the table when entering a specific learning situation or attempting to comprehend a specific text. Sometimes

PRIOR KNOWLEDGE: all of one's prior experiences, learning, and development

prior knowledge can be erroneous or incomplete. Obviously, if there are misconceptions in a reader's prior knowledge, these must be corrected so that the reader's overall comprehension skills can continue to progress. Prior knowledge includes the accumulated positive and negative experiences that readers have acquired, both in and out of school.

Prior knowledge might come from:

- Traveling
- Watching television
- Visiting museums and libraries
- Visiting hospitals and prisons
- Surviving poverty

Whatever prior knowledge students bring to the school setting, the independent reading and writing that students do in school immeasurably expands their prior knowledge and hence broadens their reading comprehension capabilities.

As you prepare to begin any imaginative/literary text, you must consider the following concerning the students' prior knowledge:

1. What prior knowledge needs to be activated for the text or theme and for the writing to be done successfully?

2. How independent are the students in using strategies to activate their prior knowledge?

Comprehension

COMPREHENSION: occurs when the reader correctly interprets the text and constructs meaning from it

COMPREHENSION occurs when the reader correctly interprets the text and constructs meaning from it. Comprehension depends on activation of prior knowledge, the cultural and social background of the reader, and the reader's ability to use comprehension-monitoring strategies.

Cues

CUES: pieces of information used to direct or monitor reading comprehension

CUES are used to direct and monitor reading comprehension. As they self-monitor their reading comprehension, readers have to integrate various sources of information, or cues, to help them construct meaning from the text and graphic illustrations.

Context clues

Context clues help readers determine the meanings of words they are not familiar with. The CONTEXT of a word is the sentence or sentences that surround the word. Sometimes the writer offers synonyms, or words that have nearly the same meaning. Context clues can appear within the sentence itself, within the preceding and/or following sentence(s), or within the passage as a whole.

Read the following sentences and attempt to determine the meanings of the words in bold print.

> The **luminosity** of the room was so incredible that there was no need for lights.

If there was no need for lights, then one must assume that the word *luminosity* has something to do with giving off light. The definition of *luminosity*, therefore, is "the emission of light."

> Jamie could not understand Joe's feelings. His mood swings made understanding him somewhat of an **enigma.**

The fact that Joe could not be understood made him somewhat of a puzzle. The definition of *enigma* is "a mystery or puzzle."

Word forms

Sometimes a very familiar word can appear as a different part of speech.

You may have heard that *fraud* involves a criminal misrepresentation, so when the word appears in the adjective form *fraudulent* ("He was suspected of fraudulent activities") you can make an educated guess as to its meaning. You probably know that something out-of-date is *obsolete*; therefore, when you read about "built-in *obsolescence*," you can guess the meaning of the unfamiliar word.

Sentence clues

Often, a writer will actually define a difficult or particularly important word for you the first time it appears in a passage. Phrases like *that is, such as, which is,* or *is called* might announce the writer's intention to give just the definition you need. Occasionally, a writer will simply use a synonym or near-synonym joined by the word *or.* Look at the following examples:

> The **credibility**—that is to say, the believability—of the witness was called into question by evidence of previous perjury.
>
> Nothing would **assuage** or lessen the child's grief.

Punctuation

At the sentence level, punctuation is often a clue to the meaning of a word.

Commas, parentheses, quotation marks, and dashes tell the reader that a definition is being offered by the writer.

> A tendency toward **hyperbole**, extravagant exaggeration, is a common flaw among persuasive writers.
>
> Political **apathy**—lack of interest—can lead to the death of the state.

Explanation

A writer might simply give an explanation in other words that you can understand in the same sentence:

> The **xenophobic** townspeople were suspicious of every foreigner.

Writers also explain a word in terms of its opposite at the sentence level:

> His **incarceration** was ended, and he was elated to be out of jail.

Adjacent sentence clues

The context for a word goes beyond the sentence in which it appears. At times, the writer uses adjacent (adjoining) sentences to present an explanation or definition:

> The $200 for the car repair would have to come out of the **contingency** fund. Fortunately, Angela's father had taught her to keep some money set aside for just such emergencies.

Analysis: The second sentence offers a clue to the definition of *contingency* as used in this sentence: "emergencies." Therefore, a fund for contingencies would be money tucked away for unforeseen and/or urgent events.

Entire Passage Clues

On occasion, you must look at an entire paragraph or passage to figure out the definition of a word or term. In the following paragraph, notice how the word *nostalgia* undergoes a form of extended definition throughout the selection rather than in just one sentence.

*The word **nostalgia** links the Greek words for "away from home" and "pain." If you're feeling **nostalgic**, then you are probably in some physical distress or discomfort, suffering from a feeling of alienation and separation from loved ones or loved places. Nostalgia is that awful feeling you remember from the first time you went away to camp or spent the weekend with a friend's family—homesickness, or some condition even more painful than that. But in common use, **nostalgia** has come to have more sentimental associations. A few years back, for example, a nostalgia craze had to do with the 1950's. We resurrected poodle skirts and saddle shoes, built new restaurants to look like old ones, and tried to make chicken a la king just as mother probably never made it. In TV situation comedies, we recreated a pleasant world that probably never existed and relished our nostalgia, longing for a homey, comfortable lost time.*

Reading Responses

Types of responses

Reading literature involves a reciprocal interaction between the reader and the text. These responses can be emotional, interpretive, critical, or evaluative.

Emotional

In an emotional response, readers can identify with the characters and situations so as to project themselves into the story. They feel a sense of satisfaction by associating aspects of their own lives with the people, places, and events in the literature. Emotional responses are observed in readers' verbal and non-verbal reactions—laughter, comments on the story's effects, and retelling or dramatizing the action.

Interpretive

Interpretive responses lead to inferences about character development, setting, or plot; analysis of style elements—metaphor, simile, allusion, rhythm, tone; outcomes derivable from information provided in the narrative; and assessment of the author's intent. Interpretive responses are made verbally or in writing.

Critical

Critical responses involve making value judgments about the quality of a piece of literature. Reactions to the effectiveness of the writer's style and language use are observed through discussion and written reactions.

Evaluative

Some reading response theorists add a response that considers the readers' considerations of such factors as how well the piece of literature represents its genre, how well it reflects the social/ethical mores of society, and how well the author has approached the subject with regard to freshness and slant.

Learn more about reading response journals:

http://www. educationworld.com/a_ curr/profdev/profdev085. shtml

Interpreting responses

Middle school readers will exhibit both emotional and interpretive responses. Naturally, the level of interpretive response depends on the student's degree of knowledge regarding literary elements. Children show critical reactions on a fundamental level when they are able to say why a particular book was boring or why a particular poem was sad. Adolescents in ninth and tenth grades should begin to make critical responses by addressing the specific language and genre characteristics of literature.

Evaluative responses are harder to detect and are rarely made by any but a few advanced high school students. However, a teacher who knows what to listen for can recognize evaluative responses and incorporate them into discussions.

For example, if a student says, "I don't understand why that character is doing that," she is making an interpretive response to character motivation. However, if she goes on to say, "What good is that action?" she is giving an evaluative response that should be explored in terms of "What good should it do and why isn't that positive action happening?"

At the emotional level, another student might say, "I almost broke into a sweat when the author was describing the heat in the burning house." An interpretive response states, "The author used descriptive adjectives to bring his setting to life." Critically, the student adds, "The author's use of descriptive language contributes to the success of the narrative and maintains reader interest through the whole story." If he goes on to wonder why the author allowed the grandmother in the story to die in the fire, he is making an evaluative response.

Levels of response

The level of reader response will depend largely on the reader's level of social, psychological, and intellectual development. Most middle school students have progressed beyond merely retelling the events in some logical sequence or describing the feelings that the story evoked. They are aware to some degree that the feelings evoked were the result of a careful manipulation of the elements of fiction writing. They may not explain that awareness as successfully as a high school student, but they are beginning to differentiate between responding to the story itself and responding to a literary creation.

Fostering self-esteem and empathy for others

The use of literature as "bibliotherapy" enables the reader to identify with others while not feeling directly betrayed or threatened. For the high school student, the ability to empathize is an evaluative response, a much desired outcome of literature studies. The following books, read either individually or as a thematic unit of study, can be used to promote discussion or writing. The titles are grouped by theme, not by reading level.

BOOKS TO INCREASE EMPATHY	
Abuse	Blair, Maury and Doug Brendel. *Maury, Wednesday's Child* Dizenzo, Patricia. *Why Me?* Parrot, Andrea. *Coping with Date Rape and Acquaintance Rape*
Natural World Concerns	Caduto, M. and J. Bruchac. *Keepers of Earth* Gay, Kathlyn. *Greenhouse Effect* Johnson, Denis. *Fiskadaro* Madison, Arnold. *It Can't Happen to Me*
Eating Disorders	Arnold, Caroline. *Too Fat, Too Thin, Do You Have a Choice?* DeClements, Barthe. *Nothing's Fair in Fifth Grade* Snyder, Anne. *Goodbye, Paper Doll*
Family	Cormier, Robert. *Tunes for Bears to Dance to* Danzinger, Paula. *The Divorce Express* Neufield, John. *Sunday Father* Okimoto, Jean Davies. *Molly by Any Other Name* Peck, Richard. *Don't Look and It Won't Hurt* Zindel, Paul. *I Never Loved Your Mind*
Stereotyping	Baklanov, Grigory. (Trans. by Antonina W. Bouis) *Forever Nineteen* Greene, Betty. *Summer of My German Soldier* Kerr, M.E. *Gentle Hands* Reiss, Johanna. *The Upstairs Room* Taylor, Mildred D. *Roll of Thunder; Hear Me Cry* WakatsukiHouston, Jeanne and James D. Houston. *Farewell to Manzanarr*
Suicide and Death	Blume, Judy. *Tiger Eyes* Bunting, Eve. *If I Asked You, Would You Stay?* Gunther, John. *Death Be Not Proud* Mazer, Harry. *When the Phone Rings* Peck, Richard. *Remembering the Good Times* Richter, Elizabeth. *Losing Someone You Love* Strasser, Todd. *Friends Till the End*

Caution

Teachers should always use caution with reading materials of a sensitive or controversial nature. A child who has known a recent death in his family or circle of friends may need to distance himself from classroom discussion. Whenever open discussion of a topic brings pain or embarrassment, the child should not be further subjected. Older children and young adults will be able to discuss issues with greater objectivity and without making blurted, insensitive comments.

> *It is always advisable to notify parents if a particularly sensitive piece is to be studied.*

Teachers must be able to gauge the level of emotional development of the students when selecting subject matter and the strategies for studying it. Students or parents may consider some material objectionable. Should a student choose not to read an assigned title, the teacher can allow the student to select an alternate title. It is always advisable to notify parents if a particularly sensitive piece is to be studied.

Reading Emphasis in Middle School

In middle and secondary schools, reading instruction spans the range of comprehension skills: literal, inferential, and critical. Most instruction in grades five and six is based on the skills delineated in basal readers adopted for those grade levels. Reading instruction in grades seven through nine is usually part of a general language arts class instead of being a distinct subject in the curriculum, unless the instruction is remedial.

Reading for comprehension of factual material—textbooks, reference books, and newspapers—is closely related to study strategies at the middle school level.

Organized study models teach students to locate main ideas and supporting details, to recognize sequential order, to distinguish fact from opinion, and to determine cause/effect relationships. One such model is the SQ3R method, a technique that enables students to learn the content of even large amounts of text (Survey, Question, Read, Recite, and Review Studying).

> *The SQ3R study model:*
> - *Survey*
> - *Question*
> - *Read*
> - *Recite*
> - *Review*

Strategies

Teacher-guided activities that require students to organize and summarize information based on the author's explicit intent are pertinent strategies in middle grades. Evaluation techniques include oral and written responses to standardized or teacher-made worksheets.

Through reading fiction, students can develop skills for inferring meaning. Teachers can identify the skills to be studied, choose the appropriate reading resources, and develop activities to guide students' reading for meaning. To monitor acquisition of these comprehension skills, teachers have at their disposal a variety of printed materials as well as individualized computer software programs.

Older middle school students should be given opportunities for more student-centered activities, such as the individual and collaborative selection of reading choices based on student interest, small group discussions of selected works, and greater written expression. Evaluation techniques include teacher monitoring and observation of discussions and written work samples.

Certain students may begin some fundamental critical interpretation, such as

- Recognizing fallacious reasoning in news media
- Examining the accuracy of news reports and advertising
- Explaining their reasons for preferring one author's writing to another's

Development of these skills may require a more learning-centered approach, in which the teacher identifies a number of objectives and suggests resources from which the student may choose a course of study. Teachers can stress self-evaluation through a reading diary, or they can encourage peer evaluation of creative projects resulting from such a study.

Teachers should encourage one-on-one tutoring or peer-assisted reading instead of evaluating students as they read aloud before the entire class. However, occasional sharing of favorite selections by teachers and willing students is a good exercise for both parties.

Reading Emphasis in High School

Reading in tenth through twelfth grades is part of the literature curriculum—World, American, and British. Students in high school literature classes should focus on interpretive and critical reading. For example, students should learn to

- Draw conclusions
- Predict outcomes
- Recognize specific genre characteristics

Critical reading will help students judge the quality of a particular writer's work against recognized standards.

At this level, students should be able to evaluate their own progress.

Strategies

Along with the requisites of most literature courses, teachers need to encourage students to pursue independent study and enrichment reading. Enabling students to be lifelong learners is a fundamental goal of teaching.

The teacher becomes more facilitator than instructor. With the teacher's guidance, students should be able to diagnose their individual strengths and weaknesses,

> *Learn more about monitoring comprehension:*
>
> *http://www.indiana.edu/~l517/monitoring.html*

> *Occasional sharing of favorite selections by teachers and willing students is a good exercise for both parties.*

keep a record of their progress, and interact with other students and the teacher when practicing skills.

Teachers should provide ample opportunities for oral interpretation of literature, special projects in creative dramatics, writing for publication in school literary magazines or newspapers, and speech/debate activities. A student portfolio provides for teacher and peer evaluation.

Reading Assessment

ASSESSMENT is the practice of collecting information about children's progress, and **EVALUATION** is the process of judging the children's responses to determine how well they are achieving particular goals or demonstrating reading skills.

Assessment and evaluation are intricately connected in the literacy classroom. Assessment is necessary because teachers need ways to determine what students are learning and how they are progressing. In addition, assessment is a tool that can also help students take ownership of their own learning and become partners in their ongoing development as readers and writers. In this day of public accountability, clear, definite, and reliable assessment creates confidence in public education. There are two broad categories of assessment.

FORMAL ASSESSMENT is composed of standardized tests and procedures carried out under prescribed conditions. Formal assessments include state tests, standardized achievement tests, NAEP tests, and the like.

INFORMAL ASSESSMENT is the use of observation and other non-standardized procedures to compile anecdotal and observational data/evidence of children's progress. Informal assessment includes but is not limited to checklists, observations, and performance tasks.

Skills to be evaluated

- The ability to use syntactic cues when encountering an unknown word. Good readers will expect the word to fit the syntax they are familiar with. Poor readers may substitute a word that does not fit the syntax and will not correct themselves.

- The ability to use semantic cues to determine the meaning of an unknown word. Good readers will consider the meanings of all the known words in the sentence. Poor readers may read one word at a time with no regard for the other words.

- The ability to use schematic cues to connect words with prior knowledge. Good readers will incorporate what they know with what the text says or

---

ASSESSMENT: the practice of collecting information about children's progress

EVALUATION: the process of judging the children's responses to determine how well they are achieving particular goals or demonstrating reading skills

FORMAL ASSESSMENT: composed of standardized tests and procedures carried out under prescribed conditions

INFORMAL ASSESSMENT: the use of observation and other non-standardized procedures to compile anecdotal and observational data/evidence of children's progress

implies. Poor readers may think only of the word they are reading without associating it with prior knowledge.

- The ability to use phonics cues to improve ease and efficiency in reading. Good readers will apply letter and sound associations almost subconsciously. Poor readers may have one of two kinds of problems:

  A. They may have underdeveloped phonics skills, and use only an initial clue without analyzing vowel patterns before quickly guessing the word.

  B. They may use phonics skills in isolation, becoming so absorbed in the word "noises" that they ignore or forget the message of the text.

- The ability to process information from the text. Good readers should be able to get information from the text as well as store, retrieve, and integrate it for later use.

- The ability to use interpretive thinking to make logical predictions and inferences.

- The ability to use critical thinking to make decisions and have insights about the text.

- The ability to use appreciative thinking to respond to the text, whether emotionally, mentally, or ideologically.

Methods of evaluation

- Assess students at the beginning of each year to determine grouping for instruction.

- Judge whether a student recognizes that a word does not make sense.

- Monitor whether the student knows when to ignore a reading mistake and read on or when to reread a sentence.

- Look for skills such as recognizing cause and effect, finding main ideas, and using comparison and contrast techniques.

- Keep dated records to follow individual progress. Focus on a few students each day. Grade them on a scale of one to five according to how well they perform certain reading abilities (such as making logical predictions). Include informal observations such as, "Ed was able to determine the meaning of the word 'immigrant' by examining the other words in the sentence."

- Remember that evaluation is important but fostering an enjoyment of reading is the ultimate goal. Keep reading pressure-free and fun so that students do not become intimidated by reading. Even if the students are not meeting standards, if they continue to want to read each day, that is a success!

Sample Test Questions and Rationale

(Average)

1. The students in Mrs. Cline's seventh-grade language arts class were invited to attend a performance of *Romeo and Juliet* presented by the drama class at the high school. To best prepare, they should:

   A. Read the play as a homework exercise

   B. Read a synopsis of the plot and a biographical sketch of the author

   C. Examine a few main selections from the play to become familiar with the language and style of the author

   D. Read a condensed version of the story and practice attentive listening skills

   Answer: D

   Rationale: By reading a condensed version of the story, students will know the plot and therefore be able to follow the play on stage. It is also important for them to practice listening techniques such as one-on-one tutoring and peer-assisted reading.

(Average)

2. What is the best course of action when a child refuses to complete a reading/literature assignment on the grounds that it is morally objectionable?

   A. Speak with the parents and explain the necessity of studying this work

   B. Encourage the child to sample some of the text before making a judgment

   C. Place the child in another teacher's class in which they are studying an acceptable work

   D. Provide the student with alternative selections that cover the same performance standards the rest of the class is learning

   Answer: D

   Rationale: If a student finds a work offensive, it is the responsibility of the teacher to assign another title. As a general rule, it is always advisable to notify parents if a particularly sensitive piece is to be studied.

Sample Test Questions and Rationale (cont.)

(Average)

3. The English department is developing strategies to encourage all students to become a community of readers. From the list of suggestions below, which would be the least effective way for teachers to foster independent reading?

   A. Each teacher will set aside a weekly thirty-minute, in-class reading session during which the teacher and students read a magazine or book for enjoyment

   B. Teacher and students develop a list of favorite books to share with each other

   C. The teacher assigns at least one book report each grading period to ensure that students are reading from the established class list

   D. The students gather books for a classroom library so that books may be shared with each other

Answer: C

Rationale: Teacher-directed assignments such as book reports appear routine and unexciting. Students will be more excited about reading when they can actively participate. In Answer A, the teacher is modeling reading behavior and providing students with a dedicated time during which they can read independently and still be surrounded by a community of readers. In Answers B and D, students share and make available to others their reading choices.

(Average)

4. Which of the following responses to literature typically gives middle school students the most problems?

   A. Interpretive

   B. Evaluative

   C. Critical

   D. Emotional

Answer: B

Rationale: Middle school readers will exhibit both emotional and interpretive responses. In middle school, organized study models enable students to identify main ideas and supporting details, to recognize sequential order, to distinguish fact from opinion, and to determine cause/effect relationships. Also, a child's being able to say why a particular book was boring or why a particular poem made him or her sad evidences critical reactions on a fundamental level. It is a bit early for evaluative responses, however. These depend on the reader's consideration of how the piece represents its genre, how well it reflects the social/ethical mores of a given society, and how well the author has approached the subject for freshness and slant. Evaluative responses are made only by a few advanced high school students.

Sample Test Questions and Rationale (cont.)

(Average)

5. **Which of the following is a formal reading-level assessment?**

   A. A standardized reading test

   B. A teacher-made reading test

   C. An interview

   D. A reading diary

   Answer: A

   Rationale: If assessment is standardized, it has to be objective. Answers B, C, and D are all subjective assessments.

(Average)

6. **Which of the following would be the most significant factor in teaching Homer's *Iliad* and *Odyssey* to any particular group of students?**

   A. Identifying a translation at the appropriate reading level

   B. Determining the students' interest level

   C. Selecting an appropriate evaluative technique

   D. Determining the scope and delivery methods of background study

   Answer: A

   Rationale: Students will learn the importance of these two works if the translation reflects both the vocabulary that they know and their reading level. Greece will always be foremost in literary assessments due to Homer's works. Homer is the most often cited author, next to Shakespeare. Greece is the cradle of both democracy and literature. This is why it is so crucial that Homer be included in the works assigned.

(Average)

7. **Which of the following definitions best describes a parable?**

   A. A short, entertaining account of some happening, usually using talking animals as characters

   B. A slow, sad poem or prose work expressing lamentation

   C. An extensive narrative work expressing universal truths concerning domestic life

   D. A short, simple story of an occurrence of a familiar kind, from which a moral or religious lesson may be drawn

   Answer: D

   Rationale: A parable is usually brief and should be interpreted as an allegory teaching a moral lesson. Jesus's forty parables are the model of the genre, but modern, secular examples exist, such as Wilfred Owen's "The Parable of the Old Man and the The Young" (1920), or John Steinbeck's prose work *The Pearl* (1948).

Sample Test Questions and Rationale (cont.)

(Average)

8. **Which teaching method would best engage underachievers in the required senior English class?**

   A. Assign glossary work and extensively foot-noted excerpts of great works

   B. Have students take turns reading aloud from the anthology selection

   C. Let students choose which readings they'll study and write about

   D. Use a chronologically arranged, traditional text, but assign group work, panel presentations, and portfolio management

   Answer: C

   Rationale: This method will encourage students to react honestly to literature. Students should take notes on what they're reading so that they will be able to discuss the material. They should not only react to literature but also experience it. Small-group work is a good way to encourage them. The other answers are not fit for middle or high school students. They should be encouraged, however, to read criticisms of works in order to understand criteria work.

(Rigorous)

9. **How will literature help students in a science class understand the following passage?**

   Just as was the case more than three decades ago, we are still sailing between the Scylla of deferring surgery for too long and risking irreversible left ventricular damage and sudden death, and the Charibdas of operating too early and subjecting the patient to the early risks of operation and the later risks resulting from prosthetic valves.

   —E. Braunwald, *European Heart Journal,*
   July 2000

   A. They will recognize the allusions to Scylla and Charibdas from Greek mythology and understand that the medical community has to select one of two unfavorable choices.

   B. They will recognize the allusion to sailing and understand its analogy to doctors as sailors navigating unknown waters.

   C. They will recognize that the allusions to Scylla and Charibdas refer to the two islands in Norse mythology on which sailors would find themselves shipwrecked and understand how the doctors feel isolated by their choices.

   D. They will recognize the metaphor of the heart and relate it to Eros, the character in Greek mythology who represents love. Eros was the love child of Scylla and Charibdas.

   Answer: A

   Rationale: Scylla and Charibdas were two sea monsters guarding a narrow channel of water. Sailors trying to elude one side would face danger by sailing too close to the other side. The allusion indicates two equally undesirable choices.

Sample Test Questions and Rationale (cont.)

(Rigorous)

10. **Which is not a Biblical allusion?**

    A. The patience of Job

    B. Thirty pieces of silver

    C. "Man proposes; God disposes"

    D. "Suffer not yourself to be betrayed by a kiss"

Answer: C

Rationale: This saying is attributed to Thomas à Kempis (1379–1471) in his *Imitation of Christ,* Book 1, Chapter 19. Anyone who exhibits the patience of Job is being compared to the Old Testament biblical figure who retained his faith despite being beset by a series of misfortunes. "Thirty pieces of silver" refers to the amount of money paid to Judas to identify Jesus. Used by Patrick Henry, the quote in D is a biblical reference to Judas's betrayal of Jesus by a kiss.

(Rigorous)

11. **Before reading a passage, a teacher gives her students an anticipation guide with a list of statements related to the topic they are about to cover in the reading material. She asks the students to indicate their agreement or disagreement with each statement on the guide. This activity is intended to:**

    A. Elicit students' prior knowledge of the topic and set a purpose for reading

    B. Help students identify the main ideas and supporting details in the text

    C. Help students synthesize information from the text

    D. Help students visualize the concepts and terms in the text

Answer: A

Rationale: Establishing a purpose for reading, the foundation for a reading unit or activity, is intimately connected to activating the students' prior knowledge in strategic ways. When the reason for reading is developed in the context of the students' experiences, they are far better prepared to succeed because they can make connections from a base they thoroughly understand. This influences motivation and, with proper motivation, students are more enthused and put forward more effort. The other choices are only indirectly supported by this activity and are more specific in focus.

(Rigorous)

12. **Recognizing empathy in literature is mostly a(n):**

    A. Emotional response

    B. Interpretive response

    C. Critical response

    D. Evaluative response

Answer: C

Rationale: In critical responses, students make value judgments about the quality and atmosphere of a text. Through class discussion and written assignments, students react to and assimilate a writer's style and language.

DOMAIN II
LANGUAGE

PERSONALIZED STUDY PLAN

COMPETENCY 2
LANGUAGE AND LINGUISTICS

> **SKILL Understanding the principles of language acquisition and 2.1 development, including social, cultural, and historical influences and the role and nature of dialects**

Language Development

Development of language skills depends on many factors, some internal (e.g., the age of the child) and some external (e.g., immigration). Teachers can use a variety of approaches to accommodate individual differences.

Learning approach

Early theories of language development were formulated from learning theory research. The assumption was that language development evolved from learning the rules of language structure and applying them through imitation and reinforcement. This approach also assumed that language and cognitive and social development were independent of each other.

Thus children were expected to learn language by patterning adults who spoke and wrote standard English. No allowance was made for communication through child jargon, idiomatic expressions, or grammatical and mechanical errors resulting from overly strict adherence to the rules of inflection ("childs" instead of "children") or conjugation ("runned" instead of "ran"). No association was made between physical and operational development and language mastery.

The learning theory approach assumes that language development evolved from learning the rules of language structure and applying them through imitation and reinforcement.

Linguistic approach

Studies spearheaded by Noam Chomsky in the 1950s formulated the theory that language ability is innate and develops through natural human maturation as environmental stimuli trigger the acquisition of syntactical structures appropriate to each exposure level. The assumption of a hierarchy of syntax downplayed the significance of semantics. Because of the complexity of syntax and the relative speed with which children acquire language, linguists attributed language development to biological rather than cognitive or social influences.

The linguistic approach holds that language ability is innate and develops through natural human maturation as environmental stimuli trigger the acquisition of syntactical structures appropriate to each exposure level.

Cognitive approach

Researchers in the 1970s proposed that language knowledge derives from both syntactic and semantic structures. Drawing on the studies of Piaget and other cognitive learning theorists, supporters of the cognitive approach maintained that children acquire knowledge of linguistic structures after they have acquired the cognitive structures necessary to process language. For example, the act of joining words to form a specific meaning necessitates sensory motor intelligence.

Children must be able to coordinate movement and recognize objects before they can identify words to name the objects or word groups to describe the actions performed with those objects.

Adolescents must be able to mentally organize concepts and concrete operations, predict outcomes, and theorize before they can assimilate and verbalize complex sentence structures, choose vocabulary for particular nuances of meaning, and examine semantic structures for tone and manipulative effect.

Sociocognitive approach

Other theorists in the 1970s proposed that language development results from sociolinguistic competence. Language, cognitive, and social knowledge are interactive elements of total human development. Emphasis on verbal communication as the medium for linguistic expression resulted in the inclusion of speech activities in most language arts curricula.

Unlike previous approaches, the sociocognitive approach allowed that determining the appropriateness of language in given situations for specific listeners is as important as understanding semantic and syntactic structures.

By engaging in conversation, children at all stages of development have opportunities to test their language skills, receive feedback, and make modifications. As a social activity, conversation is as structured by social order as grammar is structured by the rules of syntax. Conversation satisfies the learner's need to be heard and understood and to influence others. Thus, the choices of vocabulary, tone, and content are dictated by the learner's ability to assess the language knowledge of listeners. The speaker is constantly applying his cognitive skills to using language in a social interaction. Without an environment in which to practice language, children would not pass beyond grunts and gestures.

Of course, the varying degrees of environmental stimuli to which children are exposed at all age levels create a slower or faster development of language. Some children are prepared to articulate concepts and recognize symbolism by the time they enter fifth grade because they have been exposed to challenging reading and conversations with well-spoken adults at home or in their social groups. Others are still trying to master sight recognition skills and are not yet ready to combine words in complex patterns.

Benefits of the sociocognitive approach

The sociocognitive approach has tended to guide the "whole language" movement that is currently in fashion. Most basal readers use an integrated, cross-curricular approach to successfully learn grammar, vocabulary, and proper usage. Reinforcement becomes an intradepartmental responsibility.

Language incorporates diction and terminology across the curriculum. Standard usage is encouraged and supported by both the core classroom textbooks and software. Teachers need to acquaint themselves with the computer capabilities in their school district and at their individual schools. Advances in technologies require that teachers familiarize themselves with programs that would serve their students' needs. Students respond enthusiastically to technology.

Several highly effective programs are available in various formats to assist students with initial instruction or remediation. Grammar texts, such as the Warriner's series, employ various methods to accommodate individual learning styles. The school library media center should become a focal point for individual exploration.

Concerns for the teacher

Because teachers must, by virtue of tradition and the dictates of the curriculum, teach grammar, usage, and writing as well as reading and literature, the problem becomes when to teach what to whom.

The profusion of approaches to teaching grammar alone is mind-boggling. At the university level, we learn about transformational grammar, stratification grammar, sectoral grammar, and more. But in practice, most teachers, supported by presentations in textbooks and by the methods they learned themselves, keep coming back to the same traditional prescriptive approach—read and imitate—or structural approach—learn the parts of speech, the parts of the sentence, punctuation rules, and sentence patterns. After enough terminology and rules are stored in the brain, then we learn to write and speak. For some educators, the best solution is the worst: don't teach grammar at all.

The same problems occur in teaching usage. How much can we demand that students communicate in only Standard English? Different schools of thought suggest that a study of dialect and idiom and recognition of various jargons is a vital part of language development. Social pressures, especially on students in middle schools, to be accepted within their peer groups and to speak the non-standard language spoken outside of school make adolescents resistant to the corrective, remedial approach.

In many communities in which the immigrant population is high, new words are entering English from other languages even as words and expressions that were once common are becoming rare or obsolete.

Regardless of differences of opinion concerning language development, language arts teachers will be most effective using the styles and approaches with which they are most comfortable. If they subscribe to a student-centered approach, they may find that the students have a lot to teach them and each other. Moffett and Wagner, in the Fourth Edition of *Student-centered Language Arts K–12*, stress the three I's: individualization, interaction, and integration. Essentially, these authors support the sociocognitive approach to language development. By providing students with an opportunity to select their own activities and resources, the teacher is individualizing instruction. By centering on and teaching each other, students are learning interactively. The teacher's role becomes that of facilitator.

> *Learn more about student-centered learning:*
>
> *http://www.wcer.wisc.edu/step/ep301/Fall2000/Tochonites/stu_cen.html*

Geographical influences

Dialect differences are basically differences in pronunciation. Many Bostonians say "pahty" for "party," and many Southerners blend the words "you all" into the contraction "y'all." The biggest differences in spoken American English stem from minor word choice variances. Depending on where you live, when you order a carbonated, syrupy beverage most generically called a soft drink, you might ask for a "soda" in the South or a "pop" in the Midwest.

Social influences

Social influences are mostly those imposed by family, peer groups, and mass media. The economic and educational levels of families determine language use. Exposure to adults who encourage them to speak well enhances children's readiness for other areas of learning and contributes to their ability to communicate their needs. Historically, children learned language, speech patterns, and grammar from members of the extended family just as they learned rules of conduct within their family unit and community. In modern times, the mother in a nuclear family has become the dominant force in influencing children's development. With increasing social changes, many children are not receiving the proper guidance in all areas of development, especially language.

Those who are fortunate enough to be in educational day-care programs such as Head Start or in certified preschools often develop better language skills than those whose care is entrusted to untrained care providers. Once children enter elementary school, they are greatly influenced by peer language. This peer influence becomes significant in adolescence as the use of teen jargon gives teenagers a sense of identity within their chosen group(s) and independence from the influence of adults. In some lower socioeconomic groups, children use Standard English in school and street language outside of school. Some children of immigrant families become bilingual by necessity if no English is spoken in the home.

Research has shown a strong correlation between socioeconomic characteristics and all areas of intellectual development. Traditional measurement instruments rely on verbal ability to establish intelligence. Research findings and test scores reflect that children reared in nuclear families that provide cultural experiences and individual attention become more language proficient than those who are denied that security and stimulation.

Personal influences

The rate of physical development and identifiable language disabilities also influence language development. Nutritional deficiencies, poor eyesight, and conditions such as stuttering or dyslexia can inhibit a child's ability to master language. Unless diagnosed early, these conditions can hamper communication into adulthood and stymie the development of self-confidence. Children should receive proper diagnosis and positive corrective instruction.

In adolescence, children's choice of role models and decisions about their future determine the growth of identity. Rapid physical and emotional changes along with the pressures of sexual awareness make concentration on any educational pursuit difficult. The easier the transition from childhood to adulthood, the better the competence will be in all learning areas.

Middle school teachers are confronted by a student body ranging from fifth graders who are still childish to eighth or ninth graders who are, if not in fact, at least in their minds, young adults. Middle school teachers must approach language instruction as a social development tool with more emphasis on vocabulary acquisition, reading skills, and speaking/writing skills. High school teachers can deal with the more formalized instruction of grammar, usage, and literature meant for older adolescents, whose social development allows them to pay more attention to studies that will improve their chances for a better adult life.

As a tool, language must have relevance to students' real environment. Many high schools have developed practical English classes for business/vocational students whose specific needs are determined by their desire to enter the workforce upon graduation. More emphasis is placed upon accuracy of mechanics and understanding verbal and written directions because these are skills desired by employers. Writing résumés, completing forms, reading policy and operations manuals, and generating reports are some of the desired skills. In literature classes for college-bound students, more emphasis is placed on higher-level thinking skills, including inferential thinking and literary interpretation.

Middle school teachers must approach language instruction as a social development tool with more emphasis on vocabulary acquisition, reading skills, and speaking/writing skills.

Sample Test Questions and Rationale

(Average)

1. If a student has a poor vocabulary, the teacher should recommend first that:

   A. The student read newspapers, magazines, and books on a regular basis

   B. The student enroll in a Latin class

   C. The student write the words repetitively after looking them up in the dictionary

   D. The student use a thesaurus to locate synonyms and incorporate them into his or her vocabulary

   Answer: A

   Rationale: The teacher can personally influence what the student chooses to read, but the student must also be able to choose reading material independently in order to experience the reading pleasure that is indispensable for enriching vocabulary.

(Average)

2. Which of the following sentences contains a subject-verb agreement error?

   A. Both mother and her two sisters were married in a triple ceremony.

   B. Neither the hen nor the rooster is likely to be served for dinner.

   C. My boss, as well as the company's two personnel directors, have been to Spain.

   D. Amanda and the twins are late again.

   Answer: C

   Rationale: The reason for this is that the true subject of the verb is "My boss," not "two personnel directors."

(Average)

3. The synonyms *gyro, hero,* and *submarine* reflect which influence on language usage?

   A. Social

   B. Geographical

   C. Historical

   D. Personal

Answer: B

Rationale: The words are interchangeable, but their use depends on the region of the United States, not on the social class of the speaker or the historical context. The usage might be personal but will most often vary with the region.

(Rigorous)

4. Which aspect of language is innate?

   A. Biological capability to articulate sounds understood by other humans

   B. Cognitive ability to create syntactical structures

   C. Capacity for using semantics to convey meaning in a social environment

   D. Ability to vary inflections and accents

   Answer: A

   Rationale: Language ability is innate, and the biological capability to produce sounds lets children learn semantics and syntactical structures through trial and error. Linguists agree that language is first a vocal system of word symbols that enables a human to communicate his or her feelings, thoughts, and desires to other human beings.

SKILL Understanding elements of the history and development of the
2.2 English language and American English, including linguistic
change, etymology, and processes of word formation

History and Development of the English Language

History

English is an Indo-European language that evolved through several periods. The origin of English dates to the settlement of the British Isles in the fifth and sixth centuries by Germanic tribes called the Angles, the Saxons, and the Jutes. The original Britons spoke a Celtic tongue while the Angles spoke a Germanic dialect.

Modern English derives from the speech of the Anglo-Saxons, who imposed not only their language but also their social customs and laws on their new land. From the fifth to the tenth century, Britain's language was the tongue we now refer to as Old English. During the next four centuries, the many French attempts at English conquest introduced many French words to English. However, the grammar and syntax of the language remained Germanic.

Middle English, most evident in the writings of Geoffrey Chaucer, dates loosely from 1066 to 1509. William Caxton brought the printing press to England in 1474 and increased literacy. Old English words required numerous inflections to indicate noun cases and plurals as well as verb conjugations. Middle English treated these inflections as separately pronounced syllables. "English" in 1300 would have been written "Olde Anglishe," with the *e*'s at the ends of the words pronounced as our short *a* vowel. Even adjectives had plural inflections: "long dai" became "longe daies," pronounced "long-a day-as." Spelling was phonetic, and thus every vowel had multiple pronunciations, a fact that continues to affect the English language.

Modern English dates from the introduction of The Great Vowels Shift because it created guidelines for spelling and pronunciation. Before the printing press, books were copied laboriously by hand; language was subject to the individual interpretations of the scribes. Printers and subsequently lexicographers such as Samuel Johnson and America's Noah Webster influenced the guidelines. As reading matter became mass-produced, the reading public was forced to adopt the speech and writing habits of those who wrote and printed the books.

Despite many students' insistence to the contrary, Shakespeare's writings are in Modern English. Teachers should stress to students that language, like customs, morals, and other social factors, is constantly subject to change. Immigration, inventions, and cataclysmic events change language just as any other facet of life is affected by these changes.

Learn more about the history of the English language:

http://ebbs.english.vt.edu/hel/hel.html

Teachers should stress to students that language, like customs, morals, and other social factors, is constantly subject to change.

The domination of one race or nation over others can change a language significantly. Beginning with the colonization of the New World by England and Spain, English and Spanish became dominant languages in the Western hemisphere.

American English today is somewhat different in pronunciation and sometimes vocabulary from British English. The British call a truck a "lorry," a baby carriage a "pram"—short for "perambulator"—and an elevator a "lift." The two languages have very few syntactical differences, and even the tonal qualities that were once so clearly different are converging.

Though Modern English is less complex than Middle English, having lost many unnecessary inflections, it is still considered difficult to learn because of its many exceptions to the rules. It has, however, become the world's dominant language by reason of the great political, military, and social power of England from the fifteenth to the nineteenth century and of America in the twentieth century.

Modern inventions, such as the telephone, radio, television, and motion pictures, have especially affected English pronunciation. Regional dialects, once a hindrance to clear understanding, have fewer distinct characteristics. Speakers from different parts of the United States can be identified by their accents, but as educators and media personalities stress uniform pronunciations and proper grammar, the differences are diminishing.

The English language has a more extensive vocabulary than any other language. Ours is a language of synonyms, words borrowed from other languages, and coined words—many of them introduced by the rapid expansion of technology.

Students should understand that language is in constant flux. They can demonstrate this when they use language for specific purposes and audiences. Negative criticism of a student's errors in word choice or sentence structure will inhibit creativity. Positive criticism that suggests ways to enhance communication skills will encourage exploration.

How language changes

Language changes in all its manifestations. At the phonetic level, the sounds of a language will change, as will its orthography (spelling). The vocabulary level will probably manifest the greatest changes. Changes in syntax are slower and less likely to occur. For example, English has changed in response to the influences of many other languages and cultures as well as internal cultural changes such as the development of the railroad and the computer. However, English syntax still relies on word order. The English language has not shifted to an inflected system, even though many of the cultures that have impacted it do, in fact, have an inflected language—for example, Spanish.

Blending of cultures

The most significance influence on a language is the blending of cultures. The Norman Conquest that brought the English speakers in the British Isles under the rule of French speakers changed the language, but the fact that English speakers did not adopt the language of the ruling class is significant. English speakers did not become speakers of French. Even so, many vocabulary items entered the language during that period. The Great Vowel Shift that occurred between the fourteenth and sixteenth centuries is somewhat of a mystery, although it is generally attributed to the migration to Southeast England following the Plague. The Great Vowel Shift largely accounts for the discrepancy between orthography and speech in modern English.

Colonization

Colonization of other countries has also brought new vocabulary words into the language. Indian English has its own easily recognizable attributes, as do Australian and North American English. The fact that English is the most widely spoken and understood language in the world in the twenty-first century implies that it is constantly in flux.

Modern inventions

Other influences, of course, impact language. The introduction of television and its domination by the United States has had a great influence on the English that is spoken and understood all over the world. The same is true of the computerization of the world (Tom Friedman called it "flattening" in his *The World is Flat: A Brief History of the Twenty-first Century*). New terms have been added ("blog"), old terms have changed meaning ("mouse"), and nouns have been verb-ized ("prioritize").

Identification of common morphemes, prefixes, and suffixes

Students should learn to look for structural elements within words that they can use independently to help them determine meaning. The terms listed below are generally recognized as the key structural components of words.

ROOT WORD: word from which another word is developed

BASE WORD: stand-alone linguistic unit that cannot be broken down into smaller words

CONTRACTION: shortened forms of two words in which a letter or letters have been deleted

PREFIX: beginning unit of meaning that can be added to a base or root word

SUFFIX: ending unit of meaning that can be "affixed" or added onto the ends of root or base words

INFLECTIONAL ENDINGS: suffixes that impart a new meaning to the base or root word

COMPOUND WORDS: when two or more base words are connected to form a new word

Learn more about word analysis:

http://www.orangeusd.k12.ca.us/yorba/word_analysis.htm

KEY STRUCTURAL COMPONENTS OF WORDS	
Root Words	A **ROOT WORD** is a word from which another word is developed. The second word can be said to have its "root" in the first. This structural component nicely lends itself to an illustration a tree with roots. Students can use this concrete image to understand an abstract concept. An example of a root word is "bene," which means "good" or "well." English words derived from this Latin root include "benefit," "beneficial," "beneficent," and "beneficiary." Students may want to construct root words literally by using cardboard trees and/or actual roots from plants to create word family models. This is an effective way to help students own their root words.
Base Words	A **BASE WORD** is a stand-alone linguistic unit that cannot be deconstructed or broken down into smaller words. For example, in the word "re-tell," the base word is "tell."
Contractions	A **CONTRACTION** is a shortened forms of two words in which a letter or letters have been deleted. These deleted letters have been replaced by an apostrophe. For example, "hasn't" is the contraction for "has not."
Prefixes	A **PREFIX** is a beginning unit of meaning that can be added (the proper term for this type of structural adding is "affixed") to a base word or root word. Prefixes cannot stand alone. They are also sometimes known as "bound morphemes," meaning that they cannot stand alone as a base word. Some examples of prefixes are "pre-," "ex-," "trans-," and "sub-."
Suffixes	A **SUFFIX** is an ending unit of meaning that can be "affixed" or added onto the ends of root or base words. Suffixes transform the original meanings of base and root words. Like prefixes, they are also known as "bound morphemes" because they cannot stand alone as words. Some examples of suffixes are "-ing," "-ful," "-ness," and "-er."
Inflectional Endings	**INFLECTIONAL ENDINGS** are suffixes that impart a new meaning to the base or root word. These endings in particular change the gender, number, tense, or form of the base or root words. Just like other suffixes, these are also termed "bound morphemes." Some examples are "-ette," "-es," and "-ed."
Compound Words	**COMPOUND WORDS** occur when two or more base words are connected to form a new word. The meaning of the new word is in some way connected with that of the base word. "Bookkeeper," besides being the only English word with three double letters in a row, is an example of a compound word.

Origins of English words

Just as countries and families have histories, so do words. Knowing and understanding the origin of a word—where and how it has been used through the years—and the history of its meaning as it has changed are important components of the writing and language teacher's toolkit.

Never before in the history of the English language, or any other language for that matter, have the forms and meanings of words changed so rapidly. When America was settled originally, immigration from many countries made it a "melting pot." Immigration accelerated rapidly within the first hundred years, resulting in pockets of language throughout the country.

When trains began to make transportation available and affordable, individuals from those various pockets came in contact with each other, shared vocabularies, and attempted to converse. From that time forward, every generation brought the introduction of a technology that made language interchange not only more possible but also more necessary.

The trend to standardize dialects began with radio. A Bostonian might not be understood by a Houstonian, who therefore might hesitate in turning the dial to hear the advertisements of vendors that had a vested interest in being heard and understood. Soap and soup producers knew a gold mine when they saw it and created a market for radio announcers and actors who spoke without a pronounced dialect. In return, listeners began to hear the English language in a dialect very different from the one they spoke, and as it settled into their thinking processes, it eventually made its way to their tongues; consequently, spoken English began to lose some of its local peculiarities.

This change has been a slow process, but most Americans can easily understand other Americans, no matter where they come from. They can even converse with a native of Great Britain with little difficulty. The introduction of television carried the evolution further, as did the explosion of electronic communication devices.

An excellent example of the changes that have occurred in English is a comparison of Shakespeare's original works with modern translations. Without help, twenty-first century Americans are unable to read the Folio.

On the other hand, teachers must constantly be mindful of the vocabularies and etymologies of their students, who are on the receiving end of the escalation brought about by technology and increased global influence.

In the past, the *Oxford English Dictionary* has been one of the most reliable sources for etymologies. Some of the collegiate dictionaries are also useful. *Merriam-Webster's 3rd Unabridged Dictionary* is useful in tracing the sources of words in American English. *Merriam-Webster's Unabridged Dictionary* may be out

Check out the learning resources of the OED:

http://www.oed.com/learning/

of date, so a teacher should also have a *Merriam-Webster's Collegiate Dictionary*, which is updated regularly.

In addition to etymologies, knowing how and when to label a usage "jargon" or "colloquial" is important. The teacher must be aware of the possibility that a word that was previously considered "jargon" is now accepted as standard. To be on top of this, teachers must continually keep up with the etymological aids that are available, particularly online.

If you google "etymology," for instance, or any word you're unsure of, you can find a multitude of information. Don't trust a single source. Any information should be validated by at least three sources. Wikipedia is very useful, but it can be changed by anyone who chooses, so any information on it should be backed up by other sources. If you go to http://www.etymonline.com/sources.php, you will find a long list of resources on etymology.

Spelling

Spelling in English is complicated because it is not phonetic—that is, it is not based on the one sound/one letter formula used by many other languages. It is based on the Latin alphabet, which originally had twenty letters, consisting of the present English alphabet minus J, K, V, W, Y, and Z. The Romans added K to be used in abbreviations and Y and Z in words that came from the Greek. This twenty-three-letter alphabet was adopted by the English, who developed W as a ligatured doubling of U and later J and V as consonantal variants of I and U. The result was our alphabet of twenty-six letters with upper case (capital) and lower case forms.

Spelling is based primarily on fifteenth-century English. The problem is that pronunciation has changed drastically since then, especially pronunciation of long vowels and diphthongs. This Great Vowel Shift affected the seven long vowels.

For a long time, spelling was erratic—there were no standards. As long as the meaning was clear, spelling was not considered very important. Samuel Johnson tackled this problem, and his *Dictionary of the English Language* (1755) brought standards to spelling. These standards became important once printing presses were invented. There have been some changes, of course, through the years, but spelling is still not strictly phonetic.

Despite many attempts to nudge spelling into a more phonetic representation of sounds, all have failed for the most part. A good example is Noah Webster's *Spelling Book* (1783), which was a precursor to the first edition (1828) of his *American Dictionary of the English Language*. While there are rules for spelling, and it's important that students learn the rules, there are also many exceptions. Memorizing exceptions and giving plenty of opportunities for practicing them seems the only solution for the teacher of English.

Sample Test Questions and Rationale

(Easy)

1. **To understand the origins of a word, one must study the:**

   A. Synonyms

   B. Inflections

   C. Phonetics

   D. Etymology

Answer: D

Rationale: Etymology is the study of word origins. A synonym is an equivalent of another word and can substitute for it in certain contexts. Inflection is a modification of words according to their grammatical functions, usually by employing variant word endings to indicate such qualities as tense, gender, case, and number. Phonetics is the science devoted to the physical analysis of the sounds of human speech, including their production, transmission, and perception.

(Easy)

2. **The Elizabethans wrote in:**

   A. Celtic

   B. Old English

   C. Middle English

   D. Modern English

Answer: D

Rationale: There is no document written in Celtic in England, and a work such as *Beowulf* is representative of Old English in the eighth century. Before the fourteenth century, little literature is known to have appeared in Middle English, which had absorbed many words from the Norman French spoken by the ruling class. At the end of the fourteenth century, the works of Chaucer and John Gower and the novel *Sir Gawain and the Green Knight* appeared on the scene. The Elizabethans wrote in modern English. They imported the Petrarchan, or Italian, sonnet, which Sir Thomas Wyatt and Sir Philip Sydney illustrated in their works. Sir Edmund Spenser invented his own version of the Italian sonnet and wrote *The Faerie Queene*. Other literature of the time includes the hugely important works of Shakespeare and Marlowe.

(Average)

3. **Which event triggered the beginning of Modern English?**

   A. Conquest of England by the Normans in 1066

   B. Introduction of the printing press to the British Isles

   C. Publication of Samuel Johnson's lexicon

   D. American Revolution

Answer: B

Rationale: With the arrival of the printed word, reading matter became mass-produced, and so the public tended to adopt the speech and writing habits printed in books. Language became more stable.

Sample Test Questions and Rationale

(Average)

4. **Which of the following is not true about the English language?**

   A. English is the easiest language to learn

   B. English is the least inflected language

   C. English has the most extensive vocabulary of any language

   D. English originated as a Germanic tongue

Answer: A

Rationale: Just like any other language, English has inherent peculiarities that make it difficult to learn, even though English has no declensions such as those found in Latin, Greek, or contemporary Russian, and no tonal system such as is found in Chinese.

(Rigorous)

5. **Which word in the following sentence contains or is itself a bound morpheme: "The quick brown fox jumped over the lazy dog"?**

   A. The

   B. fox

   C. lazy

   D. jumped

Answer: D

Rationale: The suffix "-ed" is an affix that cannot stand alone as a unit of meaning. Thus it is bound to the free morpheme "jump." "The" is always an unbound morpheme because no suffix or prefix can alter its meaning. As written, "fox" and "lazy" are unbound, although their meanings can be changed with affixes, such as "foxes" or "laziness."

(Rigorous)

6. **What was responsible for the standardizing of dialects across America in the twentieth century?**

   A. With the immigrant influx, American became a melting pot of languages and cultures

   B. Trains enabled people to meet other people of different languages and cultures

   C. Radio, and later television, used actors and announcers who spoke without pronounced dialects

   D. Newspapers and libraries developed programs to teach people to speak English with an agreed-upon common dialect

Answer: C

Rationale: The growth of immigration in the early part of the twentieth century created pockets of language throughout the country. Coupled with regional differences already in place, the number of dialects grew. Transportation enabled people to move to different regions, where languages and dialects continued to merge. With the growth of radio and television, however, people were introduced to a standardized dialect through actors and announcers who spoke so that anyone across American could understand them. Newspapers and libraries never developed programs to standardize spoken English.

Sample Test Questions and Rationale

(Rigorous)

7. Latin words that entered the English language during the Elizabethan age include:

   A. *Allusion*, *education*, and *esteem*

   B. *Vogue* and *mustache*

   C. *Canoe* and *cannibal*

   D. *Alligator*, *cocoa*, and *armadillo*

Answer: A

Rationale: These words reflect the Renaissance interest in the classical world and the study of ideas. The words in answer B are of French derivation, and the words in answers C and D are more modern with younger etymologies.

SKILL 2.3 **Understanding and applying the elements of traditional grammar** *(e.g., syntax, sentence types, sentence structure, parts of speech, modifiers, sentence combining, phrases and clauses, capitalization, and punctuation)*

Writers strive to craft sentences that convey their thoughts precisely. One of the first rules of grammar is to use complete sentences, so a review of sentence structure is a must for students.

Sentence Completeness

Students should recognize the sentence elements necessary to form a complete thought and use independent and dependent clauses properly. Proper punctuation will often correct an error.

Sentence structure

Students should recognize simple, compound, complex, and compound-complex sentences. Use dependent (subordinate) and independent clauses correctly to create these sentence structures.

Simple	Joyce wrote a letter.
Compound	Joyce wrote a letter, and Dot drew a picture.

Table continued on next page

Complex	While Joyce wrote a letter, Dot drew a picture.
Compound-Complex	When Mother asked the girls to demonstrate their new-found skills, Joyce wrote a letter, and Dot drew a picture.

Note: Do not confuse compound sentence elements with compound sentences.

Simple sentence with compound subject:

Joyce and Dot wrote letters.

The girl in row three and the boy next to her were passing notes across the aisle.

Simple sentence with compound predicate:

Joyce wrote letters and drew pictures.

The captain of the high school debate team graduated with honors and studied broadcast journalism in college.

Simple sentence with compound object of preposition:

Coleen graded the students' essays for style and mechanical accuracy.

Clauses and phrases

CLAUSES are connected word groups that are composed of *at least* one subject and one verb. (A subject is the doer of an action or the element that is being joined. A verb conveys either the action or the link.)

CLAUSES: connected word groups that are composed of at least one subject and one verb

Students are waiting for the start of the assembly.

  Subject   Verb

At the end of the play, students wait for the curtain to come down.

            Subject Verb

INDEPENDENT CLAUSE: clause that can stand alone as a sentence or be joined to another clause

Clauses can be independent or dependent. **INDEPENDENT CLAUSES** can stand alone or can be joined to other clauses. Connect independent clauses with the coordinating conjunctions—*and, but, or, for,* or *nor*—when their content is of equal importance. Use subordinating conjunctions—*although, because, before, if, since, though, until, when, whenever, where*—and relative pronouns—*that, who, whom, which*—to introduce clauses that express ideas that are subordinate to the main ideas expressed in independent clauses.

CONNECTING CLAUSES		
Comma and coordinating conjunction		
Independent clause	, for	Independent clause
	, and	Independent clause
	, nor	Independent clause
	, but	Independent clause
	, or	Independent clause
	, yet	Independent clause
	, so	Independent clause
Semicolon		
Independent clause	;	Independent clause
Subordinating conjunction, dependent clause, and comma		
Dependent clause	,	Independent clause
Independent clause followed by a subordinating conjunction that introduces a dependent clause		
Independent clause		Dependent clause

DEPENDENT CLAUSES, by definition, contain at least one subject and one verb. However, they cannot stand alone as a complete sentence. They are structurally dependent on the main clause.

There are two types of dependent clauses: (1) those with a subordinating conjunction, and (2) those with a relative pronoun.

Sample subordinating conjunctions: *although, when, if, unless, because*

> *Unless a cure is discovered, many more people will die of the disease.*
>
> (*Coordinating conjunction* + *dependent clause* + *independent clause*)

DEPENDENT CLAUSES: clauses that contain at least one subject and one verb but cannot stand alone as a complete sentence

Sample relative pronouns: *who, whom, which, that*

> The White House has an official website, <u>which</u> contains press releases, news updates, and biographies of the president and vice president.
>
> (Independent clause + relative pronoun + relative dependent clause)

Be sure to place the conjunctions so that they express the proper relationship between ideas (cause/effect, condition, time, space).

Incorrect: *Because mother scolded me, I was late.*

Correct: *Mother scolded me because I was late.*

Incorrect: *The sun rose after the fog lifted.*

Correct: *The fog lifted after the sun rose.*

Notice that placement of the conjunction can completely change the meaning of the sentence. The main emphasis is shifted by the change.

> Although Jenny was pleased, the teacher was disappointed.
>
> Although the teacher was disappointed, Jenny was pleased.
>
> The boys who had written the essay won the contest.
>
> The boys who won the contest had written the essay.

While not syntactically incorrect, the last sentence makes it appear that the boys won the contest for something else before they wrote the essay.

Misplaced and dangling modifiers

Misplaced modifiers occur when particular phrases are not placed near the word they modify. Dangling modifiers occur when particular phrases do not relate to the subject being modified.

Error: *Weighing the options carefully, a decision was made regarding the punishment of the convicted murderer.*

Problem: Who is weighing the options? No one capable of weighing is named in the sentence; thus, the participle phrase "weighing the options carefully" dangles. This problem can be corrected by adding a subject capable of doing the action.

Correction: *Weighing the options carefully, the judge made a decision regarding the punishment of the convicted murderer.*

Error: *Returning to my favorite watering hole brought back many fond memories.*

Problem: The person who returned is never indicated, and the participle phrase dangles. This problem can be corrected by creating a dependent clause from the modifying phrase.

Correction: *When I returned to my favorite watering hole, many fond memories came back to me.*

Error: *One damaged house stood only to remind townspeople of the hurricane.*

Problem: The placement of the misplaced modifier "only" suggests that the sole reason the house remained was to serve as a reminder. The faulty modifier creates ambiguity.

Correction: *Only one damaged house stood, reminding townspeople of the hurricane.*

Parallelism

Students should recognize parallel structures using phrases (prepositional, gerund, participial, and infinitive) and omissions from sentences that create a lack of parallelism. Parallelism provides balance between the grammar and the ideas.

Prepositional phrase/single modifier

Incorrect: *Coleen ate the ice cream with enthusiasm and hurriedly.*

Correct: *Coleen ate the ice cream with enthusiasm and in a hurry.*

Correct: *Coleen ate the ice cream enthusiastically and hurriedly.*

Participial phrase/infinitive phrase

Incorrect: *After hiking for hours and to sweat profusely, Joe sat down to rest and drinking water.*

Correct: *After hiking for hours and sweating profusely, Joe sat down to rest and drink water.*

> *Learn more about parallel structure vs. faulty parallelism:*
>
> *http://jerz.setonhill.edu/writing/grammar/parallel.html*

Recognition of syntactical redundancy or omission

Redundancy and omission errors occur when superfluous words are added to a sentence or key words are omitted from a sentence.

Redundancy

Incorrect: *Joyce made sure that when her plane arrived that she retrieved all of her luggage.*

Correct: *Joyce made sure that when her plane arrived she retrieved all of her luggage.*

Incorrect: *He was a mere skeleton of his former self.*

Correct: *He was a skeleton of his former self.*

Omission

Incorrect: *Dot opened her book, recited her textbook, and answered the teacher's subsequent question.*

Correct: *Dot opened her book, recited from the textbook, and answered the teacher's subsequent question.*

Avoidance of double negatives

A double negative occurs when two negatives cancel each other in meaning.

Incorrect: *Dot didn't have no double negatives in her paper.*

Correct: *Dot didn't have any double negatives in her paper.*

Parts of Speech

The eight parts of speech form the syntactical framework of our language. While the study of grammar can be detailed, let's review some of the basics.

- Noun: names a person, place, or thing
- Pronoun: takes the place of one or more nouns
- Verb: expresses action or state of being
- Adjective: describes or modifies a noun or pronoun
- Adverb: modifies a verb, an adjective, or another adverb
- Conjunction: is a connecting word
- Preposition: relates a noun or pronoun to another word in a sentence
- Interjection: expresses emotion

Nouns

A NOUN names a person, place, or thing/idea. A COMMON NOUN names *any* person, place, or thing/idea; a PROPER NOUN names a *particular* person, place, or thing/idea. A proper noun is capitalized.

	Person	Place	Thing	Idea
Common Noun	Actor	museum	ship	bravery
Proper Noun	Meryl Streep	The Smithsonian	*Titanic*	

Plural nouns

A good dictionary is an invaluable resource that can replace the need to learn complex spelling rules based on phonics or letter doubling, especially when the exceptions to these rules have not been mastered by adulthood. Learning to use a dictionary and thesaurus will be a rewarding use of time.

Most plurals of nouns that end in hard consonants or hard consonant sounds followed by a silent *e* are made by adding -*s*. Plurals of some words ending in vowels are formed by adding only -*s*.

> *fingers, numerals, banks, bugs, riots, homes, gates, radios, bananas*

For nouns that end in soft consonant sounds—*s, j, x, z, ch,* and *sh*—the plurals are formed by adding -*es*. Plurals of some nouns ending in *o* are formed by adding -*es*.

> *dresses, waxes, churches, brushes, tomatoes*

For nouns ending in *y* preceded by a vowel, just add -*s*.

> *boys, alleys*

For nouns ending in *y* preceded by a consonant, change the *y* to *i* and add -*es*.

> *babies, corollaries, frugalities, poppies*

Some nouns' plurals are formed irregularly or remain the same.

> *sheep, deer, children, leaves, oxen*

NOUN: part of speech that names a person, place, or thing/idea

COMMON NOUN: names any person, place, or thing/idea

PROPER NOUN: names a particular person, place, or thing/idea and is capitalized

Some nouns derived from foreign words, especially Latin words, are made plural in two different ways. Sometimes the meanings are the same; other times the two plural forms are used in slightly different contexts. It is always wise to consult the dictionary.

> appendices, appendixes   criterion, criteria
> indexes, indices   crisis, crises

Make the plurals of closed (solid) compound words in the usual way.

> timelines, hairpins

Make the plurals of open or hyphenated compounds by adding the change in inflection to the word that changes in number.

> fathers-in-law, courts-martial, masters of art, doctors of medicine

Make the plurals of letters, numbers, and abbreviations by adding -*s*.

> fives and tens, IBMs, 1990s, ps and qs (Note that letters are italicized.)

Possessive nouns

Make the possessives of singular nouns by adding an apostrophe followed by the letter *s* ('*s*).

> baby's bottle, father's job, elephant's eye, teacher's desk, sympathizer's protests, week's postponement

Make the possessives of singular nouns ending in *s* by adding either an apostrophe or an ('*s*), depending on common usage or sound. When the possessive sounds awkward, use a prepositional phrase instead. Even with the sibilant ending, with a few exceptions, it is advisable to use the ('*s*) construction.

> dress's color, species' characteristics or characteristics of the species, James' hat or James's hat, Delores's shirt.

Make the possessives of plural nouns ending in *s* by adding the apostrophe after the *s*.

> *horses' coats, jockeys' times, four days' time*

Make the possessives of plural nouns that do not end in *s* by adding *'s*, just as with singular nouns.

> *children's shoes, deer's antlers, cattle's horns*

Make the possessives of compound nouns by adding the inflection at the end of the word or phrase.

> *the mayor of Los Angeles' campaign, the mailman's new truck, the mailmen's new trucks, my father-in-law's first wife, the keepsakes' values, several daughters-in-law's husbands*

Note: Because a gerund functions as a noun, any noun preceding it and operating as a possessive adjective must reflect the necessary inflection. However, if the gerundive following the noun is a participle, no inflection is added.

> *The general was perturbed by the private's sleeping on duty. (The word **sleeping** is a gerund, the object of the preposition **by**.)*
>
> *but*
>
> *The general was perturbed to see the private sleeping on duty. (The word **sleeping** is a participle modifying **private**.)*

Pronoun

A **PRONOUN** takes the place of one or more nouns and must agree with that noun in case and number. The noun to which a pronoun refers is called the **ANTECEDENT**.

> **PRONOUN:** takes the place of one or more nouns and must agree with that noun in case and number

> **ANTECEDENT:** the noun to which a pronoun refers

Proper case forms

Pronouns, unlike nouns, change case forms. Pronouns must be in the subjective, objective, or possessive form according to their function in the sentence.

PERSONAL PRONOUNS					
	SUBJECTIVE (NOMINATIVE)		POSSESSIVE		OBJECTIVE	
	Singular	Plural	Singular	Plural	Singular	Plural
1st Person	I	we	my	our	me	us
2nd Person	you	you	your	your	you	you
3rd Person	he she it	they	his her its	their	him her it	them

RELATIVE PRONOUNS	
Who	Subjective/Nominative
Whom	Objective
Whose	Possessive

Rules for clearly identifying pronoun reference

Misuse of pronouns creates agreement errors and clouds the meaning of the sentence. Here are a few tips to correct this common grammatical error.

Make sure that the antecedent reference is clear and cannot refer to something else

A "distant relative" is a relative pronoun or a relative clause that has been placed too far away from the antecedent to which it refers. It is a common error to place a verb between the relative pronoun and its antecedent.

Error:	*Return the books to the library that are overdue.*
Problem:	The relative clause "that are overdue" refers to the "books" and should be placed immediately after the antecedent.
Correction:	*Return the books that are overdue to the library.* *or* *Return the overdue books to the library.*

A pronoun should not refer to adjectives or possessive nouns

Adjectives, nouns, or possessive pronouns should not be used as antecedents. This will create ambiguity in sentences.

Error: *In Todd's letter he told his mom he'd broken the priceless vase.*

Problem: In this sentence the pronoun "he" seems to refer to the noun phrase "Todd's letter," though it was probably meant to refer to the possessive noun "Todd's."

Correction: *In his letter, Todd told his mom that he had broken the priceless vase.*

A pronoun should not refer to an implied idea

A pronoun must refer to a specific antecedent rather than to an implied antecedent. When an antecedent is not stated specifically, the reader has to guess or assume the meaning of a sentence. Pronouns that do not have antecedents are called expletives. "It" and "there" are the most common expletives, though other pronouns can also become expletives as well. In informal conversation, expletives allow for casual presentation of ideas without supporting evidence. However, in more formal writing, it is best to be more precise.

Error: *She said that it is important to floss every day.*

Problem: The pronoun "it" refers to an implied idea.

Correction: *She said that flossing every day is important.*

Error: *They returned the book because there were missing pages.*

Problem: The pronouns "they" and "there" do not refer to the antecedent.

Correction: *The customer returned the book with missing pages.*

Using who, that, and which

Who, whom, and *whose* refer to human beings and can introduce either essential or nonessential clauses. *That* refers to things other than humans and is used to introduce essential clauses. *Which* refers to things other than humans and is used to introduce nonessential clauses.

Error: *The doctor that performed the surgery said the man would recover fully.*

Problem: Since the relative pronoun is referring to a human, *who* should be used.

Correction: *The doctor who performed the surgery said the man would recover fully.*

Error: *That ice cream cone that you just ate looked really delicious.*

Problem: *That* has already been used, so you must use *which* to introduce the next clause, whether it is essential or nonessential.

Correction: *That ice cream cone, which you just ate, looked really delicious.*

Error: *Tom and me have reserved seats for next week's baseball game.*

Problem: The pronoun *me* is the subject of the verb *have reserved* and should be in the subjective form.

Correction: *Tom and I have reserved seats for next week's baseball game.*

Error: *Who's coat is this?*

Problem: The interrogative possessive pronoun is *whose; who's* is the contraction for *who is.*

Correction: *Whose coat is this?*

Error: *The voters will choose the candidate whom has the best qualifications for the job.*

Problem: The case of the relative pronoun *who* or *whom* is determined by the pronoun's function in the clause in which it appears. The word *who* is in the subjective case, and *whom* is in the objective. Analyze how the pronoun is being used within the sentence.

Correction: *The voters will choose the candidate who has the best qualifications for the job.*

Verbs

A **VERB** expresses action or state of being. Most verbs show time (tense) by an inflectional ending to the word. Other, irregular verbs take completely different forms.

VERB: expresses action or state of being

Both regular and irregular verbs must appear in their standard forms for each tense. Note: the *-ed* or *-d* ending is added to regular verbs in the past tense and for past participles.

REGULAR VERB FORMS		
Infinitive	Past Tense	Past Participle
bake	baked	baked

IREGULAR VERB FORMS		
Infinitive	Past Tense	Past Participle
be	was, were	been
become	became	become
break	broke	broken
bring	brought	brought
choose	chose	chosen
come	came	come
do	did	done
draw	drew	drawn
eat	ate	eaten
fall	fell	fallen
forget	forgot	forgotten
freeze	froze	frozen
give	gave	given
go	went	gone
grow	grew	grown

Table continued on next page

Infinitive	Past Tense	Past Participle
have/has	had	had
hide	hid	hidden
know	knew	known
lay	laid	laid
lie	lay	lain
ride	rode	ridden
rise	rose	risen
run	ran	run
see	saw	seen
steal	stole	stolen
take	took	taken
tell	told	told
throw	threw	thrown
wear	wore	worn
write	wrote	written

Error: *She should have went to her doctor's appointment at the scheduled time.*

Problem: The past participle of the verb *to go* is *gone. Went* expresses the simple past tense.

Correction: *She should have gone to her doctor's appointment at the scheduled time.*

Error: *My train is suppose to arrive before two o'clock.*

Problem: The verb following *train* is a present tense passive construction, which requires the present tense verb *to be* and the past participle.

Correction: *My train is supposed to arrive before two o'clock.*

Error: *Linda should of known that the car wouldn't start after leaving it out in the cold all night.*

Problem: *Should of* is a nonstandard expression. *Of* is not a verb.

Correction: *Linda should have known that the car wouldn't start after leaving it out in the cold all night.*

Subject-verb agreement

A verb must agree in number with its subject. The subject must be correctly identified to ensure agreement.

> *One of the boys was playing too rough.*
>
> *No one in the class, neither the teacher nor the students, was listening to the message from the intercom.*
>
> *The candidates, including a grandmother and a teenager, are debating some controversial issues.*

If two singular subjects are connected by *and*, the verb must be plural.

> *A man and his dog were jogging on the beach.*

If two singular subjects are connected by *or* or *nor*, a singular verb is required.

> *Neither Dot nor Joyce has missed a day of school this year.*
>
> *Either Fran or Paul is missing.*

If one singular subject and one plural subject are connected by *or* or *nor*, the verb agrees with the subject nearest to the verb.

> *Neither the coach nor the players were able to sleep on the bus.*

If the subject is a collective noun, its sense of number in the sentence determines the verb: singular if the noun represents a group or unit and plural if the noun represents individuals.

> *The House of Representatives has adjourned for the holidays.*
>
> *The House of Representatives have failed to reach agreement on the subject of adjournment.*

Use of verbs: tense

PRESENT TENSE is used to express that which is currently happening or is always true.

> *Randy is playing the piano.*
> *Randy plays the piano like a pro.*

PAST TENSE is used to express action that occurred in a past time.

> *Randy learned to play the piano when he was six years old.*

FUTURE TENSE is used to express action or a condition of future time.

> *Randy will probably earn a music scholarship.*

PRESENT PERFECT TENSE is used to express action or a condition that started in the past and is continued or completed in the present.

> *Randy has practiced the piano every day for the last ten years.*
> *Randy has never been bored with practice.*

PAST PERFECT TENSE expresses action or a condition that occurred as a precedent to some other past action or condition.

> *Randy had considered playing clarinet before he discovered the piano.*

FUTURE PERFECT TENSE expresses action that started in the past or the present and will conclude at some time in the future.

> *By the time he goes to college, Randy will have been an accomplished pianist for more than half of his life.*

Use of verbs: mood

Indicative mood is used to make unconditional statements; subjunctive mood is used for conditional clauses or wish statements that pose conditions that are untrue. Verbs in subjunctive mood are plural with both singular and plural subjects.

> *If I <u>were</u> a bird, I would fly.*
> *I wish I <u>were</u> as rich as Donald Trump.*

PRESENT TENSE: expresses that which is currently happening or is always true

PAST TENSE: expresses action that occurred in a past time

FUTURE TENSE: expresses action or a condition of future time

PRESENT PERFECT TENSE: expresses action or a condition that started in the past and is continued or completed in the present

PAST PERFECT TENSE: expresses action or a condition that occurred as a precedent to some other past action or condition

FUTURE PERFECT TENSE: expresses action that started in the past or the present and will conclude at some time in the future

Use of verbs: voice

A verb is in the **ACTIVE VOICE** when its subject is the doer of the action. A verb is in the **PASSIVE VOICE** when its subject is the receiver of the action.

> **ACTIVE VOICE:** when the subject of the verb is the doer of the action

> **PASSIVE VOICE:** when the subject of the verb is the receiver of the action

Active Voice	Passive Voice
The director adjourned the meeting. The subject, *director*, performs the action, *adjourned*.	**The meeting was adjourned by the director.** The subject, *meeting*, is not performing the action; instead, it is receiving the action, *was adjourned*.
The mechanic at the Shell station inspected Mrs. Johnson's automobile. The subject, *mechanic*, performed the action, *inspected*.	**Mrs. Johnson's automobile was inspected by the mechanic at the Shell station.** The subject, *automobile*, is not acting; it is receiving the action, *was inspected*.

How do you recognize passive voice? Look at the verb. A passive-voice verb has at least two parts:

1. A form of the verb to be (am, is, are, was, were, be, been)

> *The computer <u>was</u> installed by Datacorp.*

2. A past participle form of the main verb (thrown, driven, planted, talked)

> *The computer was <u>installed</u> by Datacorp.*

   – Sometimes the subject is in an object position in the sentence.

> *The computer was installed by <u>Datacorp</u>. (object of preposition)*

   – Watch for a "by" statement between the verb phrase and the object.

> *The computer was installed <u>by</u> Datacorp. (preposition)*

   – Sometimes the doer is not even present.

> *The computer was installed. (By whom?)*

Verb conjugation

The conjugation of verbs follows the patterns used in the discussion of tense above. However, the most common errors in verb use stem from the improper formation of the past and past participial forms.

Regular verb:	*believe, believed, (have) believed*
Irregular verbs:	*run, ran, run; sit, sat, sat; teach, taught, taught*

Other errors stem from the use of verbs that are the same in some tenses but have different forms and different meanings in other tenses.

I lie on the ground. I lay on the ground yesterday. I have lain down. I lay the blanket on the bed. I laid the blanket there yesterday. I have laid the blanket down every night.

The sun rises. The sun rose. The sun has risen.

He raises the flag. He raised the flag. He had raised the flag.

I sit on the porch. I sat on the porch. I have sat in the porch swing.

I set the plate on the table. I set the plate there yesterday. I had set the table before dinner.

Adjectives and adverbs

ADJECTIVES are words that modify or describe nouns or pronouns. Adjectives usually precede the words they modify, but not always; for example, an adjective occurs after a linking verb. Adjectives answer *what kind, how many,* or *which one.*

ADVERBS are words that modify verbs, adjectives, or other adverbs. They cannot modify nouns. Adverbs answer such questions as *how, why, when, where, how much,* or *how often.* Many adverbs are formed by adding *-ly.*

> **ADJECTIVES:** words that modify or describe nouns or pronouns

> **ADVERBS:** words that modify verbs, adjectives, or other adverbs

Error:	*The birthday cake tasted sweetly.*
Problem:	*Tasted* is a linking verb; the modifier that follows should be an adjective, not an adverb.
Correction:	*The birthday cake tasted sweet.*

Error:	*You have done good with this project.*
Problem:	*Good* is an adjective and cannot be used to modify a verb phrase such as *have done.*
Correction:	*You have done well with this project.*

Error: *The coach was positive happy about the team's chance of winning.*

Problem: The adjective positive cannot be used to modify another adjective, *happy*. An adverb is needed instead.

Correction: *The coach was positively happy about the team's chance of winning.*

Error: *The fireman acted quick and brave to save the child from the burning building.*

Problem: *Quick* and *brave* are adjectives and cannot be used to describe a verb. Adverbs are needed instead.

Correction: *The fireman acted quickly and bravely to save the child from the burning building.*

Conjunctions

A CONJUNCTION connects words, phrases, or clauses. It acts as a signal, indicating when a thought is added, contrasted, or altered.

> **CONJUNCTION:** connects words, phrases, or clauses

Meet the FANBOYS! This mnemonic device will help students remember the seven coordinating conjunctions.

> *For, And, Nor, But, Or, Yet, So*

COORDINATING CONJUNCTIONS join similar elements.

> **COORDINATING CONJUNCTIONS:** join similar elements

> *Strong and tall (adjectives)*
> *Easily and quickly (adverbs)*
> *Over the river and through the woods (prepositional phrases)*
> *We disagreed, but we reached a compromise. (sentences)*

SUBORDINATING CONJUNCTIONS connect clauses (subject-verb combinations) in a sentence. They signal that the clause is subordinate and cannot stand alone.

> **SUBORDINATING CONJUNCTIONS:** connect clauses (subject-verb combinations) in a sentence and signal that the clause is subordinate and cannot stand alone

SUBORDINATING CONJUNCTIONS			
after	because	though	whenever
although	before	till	where

Table continued on next page

as	if	unless	whereas
as if	since	until	wherever
as though	than	when	while

Check out this guide to grammar and writing:

http://grammar.ccc.commnet.edu/grammar/

*I will be grateful **if you will work on this project with me**.*

***Because I am running late**, you will need to cover for me.*

: relates a noun or pronoun to another word in a sentence

Prepositions

A **PREPOSITION** relates a noun or pronoun to another word in a sentence. Think of prepositions as words that show relationships. Below is a partial list.

about	above	according to	across	after	against
along	along with	among	apart from	around	as/as for
at	because of	before	behind	below	beneath
beside	between	beyond	by	by means of	concerning
despite	down	during	except	except for	excepting
for	from	in	in addition to	in back of	in case of
in front of	in place of	inside	in spite of	instead of	into
like	near	next	of	off	on
onto	on top of	out/out of	outside	over	past
regarding	round	since	through	throughout	till
to	toward	under	underneath	unlike	until
up/upon	up to	with	within	without	

PREPOSITION GUIDELINES	
Include necessary prepositions.	*I graduated from high school. (not I graduated high school.)*
Omit unnecessary prepositions.	*Both printers work well. (Not Both of the printers work well.)* *Where are the printers? (Not Where are the printers at?)*
Avoid the overuse of prepositions.	*Error: We have received your application for credit at our branch in the Fresno area.* *Correction: We have received your credit application at our Fresno branch.*

Interjections

An **INTERJECTION** is a word or group of words that express emotion, surprise, or disbelief. An interjection has no grammatical connection to other words in a sentence.

> **INTERJECTION:** word or group of words that express emotion, surprise, or disbelief

SOME COMMON INTERJECTIONS			
aha	great	my	ouch
alas	ha	no	well
gee	hey	oh	wow
good grief	hooray	oops	yes

INTERJECTION GUIDELINES	
When an interjection expresses strong emotion, it usually stands alone. It begins with a capital letter and ends with an exclamation point.	*Ouch! That paper cut really hurts.* *Good grief! My favorite store has closed.*
When an interjection expresses mild feeling, it is written as part of the sentence and is set off with commas.	*Yes, we will comply with your request.*

Capitalization

Capitalize all proper names of persons (including specific organizations or agencies of government), places (countries, states, cities, parks, and specific geographical areas), things (political parties, structures, historical and cultural terms, and calendar and time designations), and religious terms (deities, revered persons or groups, and sacred writings).

> *Percy Bysshe Shelley, Argentina, Mount Rainier National Park, Grand Canyon, League of Nations, the Sears Tower, Birmingham, Lyric Theater, Americans, Midwesterners, Democrats, Renaissance, Boy Scouts of America, Easter, God, Bible, Dead Sea Scrolls, Koran*

Capitalize proper adjectives and titles used with proper names.

> *California gold rush, President John Adams, French fries, Homeric epic, Romanesque architecture, Senator John Glenn*

Note: Some words that represent titles and offices are not capitalized unless used with a proper name.

Capitalized	Not Capitalized
Congressman McKay	*the congressman from Florida*
Commander Alger	*commander of the Pacific Fleet*
Queen Elizabeth	*the queen of England*

Capitalize all main words in titles of works of literature, art, and music.

Punctuation

A basic way to show relationships between ideas in sentences is to use punctuation correctly and effectively. Competency exams will generally test the ability to apply the more advanced skills; thus, a limited number of more frustrating rules are presented here. Rules should be applied according to the American style of English, e.g., placing terminal marks of punctuation almost exclusively within other marks of punctuation.

Quotation marks

The more troublesome punctuation marks involve the use of quotations.

Using terminal punctuation in relation to quotation marks

In a quoted statement that is either declarative or imperative, place the period inside the closing quotation marks.

> *"The airplane crashed on the runway during takeoff."*

If the quotation is followed by other words in the sentence, place a comma inside the closing quotations marks and a period at the end of the sentence.

"The airplane crashed on the runway during takeoff," said the announcer.

In most instances in which a quoted title or expression occurs at the end of a sentence, the period is placed before either the single or double quotation marks.

The educator worried, "The middle school readers were unprepared to understand Bryant's poem 'Thanatopsis.'"

Early book-length adventure stories like Don Quixote *and* The Three Musketeers *are known as "picaresque novels."*

There is an instance in which the final quotation mark precedes the period: if the content of the sentence is about a speech or quote, and the understanding of the meaning might be confused by the placement of the period.

The first thing out of his mouth was "Hi, I'm home."

but

The first line of his speech began "I arrived home to an empty house".

In sentences that are interrogatory or exclamatory, the question mark or exclamation point should be positioned outside the closing quotation marks if the quote itself is a statement or command or a cited title.

Who decided to lead us in the recitation of the "Pledge of Allegiance"?

Why was Tillie shaking as she began her recitation, "Once upon a midnight dreary..."?

I was embarrassed when Mrs. White said, "Your slip is showing"!

In sentences that are declarative but in which the quotation is a question or an exclamation, place the question mark or exclamation point inside the quotation marks.

The hall monitor yelled, "Fire! Fire!"

"Fire! Fire!" yelled the hall monitor.

Cory shrieked, "Is there a mouse in the room?" (In this instance, the question supersedes the exclamation.)

Using double quotation marks with other punctuation

Quotations—whether words, phrases, or clauses—should be punctuated according to the rules of the grammatical function they serve in the sentence.

> *The works of Shakespeare, "the bard of Avon," have been contested as originating with other authors.*
>
> *"You'll get my money," the old man warned, "when 'Hell freezes over'."*
>
> *Sheila cited the passage that began "Four score and seven years ago...." (Note the ellipsis followed by an enclosed period.)*
>
> *"Old Ironsides" inspired the preservation of the U.S.S. Constitution.*

Use quotation marks to enclose the titles of shorter works: songs, short poems, short stories, essays, and chapters of books. (See "Using Italics" for rules on punctuating longer titles.)

> *"The Tell-Tale Heart" (short story)*
>
> *"Casey at the Bat" (poem)*
>
> *"America the Beautiful" (song)*

Using commas

Use commas to separate two or more coordinate adjectives modifying the same word and three or more nouns, phrases, or clauses in a list.

> *Maggie's hair was dull, dirty, and lice-ridden.*
>
> *Dickens portrayed the Artful Dodger as skillful pickpocket, loyal follower of Fagin, and defendant of Oliver Twist.*
>
> *Ellen daydreamed about getting out of the rain, taking a shower, and eating a hot dinner.*
>
> *In Elizabethan England, Ben Jonson wrote comedy, Christopher Marlowe wrote tragedies, and William Shakespeare composed both.*

Use commas to separate antithetical or complimentary expressions from the rest of the sentence.

> *The veterinarian, not his assistant, would perform the delicate surgery.*
>
> *The more he knew about her, the less he wished he had known.*
>
> *Randy hopes to, and probably will, get an appointment to the Naval Academy.*

Using semicolons

Use semicolons to separate independent clauses when the second clause is introduced by a transitional adverb. (These clauses may also be written as separate sentences, preferably by placing the adverb within the second sentence.)

The Elizabethans modified the rhyme scheme of the sonnet; thus, it was called the English sonnet.

or

The Elizabethans modified the rhyme scheme of the sonnet. It thus was called the English sonnet.

Use semicolons to separate items in a series that are long and complex or have internal punctuation.

The Italian Renaissance produced masters in the fine arts: Dante Alighieri, author of the Divine Comedy; Leonardo da Vinci, painter of The Last Supper; *and Donatello, sculptor of the* Quattro Coronati, *the Four Saints.*

The leading scorers in the WNBA were Haizhaw Zheng, averaging 23.9 points per game; Lisa Leslie, 22; and Cynthia Cooper, 19.5.

Using colons

Place a colon at the beginning of a list of items. (Note its use in the sentence about Renaissance Italians previously.)

The teacher directed us to compare Faulkner's three symbolic novels: Absalom, Absalom; As I Lay Dying; *and* Light in August.

Do *not* use a comma if the list is preceded by a verb.

Three of Faulkner's symbolic novels are Absalom, Absalom; As I Lay Dying; *and* Light in August.

Using dashes

Place dashes (called "em" dashes) to denote sudden breaks in thought.

Some periods in literature—the Romantic Age, for example—spanned different time periods in different countries.

Use dashes instead of commas if commas are already used elsewhere in the sentence for amplification or explanation.

The Fireside Poets included three Brahmans—James Russell Lowell, Henry David Wadsworth, and Oliver Wendell Holmes—and John Greenleaf Whittier.

Using italics

Use italics to punctuate the titles of long works of literature and the names of periodical publications, musical scores, works of art, and motion picture, television, and radio programs. (If italic type is not available, you can instruct students to underline text that should be italicized.)

The Idylls of the King	*Hiawatha*	*The Sound and the Fury*
Mary Poppins	*Newsweek*	*The Nutcracker Suite*

Sample Test Questions and Rationale

(Easy)

1. **Which of the following sentences is properly punctuated?**

    A. The more you eat; the more you want.

    B. The authors—John Steinbeck, Ernest Hemingway, and William Faulkner—are staples of modern writing in American literature textbooks.

    C. Handling a wild horse, takes a great deal of skill and patience.

    D. The man who replaced our teacher, is a comedian.

    Answer: B

    Rationale: Dashes should be used instead of commas when commas are used elsewhere in the sentence for amplification or explanation—here within the dashes.

(Rigorous)

2. **Which sentence below best minimizes the impact of bad news?**

    A. We have denied you permission to attend the event.

    B. Although permission to attend the event cannot be given, you are encouraged to buy the video.

    C. Although you cannot attend the event, we encourage you to buy the video.

    D. Although attending the event is not possible, watching the video is an option.

    Answer: B

    Rationale: Subordinating the bad news and using passive voice minimizes the impact of the bad news. In Answer A, the sentence is active voice and thus too direct. The word *denied* sets a negative tone. In Answer C, the bad news is subordinated but it is still active voice with negative wording. In Answer D, the sentence is too unclear.

Sample Test Questions and Rationale (cont.)

(Rigorous)

3. The arrangement and relationships of words in sentences or sentence structures best describes:

   A. Style

   B. Discourse

   C. Thesis

   D. Syntax

Answer: D

Rationale: Syntax is the grammatical structure of sentences. Style is the manner of expression of writing or speaking. Discourse is an extended expression of thought through either oral or written communication. A thesis is the unifying main idea, which can be either explicit or implicit.

(Rigorous)

4. Which of the following sentences contains a capitalization error?

   A. The commander of the English navy was Admiral Nelson.

   B. Napoleon was the president of the French First Republic.

   C. Queen Elizabeth II is the Monarch of the British Empire.

   D. William the Conqueror led the Normans to victory over the British.

Answer: C

Rationale: Words that represent titles and offices are not capitalized unless used with a proper name. This is not the case here.

DIRECTIONS: In sentences 5–12, circle the choice that best corrects the error (underlined) without changing the meaning of the original sentence.

(Easy)

5. Joe <u>didn't hardly know his cousin Fred</u>, who'd had a rhinoplasty.

   A. hardly did know his cousin Fred

   B. didn't know his cousin Fred hardly

   C. hardly knew his cousin Fred

   D. didn't know his cousin Fred

   E. didn't hardly know his cousin Fred

Answer: C

Rationale: Using the adverb "hardly" to modify the verb creates a negative, and adding "not" creates the dreaded double negative.

(Average)

6. <u>Mixing the batter for cookies</u>, the cat licked the Crisco from the cookie sheet.

   A. While mixing the batter for cookies

   B. While the batter for cookies was mixing

   C. While I mixed the batter for cookies

   D. While I mixed the cookies

   E. Mixing the batter for cookies

Answer: C

Rationale: Answers A and E give the impression that the cat was mixing the batter (the underlined phrase is a dangling modifier). Answer B implies that the batter was mixing itself, and Answer D lacks precision: it is the batter that was being mixed, not the cookies themselves.

Sample Test Questions and Rationale (cont.)

(Average)

7. Mr. Smith <u>respectfully submitted his resignation and had</u> a new job.

   A. respectfully submitted his resignation and has

   B. respectfully submitted his resignation before accepting

   C. respectfully submitted his resignation because of

   D. respectfully submitted his resignation and had

Answer: C

Rationale: Answer A eliminates any relationship of causality between submitting the resignation and having the new job. Answer B just changes the sentence and, by omission, does not indicate the fact that Mr. Smith had a new job before submitting his resignation. Answer D means that Mr. Smith first submitted his resignation, and then got a new job.

(Average)

8. Wally <u>groaned</u>, "Why do I have to do an oral interpretation of "The Raven."

   A. groaned, "Why… of 'The Raven'?"

   B. groaned, "Why… of "The Raven"?

   C. groaned ", Why… of "The Raven?"

   D. groaned, "Why… of "The Raven."

Answer: A

Rationale: The question mark in a quotation that is an interrogation should be within the quotation marks. Also, when quoting a work of literature within another quotation, one should use single quotation marks ('…') for the title of this work, and they should close before the final quotation mark.

(Rigorous)

9. <u>The coach offered her assistance but</u> the athletes wanted to practice on their own.

   A. The coach offered her assistance, however, the athletes wanted to practice on their own.

   B. The coach offered her assistance: furthermore, the athletes wanted to practice on their own.

   C. Having offered her assistance, the athletes wanted to practice on their own.

   D. The coach offered her assistance; however, the athletes wanted to practice on their own.

   E. The coach offered her assistance, and the athletes wanted to practice on their own.

Answer: D

Rationale: A semicolon precedes a transitional adverb that introduces an independent clause. Answer A is a comma splice. In Answer B, the colon is used incorrectly since the second clause does not explain the first. In Answer C, the opening clause confuses the meaning of the sentence. In Answer E, the conjunction *and* is weak because the two ideas show contrast rather than an additional thought.

Sample Test Questions and Rationale (cont.)

(Rigorous)

10. The Taj Mahal has been designated one of the Seven Wonders of the World, and people know it for its unique architecture.

   A. The Taj Mahal has been designated one of the Seven Wonders of the World, and it is known for its unique architecture.

   B. People know the Taj Mahal for its unique architecture, and it has been designated one of the Seven Wonders of the World.

   C. People have known the Taj Mahal for its unique architecture, and it has been designated of the Seven Wonders of the World.

   D. The Taj Mahal has designated itself one of the Seven Wonders of the World.

Answer: A

Rationale: In the original sentence, the first clause is passive voice and the second clause is active voice, causing a voice shift. Answer B merely switches the clauses but does not correct the voice shift. In Answer C, only the verb tense in the first clause has been changed, but it is still active voice. Answer D changes the meaning. In Answer A, both clauses are passive voice.

(Rigorous)

11. Walt Whitman was famous for his composition *Leaves of Grass*, serving as a nurse during the Civil War, and a devoted son.

   A. for his composition *Leaves of Grass*, his service as a nurse during the Civil War, and a devoted son.

   B. for composing *Leaves of Grass*, serving as a nurse during the Civil War, and being a devoted son.

   C. for his composition *Leaves of Grass*, his nursing during the Civil War, and his devotion as a son.

   D. for his composition *Leaves of Grass*, serving as a nurse during the Civil War and a devoted son.

   E. for his composition *Leaves of Grass*, serving as a nurse during the Civil War, and a devoted son.

Answer: B

Rationale: In order to be parallel, the sentence needs three gerunds. The other sentences use both gerunds and nouns, which demonstrates a lack of parallelism.

(Rigorous)

12. A teacher must know not only her subject matter but also the strategies of content teaching.

   A. must not only know her subject matter but also the strategies of content teaching.

   B. not only must know her subject matter but also the strategies of content teaching.

   C. must not know only her subject matter but also the strategies of content teaching.

   D. must know not only her subject matter but also the strategies of content teaching.

Answer: D

Rationale: The correlative conjunction "not only" must come directly after "know" because the intent is to create the clearest meaning link with the "but also" predicate section later in the sentence.

SKILL 2.4 Understanding the elements of semantics, including ambiguity, euphemism, doublespeak, connotation, and jargon, and how these elements affect meaning

Levels of Language

Informal language and formal language are distinguished on the basis of the occasion as well as the audience. At a formal occasion—for example, a meeting of executives or of government officials—even conversational exchanges are likely to be more formal. Cocktail parties or golf games are examples of venues where the language is likely to be informal. FORMAL LANGUAGE uses few or no contractions, less slang, longer sentences, and more organization in longer segments.

Speeches delivered to executives, college professors, government officials, and similar groups are likely to be formal. Speeches made to fellow employees are likely to be informal. Sermons tend to be formal; Bible lessons tend to be informal.

Slang comes about for many reasons. Amelioration is an important one that often results in euphemisms. Examples are "passed away" for "dying" or "senior citizens" for "elderly people." Some usages have become so embedded in the language that their sources are long forgotten. For example, "fame" originally meant "rumor." Some words originally intended as euphemisms, such as "mentally retarded" and "moron" to avoid using "idiot," have themselves become pejorative.

Slang is lower in prestige than Standard English and tends to first appear in the language of groups with low status. Slang tends to displace conventional terms, either as shorthand or as a defense against perceptions associated with the conventional term.

Jargon is a specialized vocabulary. It may be the vocabulary peculiar to a particular industry, such as computers ("firewall"), or to a field, such as religion ("vocation"). For example, bloggers have developed a whole new vocabulary that even has its own dictionaries.

Jargon may also be the vocabulary of a social group. Black English is a good example. At one time a television ad showed two young men on the streets of Philadelphia discussing the merits of one of their sandwiches, and captions were "required" so that others could understand what they were saying.

Technical language is a form of jargon. It is usually specific to an industry, profession, or field of study.

> **FORMAL LANGUAGE:** uses few or no contractions, less slang, longer sentences, and more organization in longer segments

> *Check out this link—Do you speak American?:*
>
> *http://www.pbs.org/ speak/seatosea/ standardamerican/hamlet/*

Regionalisms are those usages that are peculiar to a particular part of the country. A good example is the second person plural pronoun *you*. Because the plural is the same as the singular, various parts of the country have developed their own solutions to be sure they are understood when they are speaking to more than one "you." In the South, "you-all" or "y'all" is common. In the Northeast, one often hears "youse." In some areas of the Middle West, "you'ns" can be heard.

Vocabulary also varies from region to region. A small stream is a "creek" in some regions but a "crick" in others. In Boston, soft drinks are sometimes called "tonic," but they become "soda" in other parts of the Northeast. The word is "liqueur" in Canada, and "pop" when you get very far west of New York.

The speaker must be knowledgeable about and sensitive to the jargon peculiar to his or her particular audience. Such knowledge may require some research and vocabulary development on the speaker's part.

Euphemism and doublespeak

Both euphemism and doublespeak substitute an agreeable or inoffensive term for one that might offend or suggest something unpleasant. It is the reason for the substitution that differentiates the terms.

Often, euphemisms are used to maintain a more positive tone or to prevent offense. For example, *death* might be referred to as *passed away*, *crossed over*, or nowadays *passed*. The word *death* might be too hard for people to face. On the other hand, doublespeak connotes a deliberate obfuscation or confusion of meaning. For example, the killing of innocent civilians in time of war is called *collateral damage*. Here, *death* is so minimized that it disappears.

Semantic connotations

To teach language effectively, we need to understand that as human beings acquire language, they realize that words have denotative and connotative meanings. Generally, denotative words identify things and connotative words deal with the mental suggestions that the words convey.

The word *skunk* has a denotative meaning if the speaker can point to the actual animal as he speaks the word and intends the word to identify the animal. *Skunk* has connotative meaning depending on the tone of delivery, the social attitudes about the animal, and the speaker's personal feelings about the animal.

Informative connotations

INFORMATIVE CONNOTATIONS are definitions that are agreed upon by the society in which the speaker operates. A *skunk* is "a black and white mammal of the

Learn more about connotation and denotation in "Elements of Poetry":

http://bcs. bedfordstmartins.com/ Virtualit/poetry/denotate_ def.html

INFORMATIVE CONNOTATIONS: definitions that are agreed upon by the society in which the speaker operates

weasel family with a pair of perineal glands which secrete a pungent odor." The *Merriam Webster Collegiate Dictionary* adds "...and offensive" odor. Identification of the color, species, and glandular characteristics is informative. The interpretation of the odor as *offensive* is affective (see below).

Affective connotations

> **AFFECTIVE CONNOTATIONS:** the personal feelings a word arouses

AFFECTIVE CONNOTATIONS are the personal feelings a word arouses. A child who has no personal experience with a skunk and its odor or who has had a pet skunk will feel differently about the word *skunk* than a child who has smelled a skunk's spray or been conditioned to associate offensiveness with the animal denoted *skunk.*

The very fact that our society views a skunk as an animal to be avoided will affect the child's interpretation of the word. In fact, one doesn't actually have to have seen a skunk (that is, have a denotative understanding) to use the word in either connotative form. For example, one child might call another child a skunk, connoting an unpleasant reaction (affective use). Another child might see a small black-and-white animal and call it a skunk based on the definition (informative use).

Using connotations

In everyday language, we attach affective meanings to words unconsciously; we exercise more conscious control of informative connotations. In the process of language development, the learner must not only grasp the definitions of words but also become conscious of the affective connotations and how listeners process these connotations. Gaining this conscious control over language makes it possible to use language appropriately in various situations and to evaluate its uses in literature and other forms of communication.

One goal of language instruction is to teach students how to manipulate language for a variety of purposes. Advertisers and satirists are especially conscious of the effect word choice has on their audiences. By evoking the proper responses from readers/listeners, the writer/speaker can prompt them to take action.

Choice of the medium through which the message is delivered to the receiver is a significant factor in controlling language. Spoken language relies as much on the gestures, facial expression, and tone of voice of the speaker as on the words that are spoken. Slapstick comics can evoke laughter without speaking a word. Young children use body language overtly and older children more subtly to convey messages. These refinements of body language are paralleled by an ability to recognize and apply the nuances of spoken language. To work strictly with the written work, the writer must use words that imply the body language.

Ambiguity

AMBIGUITY refers to any writing whose meaning cannot be determined by its context. Ambiguity may be introduced accidentally, confusing the reader and disrupting the flow of reading. If a sentence or paragraph jars upon reading, there is lurking ambiguity. It is particularly difficult to spot one's own ambiguities, since authors tend to see what they mean rather than what they say.

For example, when Robert Frost writes "Good fences make good neighbors" in the poem "Mending Wall," students can spend much time discussing what these words mean in the context of the poem as well as in the context of their own lives.

Commonly misused words

Because of the richness of the English language and the immensity of its vocabulary, words with similar sounds are sometimes confused. Here is a partial list of commonly misused words. Used incorrectly, these words may cause misunderstanding.

> **AMBIGUITY:** refers to any writing whose meaning cannot be determined by its context

> *Read "Mending Wall" by Robert Frost:*
>
> *http://www.writing.upenn. edu/~afilreis/88/frost-mending.html*

COMMONLY MISUSED WORDS		
Accept is a verb meaning "to receive" or "to tolerate." "	**Except** is usually a preposition meaning "excluding."	**Except** is also a verb meaning "to exclude.
Advice is a noun meaning "recommendation."	**Advise** is a verb meaning "to recommend."	
Affect is usually a verb meaning "to influence."	**Effect** is usually a noun meaning "result."	**Effect** can also be a verb meaning "to bring about."
An **allusion** is an indirect reference.	An **illusion** is a misconception or false impression.	
Add is a verb meaning "to put together."	**Ad** is a noun that is the abbreviation for the word "advertisement."	
Ain't is a common nonstandard contraction for "are not" and "is not"		
Allot is a verb meaning "to distribute."	**A lot** can be an adverb that means "often" or "to a great degree." It can also mean a large quantity.	
Allowed is an adjective that means "permitted."	**Aloud** is an adverb that means "audibly."	

Table continued on next page

Bare is an adjective that means "naked or exposed." It can also indicate a minimum.	As a noun, **bear** is a large mammal.	As a verb, **bear** means "to carry a heavy burden."
Capital refers to a city; **capitol** to a building where lawmakers meet.	**Capital** also refers to wealth or resources.	
A **chord** is a noun that refers to a group of musical notes.	**Cord** is a noun meaning "rope" or "a long electrical line."	
Compliment is a noun meaning "a praising or flattering remark."	**Complement** is a noun that means "something that completes or makes perfect."	
Climactic is derived from *climax*, the point of greatest intensity in a series or progression of events.	**Climatic** is derived from *climate*; it refers to meteorological conditions.	
Discreet is an adjective that means "tactful or diplomatic"; **discrete** is an adjective that means "separate or distinct."		
Dye is a noun or verb used to indicate that something has been artificially colored something.	**Die** is a verb that means "to pass away."	**Die** is also a noun that means "a cube-shaped game piece."
Elicit is a verb meaning "to bring out or to evoke."	**Illicit** is an adjective meaning "unlawful."	
Emigrate means "to leave one country or region to settle in another."	**Immigrate** means "to enter another country and reside there."	
Fewer is used for countable items, such "fewer minutes."	**Less** is used for amounts and quantities, such "less time."	
Hoard is a verb that means "to accumulate or store up."	**Horde** is a large group.	

Table continued on next page

Imply is to direct an interpretation toward other people.	**Infer** is to deduce an interpretation from someone else's discourse.	
Lead /lēd/ is a verb that means "to guide or serve as the head of." It is also a noun /lĕd/ that is a type of metal.		
Medal is a noun that refers to an award that is strung round the neck.	**Metal** is an element such as silver or gold.	
Meddle is a verb that means "to involve oneself in a matter without right or invitation."	**Mettle** is a noun meaning "toughness or guts."	
Morning is a noun indicating the time between midnight and midday.	**Mourning** is a verb or noun pertaining to the period of grieving after a death.	
Past is a noun meaning "a time before now" (past, present and future).	**Passed** is the past tense of the verb "to pass."	
Piece is a noun meaning "a portion."	**Peace** is a noun meaning "the opposite of war."	
Peak is a noun meaning "the top" or a verb meaning "to reach the highest point."	**Peek** is a verb that means "to take a brief look."	**Pique** is a verb meaning "to incite or raise interest."
Principal is a noun meaning "the head of a school or an organization" or "a sum of money."	**Principle** is a noun meaning "a basic truth or law."	
Rite is a noun meaning "a special ceremony."	**Right** is an adjective meaning "correct" or "direction."	**Write** is a verb meaning "to compose in writing."
Than is a conjunction used in comparisons; Example: That pizza is more <u>than</u> I can eat.	**Then** is an adverb denoting time. Example: Tom laughed, and <u>then</u> we recognized him.	Here's a mnemonic device to remember the difference. *Than* is used to *compare*; both words have the letter *a* in them. *Then* tells *when*; both words are spelled the same except for the first letter.

Table continued on next page

There is an adverb specifying place; it is also an expletive. Examples: Adverb: Sylvia is lying <u>there</u> unconscious. Expletive: *There* are two plums left.	**Their** is a possessive pronoun. Example: Fred and Jane finally washed *their* car.	**They're** is a contraction of "they are." Example: *They're* later than usual today.
To is a preposition	**Too** is an adverb	**Two** is a number
Your is a possessive pronoun	**You're** is a contraction of "you are"	

Other confusing words

Among is a preposition to be used with three or more items. **Between** is to be used with two items.

> *Between you and me, I cannot tell the difference among those three Johnson sisters.*

As is a subordinating conjunction used to introduce a subordinating clause; **like** is a preposition and is followed by a noun or a noun phrase.

> *As I walked to the lab, I realized that the recent experiment findings were much like those we found last year.*

Can is a verb that means "to be able." **May** is a verb that means "to have permission." They are only interchangeable in cases of possibility.

> *I can lift 250 pounds.*
> *May I go to Alex's house?*

Set is a transitive verb meaning "to put or to place." Its principal parts are set, set, set. **Sit** is an intransitive verb meaning "to be seated." Its principal parts are sit, sat, sat.

> *I set my backpack down near the front door.*
> *They sat in the park until the sun went down.*

PROBLEM PHRASES	
Correct	**Incorrect**
Anyway	Anyways
Come to see me	Come and see me
Could have, would have, should have	Could of, would of, should of
Couldn't care less	Could care less
En route	In route
For all intents and purposes	For all intensive purposes
Regardless	Irregardless
Second, Third	Secondly, Thirdly
Supposed to	Suppose to
Toward	Towards
Try to	Try and
Used to	Use to

Sample Test Questions and Rationale

(Easy)

1. The substitution of *went to his rest* for *died* is an example of a(n):

   A. Bowdlerism

   B. Jargon

   C. Euphemism

   D. Malapropism

Answer: C

Rationale: A euphemism replaces an unpleasant or offensive word or expression with a more agreeable one. A euphemism also alludes to distasteful things in a pleasant manner, and it can even be used to paraphrase offensive texts. Bowdlerism is named after Thomas Bowdler, who excised from Shakespeare what he considered vulgar and offensive. Jargon is a specialized language used by a particular group. What was groovy to one generation has become awesome to another. Named after Mrs. Malaprop, a character in a play by Richard Sheridan, a malapropism is a misuse of words, often to comical effect. Mrs. Malaprop once said "...she's as headstrong as an allegory on the banks of the Nile," misusing *allegory* for *alligator*.

(Average)

2. If students use slang and expletives, what is the best course of action to take in order to improve their formal communication skills?

   A. Ask the students to paraphrase their writing, that is, translate it into language appropriate for the school principal to read

   B. Refuse to read the students' papers until they conform to a more literate style

   C. Ask the students to read their work aloud to the class for peer evaluation

   D. Rewrite the flagrant passages to show the students the right form of expression

Answer: A

Rationale: Asking the students to write for a specific audience will help them become more involved in their writing. If they continue writing to the same audience—the teacher—they will continue seeing writing as just another assignment, and they will not apply grammar, vocabulary, and syntax the way they should. By rephrasing their own writing, they will learn to write for a different public.

(Rigorous)

3. Which level of meaning is the hardest aspect of a language to master?

   A. Denotation

   B. Jargon

   C. Connotation

   D. Slang

Answer: C

Rationale: Connotation refers to the meanings suggested by a word rather than the dictionary definition of the word. For example, the word "slim" means thin, and it is usually used with a positive connotation, to compliment or admire someone's figure. The word "skinny" also means thin, but its connotations are not as flattering as those of the word "slim." The connotative aspect of language is more difficult to master than the denotative aspect (dictionary definition), as the former requires a mastery of the social aspects of language, not just the linguistic rules.

Sample Test Questions and Rationale (cont.)

DIRECTIONS: In the following sentences, circle the choice that best corrects the error (underlined) without changing the meaning of the original sentence.

(Easy)

4. There were <u>few pieces</u> of evidence presented during the second trial.

   A. fewer peaces

   B. less peaces

   C. less pieces

   D. fewer pieces

   Answer: D

   Rationale: Use "fewer" for countable items; use "less" for amounts and quantities, such as in "fewer minutes but less time." "Peace" is the opposite of war, not a "piece" of evidence.

(Average)

5. The teacher <u>implied</u> from our angry words that there was conflict <u>between you and me</u>.

   A. implied… between you and I

   B. inferred… between you and I

   C. inferred… between you and me

   D. implied… between you and me

   Answer: C

   Rationale: The difference between the verb "to imply" and the verb "to infer" is that to imply is to direct an interpretation toward other people; to infer is to deduce an interpretation from someone else's discourse. Moreover, "between you and I" is grammatically incorrect: after the preposition "between," the object (or disjunctive with this particular preposition) pronoun form "me" is needed.

DOMAIN III
COMPOSITION

PERSONALIZED STUDY PLAN

KNOWN MATERIAL/ SKIP IT

COMPETENCY 3
COMPOSITION AND RHETORIC

A. Individual and collaborative approaches to teaching writing, *e.g., stages of the writing process (prewriting, drafting, revising, editing, publishing, evaluating) and how those stages work recursively*

The Writing Process

Writing is a recursive process. As students engage in the various stages of writing, they develop and improve not only their writing skills but their thinking skills as well. You will find varying approaches to teaching the writing process. Their goals, however, are similar. Most writers compose more efficiently and effectively if they use a step-by-step process.

Writing process: Approach 1

Prewriting strategies

In the first approach, students gather ideas before writing. Prewriting may include clustering, listing, brainstorming, mapping, free writing, and charting. If you provide many ways for students to develop ideas on a topic, you will increase their chances for success.

Listed below are the most common prewriting strategies students can use to explore, plan, and write about a topic. When teaching these strategies, remember that not all prewriting must eventually produce a finished piece of writing. In fact, for the initial lesson, you might have students practice prewriting strategies without the pressure of having to write a finished product. Here are some strategies for students:

- Keep an idea book so that you can jot down ideas that come to mind.

- Write in a daily journal.

- Write down whatever comes to mind; this is called free writing. Do not stop to make corrections or interrupt the flow of ideas. A variation of this technique is focused free writing—writing on a specific topic to prepare for an essay.

- Make a list of all ideas connected with your topic; this is called brainstorming. This technique works best when you let your mind work freely. After completing the list, analyze the list to see if a pattern or a way to group ideas emerges.

- Ask the questions *who, what, when, where, why* and *how.* Try to approach your topic from several perspectives.

- Create a visual map on paper to gather ideas. Use cluster circles and lines to show connections between ideas. Try to identify the relationships that exist among ideas. If you cannot see any relationships, pair up with another student and exchange papers. Have your partner look for some related ideas.

- Observe details of sight, hearing, taste, touch, and taste.

- Visualize by making mental images and write down the details in a list.

After they have practiced with each of these prewriting strategies, ask students to pick out the ones they prefer, and ask them to discuss how they might use the techniques to help them with future writing assignments. Remind them that they can use more than one prewriting strategy at a time. They may find that different writing situations suggest certain techniques.

Writing

During the writing stage, students compose the first draft. Encourage them to write freely. If they get their ideas down first, then they can move to revising. If they have difficulty, have them write as they speak—perhaps have them dictate to another writer or into a recorder.

Students might want to compose their first drafts on a computer so that they can quickly and easily type out their ideas. Encourage them to begin anywhere they want. Once they see their ideas on paper, they will be encouraged to continue.

Revising

The word *revise* comes from the Latin word *revidere*, meaning "to see again." During the revision stage, students examine their work and make changes in sentences, wording, details, and ideas. This step is often overlooked, or sometimes writers confuse it with proofreading. Students need to understand how important the revision process is. If they use a computer, they can move and delete text without having to rewrite the entire paper. This will eliminate some of the frustration that often comes with the revision process.

> The word revise comes from the Latin word revidere, meaning "to see again."

Editing

During the editing stage, students proofread the draft for punctuation and mechanical errors. If they are using computers, they can run grammar and spell checks; however, they should be taught not to rely on these devices. Sharing papers with their peers during this process can be worthwhile. A fresh look by another person can reveal errors the writer has overlooked.

Publishing

At the publishing stage, students may have their work displayed on a bulletin board, read aloud in class, or printed in a literary magazine or school anthology. A class blog of papers could stimulate interest in and out of the classroom. Students might keep a portfolio of their work throughout the year.

The above steps are recursive. As students engage in each aspect of the writing process, they may begin with prewriting and then write, revise, write, revise, edit, and publish. They do not engage in the writing process in a lockstep manner; the process is more circular.

Writing process: Approach 2

Here is another approach you might use with your students.

Prewriting activities

1. As a class, discuss the topic.

2. Map out ideas, questions, and graphic organizers on the chalkboard.

3. Break into small groups to discuss different ways of approaching the topic. Develop an organizational plan, and create a thesis statement.

4. Research the topic if necessary.

Drafting/revising

1. Students write the first draft in class or at home.

2. Students engage in peer response and class discussion.

3. Using checklists or a rubric, students critique each other's writing and make suggestions for revising the writing.

4. Students revise the writing.

Editing and proofreading

1. Students, working in pairs, analyze sentences for variety.

2. Students work in groups to read papers for punctuation and mechanics.

3. Students perform the final edit.

Students need to be trained to become effective at proofreading, revising, and editing strategies. Begin this process by using both desk-side and scheduled conferences. The following strategies are useful in guiding students through the final stages of the writing process:

- Provide some guide sheets or forms for students to use during peer responses.

- Allow students to work in pairs and limit the agenda.

- Model the use of the guide sheet or form for the entire class.

- Give students a time limit.

- Have students read their partners' papers and ask at least three "who, what, when, why, how" questions. The students should answer the questions and use them as a place to begin discussing the piece.

- Provide students with a series of questions that will assist them in revising their writing:

  - Do the details give a clear picture? Add details that appeal to more than just the sense of sight.

  - How effectively are the details organized? Reorder the details if necessary.

  - Are the thoughts and feelings of the writer included? Add personal thoughts and feelings about the subject.

As you discuss revision, begin by discussing the definition of the word *revise*. State that all writing must be revised in order to be improved.

You may think this stage is simply an exercise in catching errors in spelling or word use, but you should reframe your thinking about revising and editing. This is an extremely important step that often is ignored.

REVISING AND EDITING QUESTIONS	
Is the reasoning coherent?	Are the sentences too uniform in structure?
Is the point established?	Are there too many simple sentences?
Does the introduction make the reader want to read this discourse?	Do too many of the complex sentences use the same structure?
What is the thesis? Is it proven?	Are the compounds truly compounds, or are they unbalanced?

Table continued on next page

What is the purpose of the piece? Is it clear? Is it useful, valuable, and interesting?	Are parallel structures truly parallel?
Is the style of writing so wordy that it exhausts the reader and interferes with engagement?	If there are characters, are they believable?
Is the writing so spare that it is boring?	If there is dialogue, is it natural or stilted?
Is the language appropriate? Is it too formal or too informal? If jargon is used, is it appropriate?	Is the title appropriate?
Does the writing show creativity, or is it boring?	

After students have revised their writing, it is time for the final edit and proofread. It is crucial that students are not taught grammar in isolation but in the context of the writing process. At this point, a mini-lesson that focuses on common problems/errors would be appropriate.

Here are a few key points to remember when helping students learn to edit and proofread their work:

- Ask students to read their writing and check for specific errors, such as a subordinate clause used as a sentence

- Provide students with a proofreading checklist to guide them as they edit their work

Word processing is an important tool for teaching this stage in the writing process. Microsoft Word has had a "tracking" capability in its last several upgrades, which carries revision a step further. Now the teacher and student can carry on a dialogue on the paper itself. The teacher's deletions and additions can be tracked, the student can respond, and the tracking will be facilitated because each person's changes will display in a different color. The "comment" function makes it possible for both teacher and student to write notes at the relevant point in the manuscript.

While a computerized spell check is an appropriate first step, students should be reminded that they should not rely solely on spell checkers for proofreading. Noted for their failure to understand context, spell checkers will not help with incorrect homonyms or typos.

> B. Tools and response strategies for assessing student writing, *e.g., peer review, portfolios, holistic scoring, scoring rubrics, self-assessment, and conferencing*

Assessing Student Writing

Creating a supportive environment

Viewing writing as a process enables teachers and students to see the writing classroom as a cooperative workshop wherein students and teachers encourage and support each other in each writing endeavor. Listed below are some techniques that will help you create a supportive classroom environment.

Learn more about teaching and managing peer review:

http://writing.colostate.edu/guides/teaching/peer/

TECHNIQUES FOR CREATING A SUPPORTIVE CLASSROOM ENVIRONMENT
Create peer response/support groups that work on similar writing assignments. The members of the group help each other in all stages of the writing process—prewriting, writing, revising, editing, and publishing.
Provide several prompts or give students the freedom to write on a topic of their choice. Writing should be generated out of personal experience and students should be introduced to in-class journals. One effective way to generate enthusiasm for writing is to let students write often and freely about their own lives, without having to worry about grades or evaluation.
Respond to oral queries with a question whenever possible. Your response should be non-critical. Use positive, supportive language.
Respond to formal writing by acknowledging the student's strengths and focusing on the composition skills demonstrated by the writing. A response should encourage the student by offering praise for what the student has done well. Give the student a focus for revision and demonstrate that the process of revision has applications in many other writing situations.
Provide students with readers' checklists so that they can critique other students' drafts. Then they can revise their own papers at home using the checklists as a guide.
Pair students so that they can give and receive responses. Pairing students keeps them aware of the role of an audience in the composition process and in evaluating stylistic effects.
Focus critical comments on specific aspects of the writing. Comments such as "I noticed you use the word 'is' frequently" will be more helpful than "Your introduction is dull" and will not demoralize the writer.
Provide the group with a series of questions to guide them through the group writing sessions.

When assessing and responding to student writing, you might consider the following guidelines.

Responding to nongraded writing (formative)

- Avoid using a red pen. Whenever possible, use a number 2 pencil.

- Explain the criteria that will be used for assessment in advance.

- Read the writing once while asking the question, "Is the student's response appropriate for the assignment?"

- Reread the writing and note at the end whether the student met the objective of the writing task.

- Responses should be non-critical and should use supportive and encouraging language.

- Resist writing on or over the student's writing.

- Highlight the ideas you wish to emphasize, question, or verify.

- Encourage your students to take risks.

Responding to and evaluating graded writing (summative)

- Ask students to submit prewriting and rough-draft materials, including all revisions, with their final draft.

- For the first reading, use a holistic method, examining the work as a whole.

- When reading the draft for the second time, assess it using the standards previously established.

- Write your responses in the margin and use supportive language.

- Make sure you address the process as well as the product. It is important that students value the learning process as well as the final product.

- After scanning the piece a third time, write final comments at the end of the draft.

The last twenty years have seen great changes in methods of instruction in the English classroom. Gone are the days when literature is taught on Monday, grammar is taught on Wednesday, and writing is assigned on Friday. Integrating reading, writing, speaking, listening and viewing enables students to make connections between each aspect of language development during every class.

SUGGESTIONS FOR INTEGRATING LANGUAGE ARTS
Use prereading activities such as discussion, writing, research, and journals. Use writing to tap into prior knowledge before students read; engage students in class discussions about themes, issues, and ideas explored in journals, predicting the outcome and exploring related information.
Use prewriting activities such as reading model essays, researching a topic, interviewing others, and combining sentences. Remember that development of language proficiency is a recursive process that involves practice in reading, writing, thinking, speaking, listening, and viewing.
Create writing activities that are relevant to students by having them write and share with real audiences.
Connect correctness—including developing skills of conventional usage, spelling, grammar, and punctuation—to the revision and editing stage of writing. Reviews of mechanics and punctuation can be done with mini-lessons that use sentences from student papers and sentence-combining strategies. Model passages of skilled writers.
Connect reading, writing, listening, speaking, and viewing by using literature as a springboard for a variety of activities.

> C. Common research and documentation techniques, *e.g., gathering and evaluating data, using electronic and print media, and MLA and APA citations*

Research and Documentation

Whether researching for your own purposes or teaching students to research, the best place to start research is usually at a library. The library has numerous books, videos, and periodicals you can use as references, and the librarian is always a valuable resource who can help you retrieve relevant information. In spite of the abundance of online resources, researchers still need librarians.

> *Those who declared librarians obsolete when the Internet rage first appeared are now red-faced. We need them more than ever. The Internet is full of "stuff" but its value and readability is often questionable. "Stuff" doesn't give you a competitive edge; high-quality related information does.*
>
> *—Patricia Schroeder, President of the Association of American Publishers*

Gathering data

Keep content and context in mind when researching. Remember that there are multiple ways to get the information you need. Read an encyclopedia article about your topic to get a general overview, and then focus from there. Note names of important people associated with your subject, time periods, and geographic areas. Make a list of key words and their synonyms to use while searching for information. And finally, don't forget about articles in magazines and newspapers, or even personal interviews with experts related to your field of interest. As you gather information, be sure to do the following:

- Keep a record of any sources consulted during the research process

- As you take notes, avoid unintentional plagiarism

- Summarize and paraphrase in your own words without the source in front of you

To be lifelong learners, students should learn to conduct their own research. Thus, they need to know what resources are available to them and how to use them.

Dictionaries are useful for spelling, writing, and reading. Looking up a word in the dictionary should be an expected behavior, not a punishment or busy work.

Model the correct way to use the dictionary, as some students have never been taught proper dictionary skills. As the teacher, you need to demonstrate that as an adult reader and writer, you routinely and happily use the dictionary.

Encyclopedias in print or online are the beginning point for many research projects. While these entries may sometimes lack timeliness, they do provide students with general background.

Databases hold billions of records. Students should be taught effective search techniques, such as using key words and Boolean operators.

Learning that "and" and "or" will increase the number of hits while "not" or "and not" will decrease the number of hits can save researchers time and effort.

The Internet is a multi-faceted goldmine of information, but you must be careful to discriminate between reliable and unreliable sources. Use sites that are associated with an academic institution, such as a university or a scholarly organization. Typical domain names will end in "edu" or "org."

Students should evaluate any piece of information gleaned from the Internet. For example, if you google "etymology," you will find a multitude of sources. Don't trust just one. The information should be validated by at least three sources. Wikipedia is very useful, but it can be changed by anyone who chooses, so any information on it should be backed up by other sources.

Primary and secondary sources

The resources used to support a piece of writing can be divided into two major groups: primary sources and secondary sources.

PRIMARY SOURCES: works, records, and the like that were created during the period being studied or immediately after

SECONDARY SOURCES: works written significantly after the period being studied and are based on primary sources

Primary sources are the basic materials that provide raw data and information. Secondary sources are works that contain the explications of, and judgments on, this primary material.

PRIMARY SOURCES are works, records, and the like that were created during the period being studied or immediately after. **SECONDARY SOURCES** are works written significantly after the period being studied and are based on primary sources. Primary sources are the basic materials that provide raw data and information. Secondary sources are works that contain the explications of, and judgments on, this primary material.

Primary sources include the following kinds of materials:

- Documents that reflect the immediate, everyday concerns of people: memoranda, bills, deeds, charters, newspaper reports, pamphlets, graffiti, popular writings, journals or diaries, records of decision-making bodies, letters, receipts, snapshots, and so on.

- Theoretical writings that reflect care and consideration in composition and that attempt to convince or persuade. The topic will generally be deeper and more pervasive than is the case with "immediate" documents. Theoretical writings may include newspaper or magazine editorials, sermons, political speeches, or philosophical writings.

- Narrative accounts of events, ideas, and trends written with intentionality by someone contemporary with the events described.

- Statistical data, although statistics may be misleading.

- Literature and nonverbal materials, novels, stories, poetry, and essays from the period, as well as coins, archaeological artifacts, and art produced during the period.

Secondary sources include the following kinds of materials:

- Books written on the basis of primary materials about the period of time.

- Books written on the basis of primary materials about persons who played a major role in the events under consideration.

- Books and articles written on the basis of primary materials about the culture, the social norms, the language, and the values of the period.

- Quotations from primary sources.

- Statistical data on the period.

- The conclusions and inferences of other historians.

- Multiple interpretations of the ethos of the time.

Questions for analyzing sources

To determine the authenticity or credibility of your sources, consider these questions:

Learn more about assessing the credibility of online sources:

http://www.webcredible. co.uk/user-friendly-resources/web-credibility/ assessing-credibility-online-sources.shtml

1. Who created the source, and why? Was it created through a spur-of-the-moment act, a routine transaction, or a thoughtful, deliberate process?

2. Did the recorder have firsthand knowledge of the event? Or, did the recorder report what others saw and heard?

3. Was the recorder a neutral party, or did the recorder have opinions or interests that might have influenced what was recorded?

4. Did the recorder produce the source for personal use, for one or more individuals, or for a large audience?

5. Was the source meant to be public or private?

6. Did the recorder wish to inform or persuade others? Did the recorder have reasons to be honest or dishonest?

7. Was the information recorded during the event, immediately after the event, or after some lapse of time? How large a lapse of time?

Paraphrasing

PARAPHRASING is the art of rewording text. The goal is to maintain the original purpose of the statement while translating it into your own words. Your newly generated sentence can be longer or shorter than the original. Concentrate on the meaning, not on the words. Do not change concept words, special terms, or proper names. There are numerous ways to paraphrase effectively:

> **PARAPHRASING:** translating text into your own words without changing its meaning

- Change the key words' form or part of speech. Example: "American news **coverage** is frequently **biased** in favor of Western views" becomes "When American journalists **cover** events, they often display a Western **bias**."

- Use synonyms of "relationship words." Look for a relationship word, such as **contrast, cause,** or **effect,** and replace it with a word that conveys a similar meaning, thus creating a different structure for your sentence. Example: "**Unlike** many cats, Purrdy can sit on command" becomes "Most cats are not able to be trained, **but** Purrdy can sit on command."

- Use synonyms of phrases and words. Example: "The Beatnik writers were relatively unknown at **the start of the decade**" becomes "**Around the early 1950s**, the Beatnik writers were still relatively unknown."

- Change passive voice to active voice or move phrases and modifiers. Example: "Not to be outdone by the third graders, the fourth grade class added a musical medley to their Christmas performance" becomes "The fourth grade class added a musical medley to their Christmas performance to avoid being showed up by the third graders."

- Use reversals or negatives that do not change the meaning of the sentence. Example: "That burger chain is only found in California" becomes "That burger chain is not found on the East coast."

- Cite anything that is not common knowledge. This includes direct quotes as well as ideas or statistics.

Documentation

Documentation is an important skill when incorporating outside information into a piece of writing. Students must learn that research involves more than cutting and pasting from the Internet and that plagiarism is a serious academic offense.

Students must recognize that stealing intellectual property is an academic and, in some cases, a legal crime; thus students need to learn how to give credit where credit is due.

Students must recognize that stealing intellectual property is an academic and, in some cases, a legal crime; thus students need to learn how to give credit where credit is due.

Students should be aware of the rules that apply to borrowing ideas from various sources. Increasingly, the consequences for violating these rules are becoming more severe. Pleading ignorance is less and less of a defense. Such consequences include failing an assignment, losing credit for an entire course, expulsion from a learning environment, and civil penalties. Software exists that enables teachers and other interested individuals to determine quickly whether a given paper includes plagiarized material. As members of society in the information age, students are expected to recognize the basic justice of intellectual honesty and to conform to the systems meant to ensure it.

Consequences of plagiarism include failing an assignment, losing credit for an entire course, expulsion from the learning environment, and civil penalties.

There are several style guides for documenting sources. Each guide has its own particular ways of signaling that information has been directly borrowed or paraphrased, and familiarity with the relevant details of the major style guides is essential for students. Many libraries publish overviews of the major style guides, and most bookstores will carry full guides for the major systems. Relevant information is readily available on the web as well.

Documentation of sources takes two main forms. The first form applies when citing sources in the text of the document or as footnotes or endnotes. In-text documentation is sometimes called parenthetical documentation and requires specific information within parentheses placed immediately after borrowed material. Footnotes or endnotes are placed either at the bottom of relevant pages or at the end of the document.

In addition to citing sources within the text, style guides also require a bibliography, a references section, or a works cited section at the end of the document. Sources for any borrowed material are to be listed according to the rules of the particular guide. In some cases, a "works consulted" listing may be required even though no material is directly cited or paraphrased to the extent that an in-text citation is required.

The major style guides include the *Modern Language Association Handbook (MLA)*, the *Manual of the American Psychological Association (APA)*, the *Chicago Manuel of Style, Turabian*, and *Scientific Style and Format: the CBE Manual*.

Documentation of sources from the Internet is particularly involved and continues to evolve at a rapid pace. The best bet is to consult the most recent online update for a particular style guide.

Learn more about MLA works cited documentation:

http://www.studyguide.org/ MLAdocumentation.htm

Tips for documentation

- Keep a record of all sources consulted during the research process.

- As you take notes, avoid unintentional plagiarism. Summarize and paraphrase in your own words without the source in front of you. If you use a direct quote, copy it exactly as written and enclose it in quotation marks.

- Cite anything that is not common knowledge. This includes direct quotes as well as ideas or statistics.

- Within the body of your document, follow this blueprint for standard attribution following MLA style:

  1. Begin the sentence with, "According to _____..."
  2. Proceed with the material being cited, followed by the page number in parentheses.

In-text citation example

According to Steve Mandel, "our average conversational rate of speech is about 125 words per minute" (78).

Once students have mastered this basic approach, they can learn more sophisticated methods, such as embedding information.

Each source used within the document should have a complete citation in a bibliography or works cited page.

Works cited entry

Mandel, Steve. Effective Presentation Skills. Menlo Park, California: Crisp Publications, 1993.

Sample Test Questions and Rationale

(Easy)

1. Reading a piece of student writing to assess the overall impression of the product is:

   A. Holistic evaluation

   B. Portfolio assessment

   C. Analytical evaluation

   D. Using a performance system

   Answer: A

   Rationale: Holistic scoring assesses a piece of writing as a whole. Usually a paper is read through quickly once to get a general impression. The writing is graded according to the impression of the whole work rather than the sum of its parts. Often holistic scoring uses a rubric that establishes the overall criteria necessary to achieve a certain score.

(Easy)

2. What is not one of the advantages of collaborative or cooperative learning?

   A. Students who work together in groups or teams develop their skills in organization, leadership, research, communication, and problem solving

   B. Working in teams can help students overcome anxiety in distance-learning courses and contribute to the students' sense of community and belonging

   C. Students tend to learn more material and retain the information longer than when the same information is taught using different methods

   D. Teachers reduce their workload and the time spent on assignments and grading

   Answer: D

   Rationale: Teachers continue to expend time in monitoring and evaluating the students, their groups, and their activities.

(Easy)

3. Writing ideas quickly without interruption of the flow of thoughts or attention to conventions is called:

   A. Brainstorming

   B. Mapping

   C. Listing

   D. Free writing

   Answer: D

   Rationale: Free writing for ten or fifteen minutes enables students to develop ideas they are conscious of as well as ideas that are lurking in the subconscious. It is important to let the flow of ideas run through the hand. If a student gets stuck, he or she can write the last sentence over again until inspiration returns.

Sample Test Questions and Rationale (cont.)

(Easy)

4. Which of the following should not be included in the opening paragraph of an informative essay?

   A. Thesis sentence

   B. Details and examples supporting the main idea

   C. Broad general introduction to the topic

   D. A style and tone that grabs the reader's attention

Answer: B

Rationale: The introductory paragraph should introduce the topic, capture the reader's interest, state the thesis, and prepare the reader for the main points of the essay. Details and examples, however, should be given in the second part of the essay, so as to help develop the thesis presented at the end of the introductory paragraph.

(Easy)

5. In the paragraph below, which sentence does not contribute to the overall task of supporting the main idea?

1) The Springfield City Council met Friday to discuss new zoning restrictions for the land to be developed south of the city. 2) Residents who opposed the new restrictions were granted fifteen minutes to present their case. 3) Their argument focused on the dangers that increased traffic would bring to the area. 4) It seemed to me that the Mayor Simpson listened intently. 5) The council agreed to table the new zoning until studies could be performed.

   A. Sentence 2

   B. Sentence 3

   C. Sentence 4

   D. Sentence 5

Answer: C

Rationale: The other sentences provide detail for the main idea of the new zoning restrictions. Because sentence 4 provides no example or relevant detail, it should be omitted.

(Average)

6. In preparing your high school freshmen to write a research paper about a social problem, what recommendation can you make so that they can determine the credibility of their information?

   A. Assure them that information on the Internet has been peer-reviewed and verified for accuracy

   B. Tell them to find one solid source and use that source exclusively

   C. Suggest they use only primary sources

   D. Suggest they cross check their information with another credible source

Answer: D

Rationale: When researchers find the same information in multiple reputable sources, the information is considered credible. Using the Internet for research requires strong critical evaluation of the source. Nothing from the Internet should be taken without careful scrutiny of the source. To rely on only one source is dangerous and short-sighted. Most high school freshmen would have limited skills for conducting primary research for a paper about a social problem.

Sample Test Questions and Rationale (cont.)

(Average)

7. **Modeling is a practice that requires students to:**

   A. Create a style unique to their own language capabilities

   B. Emulate the writing of professionals

   C. Paraphrase passages from good literature

   D. Peer-evaluate the writings of other students

Answer: B

Rationale: Modeling has students analyze the writing of a professional writer and try to reach the same level of syntactical, grammatical, and stylistic mastery as the author whom they are studying.

(Average)

8. **Which of the following are secondary research materials?**

   A. The conclusions and inferences of other historians

   B. Literature and nonverbal materials, novels, stories, poetry, and essays from the period, as well as coins, archaeological artifacts, and art produced during the period

   C. Interviews and surveys conducted by the researcher

   D. Statistics gathered as the result of the researcher's experiments

Answer: A

Rationale: Secondary sources are works written significantly after the period being studied and are based on primary sources. In this case, historians have studied artifacts of the time and drawn their conclusions and inferences. Primary sources are the basic materials that provide raw data and information. Students or researchers may use literature and other data they have collected to draw their own conclusions or inferences.

(Average)

9. **In general, the most serious drawback of using a computer in writing is that:**

   A. The copy looks so good that students tend to overlook major mistakes

   B. The spell check and grammar programs discourage students from learning proper spelling and mechanics

   C. The speed with which corrections can be made detracts from the exploration and contemplation of composition

   D. The writer loses focus by concentrating on the final product rather than the details

Answer: C

Rationale: Because the process of revising is very quick with the computer, it can discourage contemplation, exploring, and examination, which are very important in the writing process.

Sample Test Questions and Rationale (cont.)

(Average)

10. **Which of the following is the least effective procedure for promoting consciousness of audience?**

    A. Pairing students during the writing process

    B. Reading all rough drafts before the students write their final copies

    C. Having students compose stories or articles for publication in school literary magazines or newspapers

    D. Writing letters to friends or relatives

Answer: B

Rationale: Reading all rough drafts will not encourage the students to take control of their texts and might even inhibit their creativity. On the contrary, pairing students will foster their sense of responsibility, and having them compose stories for literary magazines will boost their self-esteem as well as their organizational skills.

(Average)

11. **The new teaching intern is developing a unit on creative writing and is trying to encourage her freshman high school students to write poetry. Which of the following would not be an effective technique?**

    A. In groups, students will draw pictures to illustrate "The Love Song of J. Alfred Prufrock" by T.S. Eliot

    B. Either individually or in groups, students will compose a song, writing lyrics that use poetic devices

    C. Students will bring to class the lyrics of a popular song and discuss the imagery and figurative language

    D. Students will read aloud their favorite poems and share their opinions of and responses to the poems

Answer: A

Rationale: While drawing is creative, it will not accomplish as much as the other activities in encouraging students to write their own poetry. Furthermore, "The Love Song of J. Alfred Prufrock" is not a freshman-level poem. The other activities involve students in music and their own favorite poems.

Sample Test Questions and Rationale (cont.)

(Rigorous)

12. In this paragraph from a student essay, identify the sentence that provides a detail.

(1) The poem concerns two different personality types and the human relation between them. (2) Their approach to life is totally different. (3) The neighbor is a very conservative person who follows routines. (4) He follows the traditional wisdom of his father and his father's father. (5) The purpose in fixing the wall and keeping their relationship separate is only because it is all he knows.

A. Sentence 1

B. Sentence 3

C. Sentence 4

D. Sentence 5

Answer: C

Rationale: Sentence 4 provides a detail to sentence 3 by explaining how the neighbor follows routine. Sentence 1 is the thesis sentence, which is the main idea of the paragraph. Sentence 3 provides an example to develop that thesis. Sentence 5 is a reason that explains why.

(Rigorous)

13. To determine the credibility of information, researchers should do all of the following except:

A. Establish the authority of the document

B. Disregard documents with bias

C. Evaluate the currency and reputation of the source

D. Use a variety of research sources and methods

Answer: B

Rationale: Keep an open mind. Researchers should examine the assertions, facts, and reliability of the information.

Sample Test Questions and Rationale (cont.)

(Rigorous)

14. Which of the following situations is not an ethical violation of intellectual property?

 A. A student visits ten different websites and writes a report to compare the costs of downloading music. He uses the names of the websites without their permission.

 B. A student copies and pastes a chart verbatim from the Internet but does not document it because it is available on a public site.

 C. From an online article found in a subscription database, a student paraphrases a section on the problems of music piracy. She includes the source in her Works Cited but does not provide an in-text citation.

 D. A student uses a comment from M. Night Shyamalan without attribution, claiming the information is common knowledge.

Answer: A

Rationale: In this scenario, the student is conducting primary research by gathering the data and using it for his own purposes. He is not violating any principle by using the names of the websites. In Answer B, students who copy and paste from the Internet without documenting the sources of their information are committing plagiarism, a serious violation of intellectual property. Even when a student puts information in her own words by paraphrasing or summarizing as in Answer C, the information is still secondary and must be documented. In Answer D, while dedicated movie buffs might consider anything that M. Night Shyamalan says to be common knowledge, his comments are not necessarily known in numerous places or known by a lot of people.

(Rigorous)

15. Students have been asked to write a research paper on automobiles and have brainstormed a number of questions, which they will answer based on their research findings. Which of the following is not an interpretive question to guide research?

 A. Who were the first ten automotive manufacturers in the United States?

 B. What types of vehicles will be used fifty years from now?

 C. How do automobiles manufactured in the United States compare and contrast with each other?

 D. What do you think is the best solution for the fuel shortage?

Answer: A

Rationale: The question asks for objective facts. Answer B is a prediction that asks how something will look or be in the future, based on the way it is now. Answer C asks for similarities and differences, which is a higher-level research activity that requires analysis. Answer D is a judgment question that requires informed opinion.

Sample Test Questions and Rationale (cont.)

(Rigorous)

16. In preparing a speech for a contest, your student has encountered problems with gender-specific language. Not wishing to offend either women or men, she seeks your guidance. Which of the following is not an effective strategy?

    A. Use the generic "he" and explain that people will understand and accept the male pronoun as all-inclusive

    B. Switch to plural nouns and use "they" as the gender-neutral pronoun

    C. Use passive voice so that the subject is not required

    D. Use male pronouns for one part of the speech and then use female pronouns for the other part of the speech

Answer: A

Rationale: The male pronoun is no longer considered the universal pronoun. Speakers and writers should choose gender-neutral words and avoid nouns and pronouns that inaccurately exclude one gender or another.

(Rigorous)

17. For their research paper on the effects of the Civil War on American literature, students have brainstormed a list of potential online sources and are seeking your authorization. Which of these represent the strongest source?

    A. *http://www.wikipedia.org*

    B. *http://www.google.com*

    C. *http://www.nytimes.com*

    D. *http://docsouth.unc.edu/southlit/civilwar.html*

Answer: D

Rationale: Sites with an "edu" domain are associated with educational institutions and tend to be more trustworthy for research information. Wikipedia has an "org" domain, which means it is a nonprofit site. While Wikipedia may be appropriate for background reading, its credibility as a research site is questionable. Both Google and the *New York Times* are "com" sites, which are for profit. Even though this does not discredit the information available on these sites, each site is problematic for researchers. With Google, students will get overwhelmed with hits and may not choose the most reputable sites for their information. As a newspaper, the *New York Times* would not be a strong source for historical information.

Sample Test Questions and Rationale (cont.)

(Rigorous)

18. **A formative evaluation of student writing:**

   A. Requires thorough markings of mechanical errors with a pencil or pen

   B. Requires making comments on the appropriateness of the student's interpretation of the prompt and the degree to which the objective was met

   C. Should require that the student hand in all the materials produced during the process of writing

   D. Requires several careful readings of the text for content, mechanics, spelling, and usage

Answer: B

Rationale: It is important to give students numerous experiences with formative evaluation (evaluation as the student writes the piece). Formative evaluation assigns points to every step of the writing process, even though the final result is not graded. The criteria for the writing task should be very clear, and the teacher should read each step twice. Responses should be non-critical and supportive. The teacher should involve students in the process of defining criteria and make it clear that formative and summative evaluations are two distinct processes.

(Rigorous)

19. **In preparing a report about William Shakespeare, students are asked to develop a set of interpretive questions to guide their research. Which of the following would not be classified as an interpretive question?**

   A. What would be different today if Shakespeare had not written his plays?

   B. How will the plays of Shakespeare affect future generations?

   C. How does Shakespeare view nature in *A Midsummer Night's Dream* and *Much Ado About Nothing*?

   D. During the Elizabethan age, what roles did young boys take in dramatizing Shakespeare's plays?

Answer: D

Rationale: This question requires research into the historical facts; *Shakespeare in Love* notwithstanding, women did not act in Shakespeare's plays, and their parts were taken by young boys. Answers A and B are hypothetical questions requiring students to provide original thinking and interpretation. Answer C requires comparison and contrast, which are interpretive skills.

SKILL Understanding and evaluating rhetorical features in writing
3.2

A. Purposes for writing and speaking and the role of the audience within varying contexts

Tailoring language for a particular audience is an important skill. Writing to be read by a business associate will surely sound different from writing to be read by a younger sibling. Not only are the vocabularies different, but the formality or informality of the discourse will need to be adjusted.

Two characteristics that determine language style are degree of formality and word choice. The most formal language does not use contractions or slang, while the most informal language will probably feature a more casual use of common sayings and anecdotes. Formal language uses longer sentences and does not sound like a conversation. Informal language uses shorter sentences (not necessarily simple sentences, but shorter constructions) and may sound like a conversation.

In both formal and informal writing, there exists a tone—the writer's attitude toward the material and/or reader. The tone may be playful, formal, intimate, angry, serious, ironic, outraged, baffled, tender, serene, depressed, and so on. The overall tone of a piece of writing is dictated by both the subject matter and the audience. Tone is also related to the actual word choices that make up the document. Gaining conscious control over language makes it possible to use language appropriately in various situations. By evoking the proper responses from readers or listeners, the author can prompt them to take action.

Use the following questions to assess the audience and tone of a given piece of writing:

1. Who is your audience (friend, teacher, business person, etc.)?

2. How much does this person know about you and/or your topic?

3. What is your purpose (to prove an argument, to persuade, to amuse, to register a complaint, to ask for a raise, etc.)?

4. What emotions do you have about the topic (nervousness, happiness, confidence, anger, sadness, apathy)?

5. What emotions do you want to register with your audience (anger, nervousness, happiness, boredom, interest)?

6. What persona do you need to create in order to achieve your purpose?

7. What choice of language is best suited to achieving your purpose (slang, friendly but respectful, formal)?

8. What emotional quality do you want to transmit to achieve your purpose (matter-of-fact, informative, authoritative, inquisitive, sympathetic, angry), and to what degree do you want to express this tone?

In the past, teachers have assigned reports, paragraphs, and essays that focused on the teacher as the audience. The purpose of the writing was to explain information. However, for students to be meaningfully engaged in their writing, they must write for a variety of reasons. Writing for different audiences and aims encourages students to be more involved. If they write for the same audience and purpose, they will continue to see writing as just another assignment. Listed below are suggestions for helping students write in more creative and critical ways.

- Have students write letters to the editor, to a college, to a friend, or to another student

- Have students write stories that could be read aloud to a group (the class, a group of elementary school students) or published in a literary magazine or class anthology

- Have students write plays that could be performed

- Have students discuss the parallels between different speech styles and writing styles for different readers or audiences

- Have students write a particular piece for different audiences

As part of the prewriting exercises, have students identify the audience. Expose students to writing that covers the same topic but is meant for a different audience, and have them identify the variations in sentence structure and style. Remind your students that it is not necessary to identify all the specifics of the audience in the initial stage of the writing process, but that at some point they must make some determinations about audience.

Guidelines for assessing audience

Students must learn to assess their audience. What does their audience know, and what does it need to know? Here are some questions for students to consider:

ASSESSING AUDIENCE	
Values	What is important to this group of people? What is their background, and how will that background affect their perception of your writing?
Needs	Find out in advance what the audience's needs are. Why is the audience listening to you? Find a way to satisfy those needs.
Constraints	What might hold the audience back from being fully engaged in what you are saying, from agreeing with your point of view, or from processing what you are trying to say? For instance, political views might make the audience wary of your presentation's ideology from the start, or the audience might lack the appropriate background information to grasp your ideas. Avoid this last constraint by staying away from technical terminology, slang, or abbreviations that may be unclear to your audience.
Demographic Information	Take the audience's size into account as well as the location of the presentation. Demographics could include age, gender, education level, religion, income level, and other such countable characteristics.

> ### B. Organization in a piece of writing and the creation and preservation of coherence

In writing or speaking, you can be convincing if you follow the three basic principles of unity, coherence, and emphasis.

Unity

All ideas must relate to the controlling thesis. At the simplest level, this means that all sentences must develop the topic sentence of a paragraph. By extension, then, all paragraphs must develop the thesis statement of the essay; all chapters must develop the main idea of the book; all ideas must develop the argument.

Coherence

One way to achieve unity is to show the relationships between ideas by using transitional words, phrases, sentences, and paragraphs. Using coordinating conjunctions (for, and, nor, but, or, yet, so), subordinating conjunctions (because, since, whenever), or transitional adverbs (however, therefore) is an effective way to show logical order and thus create coherence. Another way to show relationships between ideas is to use an appropriate strategy (spatial, chronological, cause and effect, classification, comparison/contrast) to arrange details.

Emphasis

Use strategic placement of arguments to emphasize the significance of the ideas. In direct order, the main ideas are stated first and then supported by reasons or details. In indirect order, the support is provided first (in either increasing or decreasing order of importance) and leads to a well-defended argument.

Using transition

A mark of maturity in writing is the effective use of transitional devices at all levels. For example, a topic sentence can be used to establish continuity, especially if it is positioned at the beginning of a paragraph. The most common device is to refer to what has preceded, repeat it or summarize it, and then go on to introduce a new topic. An essay by W. H. Hudson uses this device:

> *Although the potato was very much to me in those early years, it grew to be more when I heard its history.*

It summarizes what has preceded, makes a comment on the author's interest, and introduces a new topic: the history of the potato.

Another example of a transitional sentence is, "Not all matters end so happily." This sentence refers to the previous information and prepares for the next paragraph, which will be about matters that do not end happily. The following transitional sentence is a little more forthright:

> *The increase in drug use in our community leads us to another general question.*

Another fairly simple and straightforward transitional device is the use of numbers:

> *First, I want to talk about the dangers of immigration; second, I will discuss the enormity of the problem; third, I will propose a reasonable solution.*

An entire paragraph may be transitional in purpose and form. In "Darwiniana," Thomas Huxley uses a transitional paragraph:

> *So much, then, by way of proof that the method of establishing laws in science is exactly the same as that pursued in common life. Let us now turn to another matter (though really it is but another phase of the same question), and that is, the method by which, from the relations of certain phenomena, we prove that some stand in the position of causes toward the others.*

The most common transitional device is a single word. Some examples: *and, furthermore, next, moreover, in addition, again, also, likewise, similarly, finally, second.* Single transitional words should be used correctly and judiciously.

COMMON TRANSITIONS	
LOGICAL RELATIONSHIP	**TRANSITIONAL EXPRESSION**
Similarity	also, in the same way, just as ... so too, likewise, similarly
Exception/Contrast	but, however, in spite of, on the one hand ... on the other hand, nevertheless, nonetheless, notwithstanding, in contrast, on the contrary, still, yet, although
Sequence/Order	first, second, third, next, then, finally, until
Time	after, afterward, at last, before, currently, during, earlier, immediately, later, meanwhile, now, presently, recently, simultaneously, since, subsequently, then
Example	for example, for instance, namely, specifically, to illustrate
Emphasis	even, indeed, in fact, of course, truly
Place/Position	above, adjacent, below, beyond, here, in front, in back, nearby, there
Cause and Effect	accordingly, consequently, hence, so, therefore, thus, as a result, because, hence, if...then, in short
Additional Support or Evidence	additionally, again, also, and, as well, besides, equally important, further, furthermore, in addition, moreover, then
Conclusion/Summary	finally, in a word, in brief, in conclusion, in the end, in the final analysis, on the whole, thus, to conclude, to summarize, in sum, in summary
Statement Support	most important, more significant, primarily, most essential
Addition	again, also, and, besides, equally important, finally, furthermore, in addition, last, likewise, moreover, too
Clarification	actually, clearly, evidently, in fact, in other words, obviously, of course, indeed

In marking student papers, teachers can encourage students to use transitions to move their writing coherently from one idea to the next. If the shift from one thought to another is too abrupt, the student can be asked to provide a transitional paragraph. Teachers can provide lists of possible transitions and encourage students to have the list at hand when composing essays. Such tools will nudge students toward more mature writing styles.

C. Strategies for the organization, development, and presentation of print, electronic, and visual media

Media's impact on today's society is immense and ever-increasing. Children watch programs on television that are amazingly fast-paced and visually rich. Parents' roles as verbal and moral teachers are diminishing as children respond to the much more stimulating guidance of the television set. Adolescence, which used to be the time for going out and exploring the world first-hand, is now consumed by the allure of networking websites, popular music, and video games. Young adults are exposed to uncensored sex and violence.

But at the same time, media's effect on society is beneficial and progressive. Its effect on education in particular provides special challenges and opportunities for teachers and students.

Thanks to satellite technology, urban classrooms and rural villages can receive instructional radio and television programs. CDs and DVDs enable students to learn information through a virtual reality experience. The Internet allows instant access to unlimited data and connects people across all cultures through shared interests. Educational media, when used in a productive way, enriches instruction and makes it more individualized, accessible, and economical.

A common classroom assignment is to view the movie version of a book, compare and contrast the two media, and then argue which did the better job of conveying the intended message(s).

It is difficult to convey the same message across different media because of the dynamics specific to those media. The degree of difficulty increases as the complexity of the message does.

A print message has both positive and negative features. For instance, print messages have longevity; they are also easily portable. Print messages appeal almost exclusively to the mind and allow students to recursively read sections that warrant more thought. On the negative side, a print message requires a skillful reader; without such a reader, print messages are not very effective. Print messages are not accessible to non-readers.

A graphic message gives a quick overview of some quantifiable situation. Some learners find that graphic information works for them better than print, and many struggling readers find graphic messages more helpful than print messages. However, compared to print, graphic messages convey a much shorter range of information. If the particular graphic is inspiring, the inspirations it conveys are subject to the descriptions of the various readers who view it. With print, the

Learn more about integrating technology in the classroom:

http://www.glencoe. com/sec/teachingtoday/ tiparchive.phtml/3

inspired scripts are already there for the reader, provided the reader is applying active reading skills.

Tips for using print media and visual aids:

- Use pictures over words whenever possible

- Present one key point per visual

- Use no more than three to four colors per visual to avoid clutter and confusion

- Use contrasting colors such as dark blue and bright yellow

- Use a maximum of twenty-five to thirty-five numbers per visual aid

- Use bullets instead of paragraphs when possible

- Make sure it is student-centered, not media-centered; delivery is just as important as the media presented

- Keep the content simple and concise (avoid too many lines, words, or pictures)

- Balance substance and visual appeal

- Make sure the text is large enough for the class to read

- Match the information to the format that will fit it best

Tips for using film and television:

- Study programs in advance

- Obtain supplementary materials such as printed transcripts of the narrative or study guides

- Provide your students with background information, explain unfamiliar concepts, and anticipate outcomes

- Assign outside readings based on student viewing

- Ask cuing questions

- Watch along with students

- Observe students' reactions

- Follow up viewing with discussions and related activities

An audio message allows for attention to prosody. Students who can't read can access the material. Audio messages invite the listener to form mental images consistent with the topic of the audio. Audio messages allow learners to close their eyes for better mental focus. Listening to an audio message is a more passive modality than reading a print message. As a rule, people read faster than normal speech patterns, so print conveys more information in a given time span.

An audiovisual message offers the easiest accessibility for learners. It has the advantages of both the graphic and the audio medium. Learners' eyes and ears are engaged. Non-readers get significant access to content. On the other hand, viewing an audiovisual presentation is an even more passive activity than listening to an audio message because information is coming to learners effortlessly through two senses.

Technology has broadened and enriched the entire communication process. Teachers and students who learn to use technological resources effectively will expand their capabilities inside and outside the classroom.

Multimedia refers to a technology for presenting material in both visual and verbal forms. This format is especially conducive to the classroom, since it reaches both visual and auditory learners.

Knowing how to select effective teaching software is the first step in efficient multimedia education. First, decide what the software will be used for (creating spreadsheets, making diagrams, or creating slideshows). Consult magazines such as *PC World, Macworld,* and *Multimedia World* to learn about the newest programs available.

Go to a local computer store and ask a customer service representative to help you find the exact equipment you need. If possible, test the programs you are interested in. Check reviews in magazines such as *Consumer Reports, PC World,* or *Multimedia Schools* to ensure the software's quality.

Check out the Language of Media Literacy: A Glossary of Terms:

http://www.medialit.org/ reading_room/article565. html

SOFTWARE PROGRAMS FOR PRODUCING TEACHING MATERIAL	
Adobe	Aldus Freehand
CorelDRAW!	DrawPerfect
Claris Works	PC Paintbrush
Harvard Graphics	Visio
Microsoft Word	Microsoft PowerPoint

MULTIMEDIA TEACHING MODEL	
Step 1	Diagnose Figure out what students need to know Assess what students already know
Step 2	Design Design tests of learning achievement Identify effective instructional strategies Select suitable media Sequence learning activities within program Plan introductory activities Plan follow-up activities
Step 3	Procure Secure materials at hand Obtain new materials
Step 4	Produce Modify existing materials Craft new materials
Step 5	Refine Conduct small-scale test of program Evaluate procedures and achievements Revise program accordingly Conduct classroom test of program Evaluate procedures and achievements Revise in anticipation of next school term

D. Discourse aims, *e.g., creative, expository, persuasive*

Written discourse

BASIC EXPOSITORY WRITING simply gives information not previously known about a topic or is used to explain or define a topic. Facts, examples, statistics, and non-emotional information are presented in a formal manner. The tone is direct and the delivery objective rather than subjective.

> **BASIC EXPOSITORY WRITING:** simply gives information not previously known about a topic or is used to explain or define a topic

DESCRIPTIVE WRITING centers on person, place, or object, using sensory words to create a mood or impression and arranging details in a chronological or spatial sequence.

NARRATIVE WRITING is developed using an incident or anecdote or a related series of events. Chronology, the five W's, topic sentence, and conclusion are essential ingredients.

PERSUASIVE WRITING implies the writer's ability to select vocabulary and arrange facts and opinions in such a way as to direct the actions of the listener/reader. Persuasive writing may incorporate exposition and narration as they illustrate the main idea.

JOURNALISTIC WRITING is theoretically free of author bias. In journalistic writing, it is essential that information about an event, a person, or a thing be factual and objective. Provide students with an opportunity to examine newspapers and create their own articles. Many newspapers have educational programs that are offered free to schools.

Oral discourse

Oral discourse includes debate, discussion, and conversation. The ability to use language and logic to convince the audience to accept your reasoning and to side with you is an art. This form of writing/speaking is extremely confined or structured and logically sequenced with supporting reasons and evidence. At its best, it is the highest form of propaganda. A position statement, evidence, reason, and evaluation and refutation are integral parts of this writing schema.

Interviewing provides opportunities for students to apply expository and informative communication. It teaches them how to structure questions to evoke fact-filled responses. Compiling the information from an interview into a biographical essay or speech helps students list, sort, and arrange details in an orderly fashion.

Speeches that encourage students to describe persons, places, or events in their own lives or oral interpretations of literature help them sense the creativity and effort used by professional writers.

The memorization and recitation of poetry give students a deeper comprehension of a poem than is available by simply reading or studying the words. The act of recitation involves projecting yourself into the poet's position, fully personifying the emotions and ideas of the poem as conveyed through language. To fully convey the meaning of a poem in recitation, students learn to make important decisions regarding style, tone of voice, projection, speed or slowness, emotional tenor, and character.

DESCRIPTIVE WRITING: centers on person, place, or object, using sensory words to create a mood or impression and arranging details in a chronological or spatial sequence

NARRATIVE WRITING: developed using an incident or anecdote or a related series of events

PERSUASIVE WRITING: writer's ability to select vocabulary and arrange facts and opinions to direct the actions of the reader

JOURNALISTIC WRITING: free of author bias; factual and objective

Learn more about oral communication skills:

http://www.glencoe. com/sec/teachingtoday/ weeklytips.phtml/88

Public speaking skills are enhanced through recitation, as students who memorize and recite poetry become cognizant of the power of words. Students also become aware of the connections between traditional poetic forms and contemporary ones, such as hip-hop, slam, song lyrics, and performance poetry, making palpable a connection between historical periods and the current moment. Memorization of poetry "classics" is an excellent way for students to study elements of prosody (rhyme, meter, conventions of open and closed form) in an active context rather than in a book, supplying them a wide range of techniques and tools for their own future writing and reading.

Delivery techniques

As a teacher, you recognize the importance of delivering your message effectively. Students should learn that both verbal and nonverbal communication can affect the way a presentation is understood. You can model the following techniques.

Posture

Maintain a straight but not stiff posture. Instead of shifting weight from hip to hip, point your feet directly at the audience and distribute your weight evenly. Keep shoulders toward the audience. If you have to turn your body to use a visual aid, turn 45 degrees and continue speaking toward the audience.

Movement

Instead of staying glued to one spot or pacing back and forth, stay within four to eight feet of the front row of your audience. Take a step or half-step to the side every once in a while. If you are using a lectern, feel free to move to the front or side of it to engage your audience more. Avoid distancing yourself from the audience; you want them to feel involved and connected.

Gestures

Gestures can help you maintain a natural atmosphere when speaking publicly. Use them just as you would when speaking to a friend. They shouldn't be exaggerated, but they should be used for added emphasis. Avoid keeping your hands in your pockets or locked behind your back, wringing your hands and fidgeting nervously, or keeping your arms crossed.

Eye contact

Many people are intimidated by using eye contact when speaking to large groups. Interestingly, eye contact usually *helps* the speaker overcome speech anxiety by connecting with the attentive audience and easing feelings of isolation. Instead of looking at a spot on the back wall or at your notes, scan the room and make eye contact for one to three seconds per person.

Memorization of poetry "classics" is an excellent way for students to study elements of prosody (rhyme, meter, conventions of open and closed form) in an active context rather than in a book, supplying them a wide range of techniques and tools for their own future writing and reading.

Successful public speaking techniques:
- *Maintain good posture*
- *Face the audience at a 45-degree angle if using a visual aid*
- *Take a step to the side every so often*
- *Use natural hand gestures to emphasize your point*
- *Make eye contact*
- *Speak at a natural pace*
- *Make sure your entire audience can hear you*

Voice

Many people fall into one of two traps when speaking: using a monotone or talking too fast. These are both caused by anxiety. A monotone restricts your natural inflection but can be remedied by releasing tension in the upper and lower body muscles. Subtle movement will keep you loose and natural.

Talking too fast, on the other hand, is not necessarily bad if you are exceptionally articulate. If you are not a strong speaker or if you are talking about very technical items, the audience will easily become lost.

When you talk too fast and begin tripping over your words, consciously pause after every sentence you say. Don't be afraid of brief silences. The audience needs time to absorb what you are saying.

Volume

Problems with volume, whether too soft or too loud, can usually be overcome with practice. If you tend to speak too softly, have someone stand in the back of the room and signal you when your volume is strong enough. If possible, have someone stand in the front of the room as well to make sure you're not overcompensating with excessive volume.

Conversely, if you have a problem with speaking too loudly, have the person in the front of the room signal you when your voice is soft enough and check with the person in the back to make sure it is still loud enough to be heard. In both cases, note your volume level for future reference. Don't be shy about asking your audience, "Can you hear me in the back?" Suitable volume is beneficial for both you and the audience.

Pitch

Pitch refers to the length, tension, and thickness of your vocal bands. As your voice gets higher, the pitch gets higher. In oral performance, pitch reflects emotional arousal level. More variation in pitch typically corresponds to more emotional arousal but can also be used to convey sarcasm or highlight specific words.

By encouraging the development of proper techniques for oral presentations, you are enabling your students to develop self-confidence for higher levels of communication.

Learn more about using your voice:

*http://www.longview.
k12.wa.us/mmhs/wyatt/
pathway/voice.html*

When you talk too fast and begin tripping over your words, consciously pause after every sentence you say. Don't be afraid of brief silences. The audience needs time to absorb what you are saying.

E. Methods of argument and types of appeals, *e.g., argumentative strategies, analogy, extended metaphor, allusion*

The art of rhetoric was first developed in Ancient Greece. Its pioneer was Socrates, who recognized the crucial role that rhetoric played in education, politics, and storytelling. Socrates argued that, presented effectively, speech could evoke any desired emotion or opinion. His method of dialectic syllogism, known today as the Socratic Method, pursued truth through a series of questions. Socrates established three types of appeals used in persuasive speech.

Types of appeals

Ethos

ETHOS refers to the credibility of the speaker. It establishes the speaker as a reliable and trustworthy authority by focusing on the speaker's credentials.

Pathos

PATHOS refers to the emotional appeal made by the speaker to the listener. It emphasizes the fact that an audience responds to ideas with emotion. For example, when a government is trying to persuade citizens to go to war for the sake of "the fatherland," it is using pathos to target the citizens' love of their country.

Logos

LOGOS refers to the logic of the speaker's argument. It uses the idea that facts, statistics, and other forms of evidence can convince an audience to accept a speaker's argument. Remember that information can be just as persuasive as appeal tactics.

Today, the structures of many governments and judicial systems reflect rhetorical tactics established by the Greeks long ago. The media has taken rhetoric to a whole new level and has refined it to a very skilled art. Every word, as well as the method of presentation, is carefully planned. The audience is taken into account and speech tailored to its needs and motivations. Though the content has changed, rhetoric has been around since Socrates contemplated it thousands of years ago.

Advertising techniques

Because students are very interested in the approaches used by advertisers, you can develop high-interest assignments requiring students to analyze commercial messages. What is powerful about Nike's "Just Do It" campaign? What is the appeal of Jessica Simpson's eponymous perfume?

> **ETHOS:** a type of rhetorical appeal that focuses on the credibility and authority of the speaker

> **PATHOS:** a type of rhetoric that appeals to the emotions of the audience

> **LOGOS:** refers to the use of logic—facts, evidence, and statistics—to persuade an audience

COMMON ADVERTISING TECHNIQUES	
Beauty Appeal	Beauty attracts us; we are drawn to beautiful people, places, and things.
Celebrity Endorsement	This technique associates product use with a well-known person. We are led to believe that by purchasing this product we will attain characteristics similar to those of the celebrity.
Compliment the Consumer	Advertisers flatter the consumer who is willing to purchase their product. By purchasing the product, the consumer is recognized by the advertiser for making a good decision with his or her selection.
Escape	"Getting away from it all" is very appealing; you can imagine adventures you might never actually experience. The idea of escape is pleasurable.
Independence/ Individuality	This technique associates a product with people who can think and act for themselves. Products are linked to individual decision making.
Intelligence	This technique associates a product with smart people who can't be fooled.
Lifestyle	This technique associates a product with a particular style of living or way of doing things.
Nurture	Every time you see an animal or a child in an advertisement, the appeal is to your paternal or maternal instincts. This technique associates products with taking care of someone.
Peer Approval	This technique associates product use with friendship and acceptance. Advertisers can also use this technique negatively to make you worry that you'll lose friends if you don't use a certain product.
Rebel	This technique associates products with behaviors or lifestyles that oppose society's norms.
Rhetorical Question	This technique poses a question to the consumer that demands a response. A question is asked, and the consumer is supposed to answer in such a way that affirms the product's value.
Scientific/ Statistical Claim	This technique provides some sort of scientific proof or experiment, very specific numbers, or an impressive-sounding mystery ingredient.
Unfinished Comparison/ Claim	This technique uses phrases such as "Works better in poor driving conditions!" Works better than what?

Deductive and inductive reasoning

The two forms of reasoning used to support an argument are *inductive* and *deductive*. INDUCTIVE REASONING goes from particular observations to a general conclusion. For example, I first observe that all the green apples I have ever tasted have been sour. (I have tasted some from my grandfather's orchard; I have tasted

> **INDUCTIVE REASONING:** the process of using particular observations to come to a general conclusion

the Granny Smiths that my mother buys in the grocery store; I have tasted the green apples in my friend's kitchen. All have been sour.) Then I can *generalize* that all green apples are sour. (This is the conclusion.) Inductive reasoning is a very prevalent aspect of the way we think and deal with each other and is essential to persuasive discourse.

DEDUCTIVE REASONING, on the other hand, reverses the order by going from general to particular. The generalization drawn in the previous illustration, "All green apples are sour," can be used to make a statement about a particular apple. Suppose a new variety of green apples has appeared in the grocery store. Arguing from the generalization that all green apples are sour, I may reject this new variety because I am sure that it is going to be sour. Deductive reasoning is based on the following syllogism:

> *All green apples are sour.*
> *This apple is green.*
> *Therefore, this apple is sour.*

A court trial is a good example of inductive reasoning. When a prosecutor presents a case in a courtroom, he or she typically first puts forth a statement of fact:

> *On November 2, in an alley between Smith and Jones Street at the 400 block, Stacy Highsmith was brutally raped and murdered. The coroner has concluded that she was bludgeoned with a blunt instrument at or around midnight, and her body was found by a shopkeeper the next morning.*

Following the outline of the facts of the case, the prosecutor will use inductive reasoning to accuse the person on trial of the crime. For example:

> *Terry Large, the accused, was seen in the neighborhood at 11:30 p.m. on November 2 (fact 1). He was carrying a carpenter's tool kit, which was later recovered (fact 2), and a hammer with evidence of blood on it was found in that tool kit (fact 3). The blood was tested and it matched the victim's DNA (fact 4).*

Ultimately, the prosecutor will use the above facts to reach the generalization that Terry Large murdered Stacy Highsmith.

Other forms of persuasive speech

Throughout history, theories of rhetoric have been developed, adopted, modified, and discarded. Here are three forms of persuasive speech.

DEDUCTIVE REASONING: the process of using a general statement or assumption to come to a particular conclusion

Fact

Similar to an informative speech, a persuasive speech on a question of fact seeks to find an answer where there isn't a clear one. The speaker evaluates evidence and attempts to convince the audience of his or her conclusion. The challenge is to persuade the audience to accept a certain, carefully crafted view of the facts presented.

Value

This kind of persuasion tries to convince the audience that a certain thing is good or bad, moral or immoral, valuable or worthless. It focuses less on knowledge and more on beliefs and values.

Policy

This type of speech is a call to action, arguing that something should be done, improved, or changed. Its goal is action from the audience, but it also seeks passive agreement with the proposition proposed. It appeals to both reason and emotion and tells listeners what they can do and how to do it.

Logical fallacies

A FALLACY is, essentially, an error in reasoning. In persuasive speech, logical fallacies are flaws in reasoning that make an argument invalid. For example, a premature generalization occurs when one forms a general rule based on only one or a few specific cases. An illustration of this is the argument "Bob Marley was a Rastafarian singer. Therefore, all Rastafarians sing."

> **FALLACY:** an error in reasoning

A common fallacy in reasoning is the *post hoc ergo propter hoc* ("after this, therefore because of this") or the false-cause fallacy. This type of fallacy occurs in cause/effect reasoning, which may go either from cause to effect or from effect to cause. The following is an example of a post hoc fallacy:

> *Our sales shot up thirty-five percent after we ran that television campaign; therefore, the campaign caused the increase in sales.*

The television campaign might have caused the increase in sales, of course, but more evidence is needed to prove so. Sales may have increased for other reasons.

A post hoc fallacy happens when an inadequate cause is offered for a particular effect, when the possibility of more than one cause is ignored, and when an

> *Learn more about post hoc fallacy:*
>
> *http://www.sjsu.edu/depts/itl/graphics/adhom/posthoc.html*

invalid connection is made between a particular cause and a particular effect. The following is an example of **an inadequate cause for a particular effect:**

> *An Iraqi truck driver reported that Iraq had nuclear weapons; therefore, Iraq is a threat to world security.*

In this case, more causes are needed to prove the conclusion.

The following is an example of **ignoring the possibility of more than one possible cause:**

> *John Brown was caught out in a thunderstorm, and his clothes got wet before he was rescued. Therefore, he developed influenza the next day because he got wet.*

Being chilled may have played a role in the illness, but Brown would have had to contract the influenza virus before he could have come down with influenza, whether or not he had gotten wet.

The following is an example of **failing to make a valid connection between a particular cause and a particular effect:**

> *Anna fell into a putrid pond on Saturday; on Monday she came down with polio. Therefore, the pond caused the polio.*

This, of course, is not an acceptable argument unless the polio virus is found in a sample of water from the pond. The connection must be proven.

Argumentation

A logical argument consists of three stages. First, state the premises of the argument. These are the propositions that are necessary for the argument to continue. They are the evidence or reasons for accepting the argument and its conclusions.

A logical argument consists of three steps:
1. *State the premises*
2. *Use the premises to derive propositions or make inferences*
3. *Conclude the argument*

Premises (or assertions) are often indicated by phrases such as "because," "since," "obviously," and so on. (The phrase "obviously" is often viewed with suspicion, as it can be used to intimidate others into accepting suspicious premises. If something doesn't seem obvious to you, don't be afraid to question it. You can always say, "Oh, yes, you're right, it is obvious" when you've heard the explanation.)

Next, use the premises to derive further propositions by a process known as inference. In inference, a proposition is arrived at on the basis of one or more other propositions already accepted. There are various forms of valid inference.

The propositions arrived at by inference may then be used in further inference. Inference is often denoted by phrases such as "implies that" or "therefore."

Finally, conclude the argument with the proposition that is affirmed on the basis of the premises and inferences. Conclusions are often indicated by phrases such as "therefore," "it follows that," "we conclude," and so on. The conclusion is often stated as the final stage of inference.

Classical argument

The classical argument structure below uses unity, coherence, and emphasis effectively. In its simplest form, the classical argument has five main parts.

FIVE PARTS OF CLASSICAL ARGUMENT	
Introduction	Warms up the audience, establishes goodwill and rapport, and announces the general theme or thesis of the argument.
Narration	Summarizes relevant background material, provides any information the audience needs to know about the environment and circumstances that produce the argument, and sets up the stakes—i.e., what's at risk in this question.
Confirmation	Lays out in a logical order (usually strongest to weakest or most obvious to most subtle) the claims that support the thesis, providing evidence for each claim.
Refutation and Concession	Considers opposing viewpoints, anticipates objections from the audience, and allows for as much of the opposing viewpoints as possible without weakening the thesis.
Summation	Provides a strong conclusion, amplifies the force of the argument, and shows the audience that the proposed solution is the best available given the circumstances.

F. Style, tone, voice, and point of view as part of rhetorical strategy

Style and tone

Writers often have an emotional stake in their subject. Their purpose is to convey those feelings, either explicitly or implicitly, to the reader. In such cases, the writing is generally subjective—that is, it stems from opinions, judgments, values, ideas, and feelings.

In literature, style refers to a distinctive manner of expression and applies to all levels of language, beginning at the phonemic level with word choices, alliteration, assonance, and so on; and moving to the syntactic level, characterized by length of sentences, choice of structure and phraseology (diction), and patterns, and even extending beyond the sentence to paragraphs and chapters. Critical readers can determine what is distinctive about the writer's use of these elements. All of the author's style choices are instrumental in creating tone.

TONE: the author's attitude toward the subject matter of a written passage, revelead through word choice and sentence structure

The TONE of a written passage is the author's attitude toward the subject matter. The tone (mood, feeling) is revealed through the qualities of the writing and is a direct product of such stylistic elements as language and sentence structure. The tone of a written passage is much like a speaker's voice; instead of being spoken, however, it is the product of words on a page.

Tone may be thought of generally as positive, negative, or neutral. Below is a statement about snakes that demonstrates tone.

> *Many species of snakes live in Florida. Some of those species, both poisonous and non-poisonous, have habitats that coincide with those of human residents of the state.*

The voice of the writer in this statement is neutral. The sentences are declarative (not exclamations or fragments or questions). The adjectives are few and nondescript—*many, some, poisonous* (balanced with *non-poisonous*). Nothing much in this brief paragraph would alert the reader to the feelings of the writer about snakes. The paragraph has a neutral, objective, detached, and impartial tone.

If the writer's attitude toward snakes involved admiration, or even affection, the tone would generally be positive:

> *Florida's snakes are a tenacious bunch. When they find their habitats invaded by humans, they cling to their home territories as long as they can, as if vainly attempting to fight off the onslaught of the human hordes.*

An additional message emerges in this paragraph: the writer quite clearly favors snakes over people. The writer uses adjectives like *tenacious* to describe feelings about snakes. The writer also humanizes the reptiles, making them brave, beleaguered creatures. Obviously, the writer is more sympathetic to snakes than to people in this paragraph.

If the writer's attitude toward snakes involved active dislike and fear, then the tone would reflect that attitude by being negative:

> *Countless species of snakes, some more dangerous than others, still lurk on the urban fringes of Florida's towns and cities. They will often invade domestic spaces, terrorizing people and their pets.*

Here, obviously, the snakes are the villains. They *lurk*, they *invade*, and they *terrorize*. The tone of this paragraph might be said to be distressed about snakes.

In the same manner, a writer can use language to portray characters as good or bad. A writer uses positive and negative adjectives, as seen above, to convey the manner of a character.

Voice and point of view

POINT OF VIEW or voice is essentially the character through whose eyes the reader sees the action. There are at least thirteen possible choices for point of view (voice) in literature, as demonstrated and explained by Wallace Hildick in his *13 Types of Narrative*. However, for purposes of helping students write essays about literature, three, or possibly four, are adequate. Students should think about how a writer's choice of voice impacts the overall effect of the work.

Third person

The most common point of view is third-person objective. If the story is seen from this point of view, the reader watches the action, hears the dialogue, reads descriptions, and from all of these deduces characterization. In this point of view, an unseen narrator tells the reader what is happening using the third person: he, she, it, they. The effect of this point of view is usually a feeling of distance from the plot. The responsibility for making judgments is given to the reader. However, the author may intrude and evaluate or comment on the characters or the action.

First person

The voice of first-person narrator is another common voice. The reader sees the action through the eyes of a character in the story who is also telling the story. In using this voice, the narrator must be analyzed as a character:

- What sort of person is he or she?
- What is this character's position in the story—observer, commentator, or actor?
- Can the narrator be believed, or is he or she biased?

The value of this voice is that, while the reader is able to see what is happening through the narrator's eyes, the reader is also able to feel what the narrator feels. For this reason, the writer can involve the reader more intensely in the story and move the reader by invoking feelings of pity, sorrow, anger, hate, confusion, disgust, and so on. Many of the most memorable novels, such as Charlotte Bronte's *Jane Eyre*, are written in this point of view.

POINT OF VIEW: the character through whose eyes the reader sees the action

Learn more about writing fiction:

http://crofsblogs.typepad.com/fiction/2003/07/narrative_voice.html

Omniscient

Another voice that is often used may best be titled omniscient, because the reader is able to get into the mind of more than one character or sometimes all the characters. This point of view can bring about greater involvement of the reader in the story. By knowing what a character is thinking and feeling, the reader is able to empathize when a character feels great pain and sorrow. Through omniscient voice, the reader may be drawn into the mind of a pathological murderer, which may elicit feelings of horror or disgust in the reader.

Omniscient voice can be broken down into third-person omniscient or first-person omniscient. In third-person omniscient, the narrator is not seen or acting in the story but is able to watch and record not only what is happening or being said but also what characters are thinking. In first-person omniscient, on the other hand, the narrator plays a role in the story and can also record what other characters are thinking.

Point of view or voice is a powerful tool in the hands of a skillful writer. The questions to be answered in writing an essay about a literary work are:

- What point of view has this author used?
- What effect does it have on the story?
- If the story had been written in a different voice, how would the story be different?

Most credible literary works are consistent in point of view, but not always. Thus consistency is another aspect that should be analyzed:

- Does the point of view change?
- Where does it vary?
- Does the variation in voice help or hurt the effect of the story?

G. Recognition of bias, distinguishing between fact and opinion, and identifying stereotypes, inferences, and assumptions

Your students will enjoy sharing their opinions. Some of them may be repeating what they have heard from others, while others are discovering their own voices. All are trying to make sense of their world. You can help your students develop critical reasoning skills by teaching them to distinguish between fact and opinion, to realize conclusions, and to make inferences.

Bias in interpretation

Everyone is biased to some degree because everyone has his or her own unique perspective on life. While objectivity is often a goal, we sometimes fall short with our subjective perceptions and attitudes. Unfair bias weakens our credibility and undercuts the force of our arguments.

What we need to do, then, is avoid conscious bias and be sensitive to unconscious bias, both of which can compromise the integrity of research. Conscious (deliberate) bias is unethical. Unconscious bias can be difficult to detect and/or control. It reflects the beliefs of the analyst. We should always be on the lookout for bias, which often can be subtle and hard to detect. The writer should avoid racial, sexist, ageist, ethnic, and religious bias whenever possible.

EXAMPLES OF BIAS	
Personal Bias	A researcher with a work-related injury may be partial when conducting a job safety study.
Cultural Bias	A person with a strong work ethic may be partial when conducting a study of the chronically unemployed.
Professional Bias	A teacher with a set work pattern may not be receptive to an alternative method of teaching.

EVALUATING SOURCES FOR BIAS	
Preliminary Checklist	Title (How relevant is it to your topic?) Date (How current is the source?) Organization (What institution is this source coming from?) Length (How in-depth does it go?)
Check for Signs of Bias	Does the author or publisher have political ties or religious views that could affect objectivity? Is the author or publisher associated with any special interest groups that might see only one side of an issue, such as Greenpeace or the National Rifle Association? How fairly does the author treat opposing views? Does the language of the piece show signs of bias?

Keep an open mind while reading, and don't let opposing viewpoints prevent you from absorbing the text. Remember that you are not judging the author's opinion; you are examining the work's assumptions, assessing its evidence, and weighing its conclusions.

Facts and opinions

Recall that facts are statements that are verifiable. Facts report what has happened or exists and comes from observation, measurement, or calculation. Opinions are statements that must be supported in order to be accepted. Facts are used to support opinions. For example, "Jane is a bad girl" is an opinion. However, "Jane hit her sister with a baseball bat" is a *fact* upon which the opinion is based. Judgments are decisions or declarations based on observation or reasoning that express approval or disapproval. Facts can be tested and verified, whereas opinions and judgments cannot. They can only be supported with facts.

It is sometimes difficult to distinguish between fact and judgment. "I believe that Jane is a bad girl" is a fact. The speaker knows what he or she believes. However, this statement obviously includes a judgment that could be disputed by another person who might believe otherwise. Judgments are not usually as firm as facts. They are, rather, plausible opinions that provoke thought or lead to factual development.

Fact vs. Opinion

Use the chart below to identify both facts and opinions in a text. Be sure to explain how you know the details you write down are either facts or opinions.

	Text Details and Direct Quotes from the Text	Explain How You Know the Details Are Facts or Opinions
Facts		
Opinions		

http://www.greece.k12.ny.us/instruction/ela/6-12/Tools/factvsopinion.pdf

Conclusions

Conclusions are drawn as a result of reasoning. Whether arrived at through inductive or deductive reasoning, a conclusion is an analysis of the data. Given all the facts, all the opinions, and all the details, the reader draws a conclusion.

Joe DiMaggio, a Yankees' center-fielder, was replaced by Mickey Mantle in 1952.

This is a fact. If necessary, evidence can be produced to support this statement.

> *First-year players are more ambitious than seasoned players.*

This is an opinion. There is no proof to support that every first-year player is more ambitious than every seasoned player.

Sample Test Questions and Rationale

(Easy)

1. **In writing a report, Hector has to explain where acid rain comes from and what it has done to the environment. What is the most likely form of organizational structure?**

   A. Cause and effect

   B. Problem and solution

   C. Exposition

   D. Definition

   Answer: A

   Rationale: This report would discuss what has caused acid rain and what effects acid rain has had on the environment. Although the report could offer a solution, the report questions do not focus on that. Most report writing is expository because it provides information and an explanation, but that is not the primary structure. While a definition might be an important detail, it would not be the major organizational structure.

(Easy)

2. **Explanatory or informative discourse is:**

   A. Exposition

   B. Narration

   C. Persuasion

   D. Description

   Answer: A

   Rationale: Exposition sets forth a systematic explanation of any subject. It can also introduce the characters of a literary work and their situations in the story. Narration relates a sequence of events (the story) told through a process of narration (discourse) in which events are recounted in a certain order (the plot). Persuasion strives to convince either a character in the story or the reader. Description uses sensory words to create a mood or impression.

(Easy)

3. **Which of the following is not a technique of prewriting?**

   A. Clustering

   B. Listing

   C. Brainstorming

   D. Proofreading

   Answer: D

   Rationale: Proofreading cannot be a method of prewriting, since it is done on texts that have already been written. Clustering, listing, and brainstorming are all prewriting strategies.

Sample Test Questions and Rationale (cont.)

(Easy)

4. The following passage is written from which point of view?

As she mused the pitiful vision of her mother's life laid its spell on the very quick of her being—that life of commonplace sacrifices closing in final craziness. She trembled as she heard again her mother's voice saying constantly with foolish insistence: *Dearevaun Seraun! Dearevaun Seraun!**

* "The end of pleasure is pain!" (Gaelic)

A. First person, narrator

B. Second person, direct address

C. Third person, omniscient

D. First person, omniscient

Answer: C

Rationale: The passage is clearly in the third person (the subject is "she"), and it is omniscient because it gives the character's inner thoughts.

(Easy)

5. Which of the following is most true of expository writing?

A. It is mutually exclusive of other forms of discourse

B. It can incorporate other forms of discourse in the process of providing supporting details

C. It should never employ informal expression

D. It should only be scored with a summative evaluation

Answer: B

Rationale: Expository writing sets forth an explanation or an argument about any subject and can use distinct or combined forms of discourse, a sign of academic literacy. This directly contradicts Answer A. Writing can use formal and informal language and can be evaluated in many subjective and objective ways.

(Easy)

6. Which of the following is not correct?

A. Because most students have wide access to media, teachers should refrain from using it in their classrooms to diminish media overload

B. Students can use CDs and DVDs to explore information using a virtual reality experience

C. Teacher can make their instruction more powerful by using educational media

D. The Internet enables students to connect with people across cultures and to share interests

Answer: A

Rationale: Teachers can use media in productive ways to enrich instruction. Rather than ignoring it, educators should use a wide assortment of media for the benefit of their students.

Sample Test Questions and Rationale (cont.)

(Easy)

7. Which of the following should students use to improve coherence of ideas within an argument?

   A. Transitional words or phrases to show relationships between ideas

   B. Conjunctions like "and" to join ideas together

   C. Direct quotes to improve credibility

   D. Adjectives and adverbs to provide stronger detail

Answer: A

Rationale: Transitional words and phrases are two-way indicators that connect the previous idea to the following idea. Sophisticated writers use transitional devices to clarify text ("for example"), to show contrast ("despite"), to show sequence ("first," "next"), and to show cause ("because").

(Average)

8. Which transition word would show contrast between the following two ideas?

   We are confident in our ability to teach English. We welcome new ideas on the subject.

   A. We are confident in our ability to teach English, and we welcome new ideas on the subject.

   B. Because we are confident in our ability to teach English, we welcome new ideas on the subject.

   C. When we are confident in our ability to teach English, we welcome new ideas on the subject.

   D. We are confident in our ability to teach English; however, we welcome new ideas on the subject.

Answer: D

Rationale: Transitional words, phrases, and sentences help clarify meanings. In Answer A, the transition word "and" introduces another equal idea. In Answer B, the transition word "because" indicates cause and effect. In Answer C, the transition word "when" indicates order or chronology. In Answer D, "however" shows that these two ideas contrast with each other.

(Average)

9. In preparing students for their oral presentations, the instructor provided all of the following guidelines except one. Which is not an effective guideline?

   A. Even if you are using a lectern, feel free to move about. This will connect you to the audience.

   B. Your posture should be natural, not stiff. Keep your shoulders toward the audience.

   C. Gestures can help you communicate as long as you don't overuse them or make them distracting.

   D. You can avoid eye contact if you focus on your notes. This will make you appear more knowledgeable.

Answer: D

Rationale: Although many people are nervous about making eye contact, they should focus on two or three people at a time. Body language, such as movement, posture, and gestures, helps the speaker connect to the audience.

Sample Test Questions and Rationale (cont.)

(Average)

10. **Which of the following statements indicates an instructional goal for using multimedia in the classroom?**

    A. Audio messages invite the listener to form mental images consistent with the topic of the audio

    B. Print messages appeal almost exclusively to the mind and push students to read with more thought

    C. Listening to an audio message is more passive than reading a print message

    D. Teachers who develop activities that foster a critical perspective on audiovisual presentation will decrease passivity

    Answer: D

    Rationale: Each of the statements is true, but only the last one establishes a goal for using multimedia in the classroom.

(Average)

11. **What is the main form of discourse in the following passage?**

    It would have been hard to find a passer-by more wretched in appearance. He was a man of middle height, stout and hardy, in the strength of maturity; he might have been forty-six or -seven. A slouched leather cap hid half his face, bronzed by the sun and wind, and dripping with sweat.

    A. Description

    B. Narration

    C. Exposition

    D. Persuasion

    Answer: A

    Rationale: A description presents a thing or a person in detail and tells the reader about the appearance of whatever it is presenting. Narration relates a sequence of events (the story) told through a process of narration (discourse) in which events are recounted in a certain order (the plot). Exposition is an explanation or an argument within the narration. It can also be the introduction to a play or a story. Persuasion strives to convince either a character in the story or the reader.

Sample Test Questions and Rationale (cont.)

(Average)

12. In literature, to evoke feelings of pity or compassion is to create

    A. Colloquy

    B. Irony

    C. Pathos

    D. Paradox

Answer: C

Rationale: A very well-known example of pathos is Desdemona's death in *Othello*, but there are many other examples of pathos. In *King Lear*, Cordelia accepts defeat with this line: "We are not the first / Who with best meaning have incurred the worst." A colloquy is a formal conversation. Irony is a discrepancy between what is expected and what occurs. A paradox is a contradictory statement.

(Average)

13. Which of the following would not be a major concern in an oral presentation?

    A. Establishing the purpose of the presentation

    B. Evaluating the audience's demographics and psychographics

    C. Creating a PowerPoint slide for each point

    D. Developing the content to fit the occasion

Answer: C

Rationale: PowerPoint slides should be kept to a minimum of one slide per minute and should not overwhelm the presentation. The slides should be a supplement so that the speaker can accomplish the purpose. To reach that goal, the speaker should understand the makeup of the audience: demographics, such as age, education level, or other quantifiable characteristics; and psychographics, such as attitudes or values. Knowing the purpose and the audience will enable the speaker to develop the content to fit the occasion.

(Rigorous)

14. Mr. Ledbetter has instructed his students to prepare a slide presentation that illustrates an event in history. Students are to include pictures, graphics, media clips, and links to resources. What competencies will students exhibit at the completion of this project?

    A. Analyze the impact of society on media

    B. Recognize the media's strategies to inform and persuade

    C. Demonstrate strategies and creative techniques to prepare presentations using a variety of media

    D. Identify the aesthetic effects of a media presentation

Answer: C

Rationale: Students will have learned how to use various media to convey a unified message.

Sample Test Questions and Rationale (cont.)

(Rigorous)

15. In the following excerpt from "Civil Disobedience," what type of reasoning does Henry David Thoreau use?

   Unjust laws exist; shall we be content to obey them, or shall we endeavor to amend them, and obey them until we have succeeded, or shall we transgress them at once? Men generally, under such a government as this, think that they ought to wait until they have persuaded the majority to alter them. They think that, if they should resist, the remedy would be worse than the evil. But it is the fault of the government itself that the remedy *is* worse than the evil. … Why does it always crucify Christ, and excommunicate Copernicus and Luther, and pronounce Washington and Franklin rebels?

   A. Ethical reasoning

   B. Inductive reasoning

   C. Deductive reasoning

   D. Intellectual reasoning

   Answer: C

   Rationale: Deductive reasoning begins with a general statement that leads to particulars. In this essay, Thoreau begins with the general question about what should be done about unjust laws. His argument leads to a condemnation of the government's role in suppressing dissent.

(Rigorous)

16. Which of the following is not a fallacy in logic?

   A. All students in Ms. Suarez's fourth-period class are bilingual.
   Beth is in Ms. Suarez's fourth-period class.
   Beth is bilingual.

   B. All bilingual students are in Ms. Suarez's class.
   Beth is in Ms. Suarez's fourth-period class.
   Beth is bilingual.

   C. Beth is bilingual.
   Beth is in Ms. Suarez's fourth-period class.
   All students in Ms. Suarez's fourth-period class are bilingual.

   D. If Beth is bilingual, then she speaks Spanish.
   Beth speaks French.
   Beth is not bilingual.

   Answer: A

   Rationale: The second statement, or premise, is tested against the first premise. Both premises are valid and the conclusion is logical. In Answer B, the conclusion is invalid because the first premise does not exclude other students. In Answer C, the conclusion cannot be logically drawn from the preceding premises; you cannot conclude that all students are bilingual based on one example. In Answer D, the conclusion is invalid because the first premise is faulty.

Sample Test Questions and Rationale (cont.)

(Rigorous)

17. Which of the following is an example of a post hoc fallacy?

    A. When the new principal was hired, student-reading scores improved; therefore, the principal caused the increase in scores.

    B. Why are we spending money on the space program when our students don't have current textbooks?

    C. You can't give your class a ten-minute break. Once you do that, we'll all have to give our students a ten-minute break.

    D. You can never believe anything he says because he's not from the same country as we are.

Answer: A

Rationale: A post hoc fallacy assumes that because one event preceded another, the first event caused the second event. In this case, student scores could have increased for other reasons. Answer B is a red herring fallacy, in which one raises an irrelevant topic to sidetrack the audience from the first topic. In this case, the space budget and the textbook budget have little effect on each other. Answer C is an example of a slippery slope, in which one event is followed precipitously by another event. Answer D is an ad hominem ("to the man") fallacy in which a person is attacked rather than the concept or interpretation.

(Rigorous)

18. Identify the type of rhetorical appeal used by Molly Ivins in this excerpt from her essay "Get a Knife, Get a Dog, But Get Rid of Guns."

    As a civil libertarian, I, of course, support the Second Amendment. And I believe it means exactly what it says: *A well regulated militia being necessary to the security of a free state, the right of the people to keep and bear arms shall not be infringed.*

    A. Ethos

    B. Pathos

    C. Logos

    D. Literary

Answer: A

Rationale: An ethical appeal involves using the credentials of a reliable and trustworthy authority. In this case, Ivins cites the Constitution. Pathos is an emotional appeal, and logos is a rational appeal. Literature might appeal to you, but it's not a type of rhetorical appeal.

Sample Test Questions and Rationale (cont.)

(Rigorous)

19. What is the common advertising technique used by the following advertising slogans?

"It's everywhere you want to be."
            —Visa

"Have it your way."
      —Burger King

"When you care enough to send the very best."   —Hallmark

"Be all you can be."
      —U.S. Army

A. Peer approval

B. Rebel

C. Individuality

D. Escape

Answer: C

Rationale: All of these ads associate products with people who can think and act for themselves. Products are linked to individual decision making. With peer approval, the ads would associate their products with friends and acceptance. With rebellion, the ads would associates products with behaviors or lifestyles that oppose society's norms. Escape would suggest the appeal of "getting away from it all."

(Rigorous)

20. In presenting a report to peers about the effects of Hurricane Katrina on New Orleans, the students wanted to use various media in their argument to persuade their peers that more needed to be done. Which of these would be the most effective?

A. A PowerPoint presentation showing the blueprints of the levees before the flood and new designs for reconstruction

B. A collection of music clips made by street performers in the French Quarter before and after the flood

C. A video showing the areas devastated by the flood and the current state of rebuilding

D. A collection of recordings of interviews made by various government officials and local citizens affected by the flooding

Answer: C

Rationale: For maximum impact, a video would offer dramatic scenes of the devastated areas. A video by its very nature is more dynamic than a static PowerPoint presentation. Further, seeing the condition of the levees would not provide as much impetus for change as seeing the devastated areas. Oral messages such as music clips and interviews provide another way of supplementing the message but, again, they are not as dynamic as video.

Sample Test Questions and Rationale (cont.)

(Rigorous)

21. Based on the excerpt below from Kate Chopin's short story "The Story of an Hour," what can students infer about the main character?

She did not stop to ask if it were or were not a monstrous joy that held her. A clear and exalted perception enabled her to dismiss the suggestion as trivial. She knew that she would weep again when she saw the kind, tender hands folded in death; the face that had never looked save with love upon her, fixed and gray and dead. But she saw beyond that bitter moment a long procession of years to come that would belong to her absolutely. And she opened and spread her arms out to them in welcome.

A. She dreaded her life as a widow

B. Although she loved her husband, she was glad that he was dead for he had never loved her

C. She worried that she was too indifferent to her husband's death

D. Although they had loved each other, she was beginning to appreciate that opportunities had opened because of her husband's death

Answer: D

Rationale: Dismissing her feeling of "monstrous joy" as insignificant, the young woman realizes that she will mourn her husband, who had been good to her and had loved her. But that "long procession of years" does not frighten her; instead she recognizes that this new life belongs to her alone and she welcomes it with open arms.

(Rigorous)

22. Which part of a classical argument is illustrated in this excerpt from the essay "What Should Be Done About Rock Lyrics?"

But violence against women is greeted by silence. It shouldn't be.

This does not mean censorship, or book (or record) burning. In a society that protects free expression, we understand a lot of stuff will float up out of the sewer. Usually, we recognize the ugly stuff that advocates violence against any group as the garbage it is, and we consider its purveyors as moral lepers. We hold our nose and tolerate it, but we speak out against the values it proffers.

A. Narration

B. Confirmation

C. Refutation and concession

D. Summation

Answer: C

Rationale: The author refutes the idea of censorship and concedes that society tolerates offensive lyrics as part of our freedom of speech. Narration provides background material to enhance an argument. In confirmation, the author details the argument with claims that support the thesis. In summation, the author concludes the argument by offering the strongest solution.

SAMPLE TEST

SAMPLE TEST

Section I: Essay Test

Several prompts are given. You are expected to exhibit a variety of writing skills. In most testing situations, you will have thirty minutes to respond to each of the prompts. For some tests you will be allowed sixty minutes, either to incorporate more than one question or for greater preparation and editing time. Read the directions carefully and organize your time wisely.

Section II: Multiple-Choice Test

This section contains 125 questions. In most testing situations, you will be expected to answer from 35 to 40 questions within 30 minutes. If you time yourself on the entire battery, take no more than 90 minutes.

Section III: Answer Key

Section I: Essay Prompts

Prompt A

Write an expository essay discussing effective teaching strategies for developing literature appreciation with a heterogeneous class of ninth graders. Select any appropriate piece(s) of world literature to use as examples in the discussion.

Prompt B

After reading the following passage from Aldous Huxley's *Brave New World*, discuss the types of reader responses possible with a group of eight graders.

He hated them all—all the men who came to visit Linda. One afternoon, when he had been playing with the other children—it was cold, he remembered, and there was snow on the mountains—he came back to the house and heard angry voices in the bedroom. They were women's voices, and they were words he didn't understand; but he knew they were dreadful words. Then suddenly, crash! something was upset; he heard people moving about quickly, and there was another crash and then a noise like hitting a mule, only not so bony; then Linda screamed. 'Oh, don't, don't, don't!' she said. He ran in. There were three women in dark blankets. Linda was on the bed. One of the women was holding her wrists. Another was lying across her legs, so she couldn't kick. The third was hitting her with a whip. Once, twice, three times; and each time Linda screamed.

Prompt C

Write a persuasive letter to the editor on any contemporary topic of special interest. Employ whatever forms of discourse, style devices, and audience appeal techniques that seem appropriate to the topic.

Section II: Multiple-Choice Test

Explanation of Rigor

Easy: The majority of test takers would get this question correct. The question requires a simple understanding of the facts, or the subject matter is part of the basics of an education for teaching English.

Average Rigor: This question represents a test item that most people would pass. It requires a particular level of analysis or reasoning, or the subject matter exceeds the basics of an education for teaching English.

Rigorous: The majority of test takers would have difficulty answering this question. It involves critical thinking skills that reflect a very high level of abstract thought, analysis, or reasoning, and it would require a very deep and broad education for teaching English.

LITERATURE

Part A

Each underlined portion of sentences 1–10 contains one or more errors in grammar, usage, mechanics, or sentence structure. Circle the choice that best corrects the error without changing the meaning of the original sentence.

(Easy) (Skill 2.3)

1. Joe <u>didn't hardly know his cousin Fred,</u> who'd had a rhinoplasty.

    A. hardly did know his cousin Fred

    B. didn't know his cousin Fred hardly

    C. hardly knew his cousin Fred

    D. didn't know his cousin Fred

    E. didn't hardly know his cousin Fred

(Average) (Skill 2.3)

2. <u>Mixing the batter for cookies,</u> the cat licked the Crisco from the cookie sheet.

    A. While mixing the batter for cookies

    B. While the batter for cookies was mixing

    C. While I mixed the batter for cookies

    D. While I mixed the cookies

    E. Mixing the batter for cookies

(Average) (Skill 2.3)

3. Mr. Smith <u>respectfully submitted his resignation and had</u> a new job.

    A. respectfully submitted his resignation and has

    B. respectfully submitted his resignation before accepting

    C. respectfully submitted his resignation because of

    D. respectfully submitted his resignation and had

(Average) (Skill 2.3)

4. Wally <u>groaned, "Why do I have to do an oral interpretation of "The Raven."</u>

    A. groaned, "Why… of 'The Raven'?"

    B. groaned, "Why… of "The Raven"?

    C. groaned ", Why… of "The Raven?"

    D. groaned, "Why… of "The Raven."

(Rigorous) (Skill 2.3)

5. <u>The coach offered her assistance but the athletes wanted to practice on their own.</u>

    A. The coach offered her assistance, however, the athletes wanted to practice on their own.

    B. The coach offered her assistance: furthermore, the athletes wanted to practice on their own.

    C. Having offered her assistance, the athletes wanted to practice on their own.

    D. The coach offered her assistance; however, the athletes wanted to practice on their own.

    E. The coach offered her assistance, and the athletes wanted to practice on their own.

(Rigorous) (Skill 2.3)

6. **The Taj Mahal has been designated one of the Seven Wonders of the World, and people know it for its unique architecture.**

    A. The Taj Mahal has been designated one of the Seven Wonders of the World, and it is known for its unique architecture.

    B. People know the Taj Mahal for its unique architecture, and it has been designated one of the Seven Wonders of the World.

    C. People have known the Taj Mahal for its unique architecture, and it has been designated of the Seven Wonders of the World.

    D. The Taj Mahal has designated itself one of the Seven Wonders of the World.

(Rigorous) (Skill 2.3)

7. **Walt Whitman was famous for his composition *Leaves of Grass*, serving as a nurse during the Civil War, and a devoted son.**

    A. for his composition *Leaves of Grass*, his service as a nurse during the Civil War, and a devoted son.

    B. for composing *Leaves of Grass*, serving as a nurse during the Civil War, and being a devoted son.

    C. for his composition *Leaves of Grass*, his nursing during the Civil War, and his devotion as a son.

    D. for his composition *Leaves of Grass*, serving as a nurse during the Civil War and a devoted son.

    E. for his composition *Leaves of Grass*, serving as a nurse during the Civil War, and a devoted son.

(Rigorous) (Skill 2.3)

8. **A teacher must know not only her subject matter but also the strategies of content teaching.**

    A. must not only know her subject matter but also the strategies of content teaching

    B. not only must know her subject matter but also the strategies of content teaching

    C. must not know only her subject matter but also the strategies of content teaching

    D. must know not only her subject matter but also the strategies of content teaching

(Easy) (Skill 2.4)

9. **There were few pieces of evidence presented during the second trial.**

    A. fewer peaces

    B. less peaces

    C. less pieces

    D. fewer pieces

(Average) (Skill 2.4)

10. **The teacher implied from our angry words that there was conflict between you and me.**

    A. Implied… between you and I

    B. Inferred… between you and I

    C. Inferred… between you and me

    D. Implied… between you and me

Part B

Directions: Select the best answer in each group.

(Easy) (Skill 1.1)

11. **The tendency to emphasize and value the qualities and peculiarities of life in a particular geographic area exemplifies:**

    A. Pragmatism

    B. Regionalism

    C. Pantheism

    D. Abstractionism

(Easy) (Skill 1.1)

12. **Charles Dickens, Robert Browning, and Robert Louis Stevenson were:**

    A. Victorians

    B. Medievalists

    C. Elizabethans

    D. Absurdists

(Easy) (Skill 1.1)

13. **Among middle school students of low-to-average reading level, which work would most likely stir reading interest?**

    A. *Elmer Gantry*, Sinclair Lewis

    B. *Smiley's People*, John Le Carre

    C. *The Outsiders*, S.E. Hinton

    D. *And Then There Were None*, Agatha Christie

(Easy) (Skill 1.1)

14. **What is considered the first work of English literature because it was written in the vernacular of the day?**

    A. *Beowulf*

    B. *Le Morte d'Arthur*

    C. *The Faerie Queene*

    D. *Canterbury Tales*

(Average) (Skill 1.1)

15. **Considered one of the first feminist plays, this Ibsen drama ends with a door slamming, symbolizing the lead character's emancipation from traditional societal norms.**

    A. *The Wild Duck*

    B. *Hedda Gabler*

    C. *Ghosts*

    D. *A Doll's House*

(Average) (Skill 1.1)

16. **Which of the following titles is known for its scathingly condemning tone?**

    A. Boris Pasternak's *Dr Zhivago*

    B. Albert Camuss' *The Stranger*

    C. Henry David Thoreau's "On the Duty of Civil Disobedience"

    D. Benjamin Franklin's "Rules by Which a Great Empire May Be Reduced to a Small One"

(Average) (Skill 1.1)

17. **American colonial writers were primarily:**

    A. Romanticists

    B. Naturalists

    C. Realists

    D. Neoclassicists

(Average) (Skill 1.1)

18. Arthur Miller wrote *The Crucible* as a parallel to what twentieth century event?

    A. Senator McCarthy's House Un-American Activities Committee Hearing

    B. The Cold War

    C. The fall of the Berlin wall

    D. The Persian Gulf War

(Average) (Skill 1.1)

19. Which of the writers below is a renowned Black memoirist?

    A. Maya Angelou

    B. Sandra Cisneros

    C. Richard Wilbur

    D. Richard Wright

(Average) (Skill 1.1)

20. Which of the following is not a theme of Native American writing?

    A. Emphasis on the hardiness of the human body and soul

    B. The strength of multicultural assimilation

    C. Contrition for the genocide of native peoples

    D. Remorse for the destruction of the Native American way of life

(Average) (Skill 1.1)

21. The writing of Russian naturalists is:

    A. Optimistic

    B. Pessimistic

    C. Satirical

    D. Whimsical

(Average) (Skill 1.1)

22. Most children's literature written prior to the development of popular literature was intended to be didactic. Which of the following would not be considered didactic?

    A. "A Visit from St. Nicholas" by Clement Moore

    B. *McGuffy's Reader*

    C. Any version of Cinderella

    D. Parables from the Bible

(Average) (Skill 1.1)

23. Written at the sixth-grade reading level, most of S. E. Hinton's novels (for instance, *The Outsiders*) have the greatest reader appeal with:

    A. Sixth graders

    B. Ninth graders

    C. Twelfth graders

    D. Adults

(Average) (Skill 1.1)

24. Children's literature became established in the:

    A. seventeenth century

    B. eighteenth century

    C. nineteenth century

    D. twentieth century

(Rigorous) (Skill 1.1)

25. After watching a movie of a train derail-ment, a child exclaims, "Wow, look how many cars fell off the tracks. There's junk everywhere. The engineer must have really been asleep." Using the facts that the child is impressed by the wreck-age and assigns blame to the engineer, a follower of Piaget's theories would estimate the child to be about:

    A. Ten years old

    B. Twelve years old

    C. Fourteen years old

    D. Sixteen years old

(Rigorous) (Skill 1.1)

26. The most significant drawback to applying learning theory research to classroom practice is that:

    A. Today's students do not acquire reading skills with the same alacrity as they did when greater emphasis was placed on reading classical literature.

    B. Development rates are complicated by geographical and cultural factors. In analyzing literature and in looking for ways to bring a work to life for an audience, the use of comparable themes and ideas from other pieces of literature and from one's own life experiences, including from reading the daily newspaper, is very important and useful.

    C. Homogeneous grouping has contrib-uted to faster development of some age groups.

    D. Social and environmental conditions have contributed to a more escalated maturity level than research done twenty or more years ago would seem to indicate.

(Rigorous) (Skill 1.1)

27. Which of the following is the best defini-tion of existentialism?

    A. The philosophical doctrine that mat-ter is the only reality and that every-thing in the world, including thought, will, and feeling, can be explained in terms of matter

    B. A philosophy that views things as they should be or as one would wish them to be

    C. A philosophical and literary move-ment, variously religious and atheistic, stemming from Kierkegaard and represented by Sartre

    D. The belief that all events are deter-mined by fate and are hence inevitable

(Rigorous) (Skill 1.1)

28. The following lines from Robert Browning's poem "My Last Duchess" come from an example of what form of dramatic literature?

    That's my last Duchess painted on the wall,
    Looking as if she were alive. I call
    That piece a wonder now: Frà Pandolf's
        hands
    Worked busily a day, and there she stands.
    Will 't please you sit and look at her?

    A. Tragedy

    B. Comic opera

    C. Dramatis personae

    D. Dramatic monologue

(Rigorous) (Skill 1.1)

29. **"Every one must pass through Vanity Fair to get to the Celestial City" is an allusion from a:**

    A. Chinese folk tale

    C. British allegory

    B. Norse saga

    D. German fairy tale

(Rigorous) (Skill 1.1)

30. **Which author did not write satire?**

    A. Joseph Addison

    B. Richard Steele

    C. Alexander Pope

    D. John Bunyan

(Rigorous) (Skill 1.1)

31. **What were two major characteristics of the first American literature?**

    A. Vengefulness and arrogance

    B. Bellicosity and derision

    C. Oral delivery and reverence for the land

    D. Maudlin and self-pitying egocentricism

(Rigorous) (Skill 1.1)

32. **Hoping to take advantage of the popularity of the Harry Potter series, a teacher develops a unit on mythology comparing the story and characters of Greek and Roman myths with the story and characters of the Harry Potter books. Which of these is a commonality that would link classical literature to popular fiction?**

    A. The characters are gods in human form with human-like characteristics

    B. The settings are realistic places in the world where the characters interact as humans would

    C. The themes center on the universal truths of love and hate and fear

    D. The heroes in the stories are young males and only they can overcome the opposing forces

(Rigorous) (Skill 1.1)

33. **In the following poem, what literary movement is reflected?**

    "My Heart Leaps Up" by William Wordsworth

    My heart leaps up when I behold
        A rainbow in the sky:
    So was it when my life began;
        So is it now I am a man;
    So be it when I shall grow old,
        Or let me die!
    The Child is father of the Man;
        And I could wish my days to be
        Bound each to each by natural piety

    A. Neoclassicism

    B. Victorian literature

    C. Romanticism

    D. Naturalism

(Average) (Skill 1.2)

34. **Sometimes readers are asked to demonstrate their understanding of a text. This might include all of the following except:**

    A. Role playing

    B. Paraphrasing

    C. Storyboarding a part of the story with dialogue bubbles

    D. Reading the story aloud

(Average) (Skill 1.2)

35. **Which of the following reading strategies calls for higher-order cognitive skills?**

    A. Making predictions

    B. Summarizing

    C. Monitoring

    D. Making inferences

(Average) (Skill 1.3)

36. **The literary device of personification is used in which example below?**

    A. "Beg me no beggary by soul or parents, whining dog!"

    B. "Happiness sped through the halls, cajoling as it went."

    C. "O wind thy horn, thou proud fellow."

    D. "And that one talent which is death to hide."

(Easy) (Skill 1.3)

37. **Which definition best defines *diction*?**

    A. The specific word choices used by an author to create a particular mood or feeling in the reader

    B. Writing that explains something thoroughly

    C. The background, or exposition, for a short story or drama

    D. Word choices that help teach a truth or moral

(Average) (Skill 1.3)

38. **In the following quotation, Marc Antony addresses the dead body of Caesar as though it were still a living being.**

    O, pardon me, thou
    Bleeding piece of earth
    That I am meek and gentle With these butchers.

    —Marc Antony from *Julius Caesar*

    This passage employs:

    A. Apostrophe

    B. Allusion

    C. Antithesis

    D. Anachronism

(Average) (Skill 1.3)

39. **An extended metaphor comparing two very dissimilar things (one lofty, one lowly) is a definition of a(n):**

    A. Antithesis

    B. Aphorism

    C. Apostrophe

    D. Conceit

(Average) (Skill 1.3)

40. Which of the following is a characteristic of blank verse?

A. Meter in iambic pentameter

B. Clearly specified rhyme scheme

C. Lack of figurative language

D. Unspecified rhythm

(Average) (Skill 1.3)

41. Which is the best definition of free verse, or *vers libre*?

A. Poetry that consists of an unaccented syllable followed by an unaccented sound

B. Short lyrical poetry written to entertain but with an instructive purpose

C. Poetry that does not have a uniform pattern of rhythm

D. A poem that tells a story and has a plot

(Rigorous) (Skill 1.3)

42. Which term best describes the form of the following poetic excerpt?

And more to lulle him in his
    slumber soft,
A trickling streake from high rock
    tumbling downe,
And ever-drizzling raine upon
    the loft.
Mixt with a murmuring winde,
    much like a swowne
No other noyse, nor peoples
    troubles cryes.
As still we wont t'annoy the
    walle'd towne,
Might there be heard: but
    careless Quiet lyes,
Wrapt in eternall silence farre
    from enemyes.

A. Ballad

B. Elegy

C. Spenserian stanza

D. Ottava rima

(Rigorous) (Skill 1.3)

43. In the phrase "The Cabinet conferred with the President," *Cabinet* is an example of a(n):

A. Metonym

B. Synecdoche

C. Metaphor

D. Allusion

(Rigorous) (Skill 1.3)

44. What syntactic device is most evident in the following excerpt from Abraham Lincoln's "Gettysburg Address"?

It is rather for us to be here dedicated to the great task remaining before us—that from these honored dead we take increased devotion to that cause for which they gave the last full measure of devotion—that we here highly resolve that these dead shall not have died in vain—that this nation, under God, shall have a new birth of freedom—and that government of the people, by the people, for the people, shall not perish from the earth.

A. Affective connotation

B. Informative denotations

C. Allusion

D. Parallelism

(Easy) (Skill 1.4)

45. A traditional, anonymous story, ostensibly having a historical basis, usually explaining some phenomenon of nature or aspect of creation, defines a(n):

   A. Proverb

   B. Idyll

   C. Myth

   D. Epic

(Easy) (Skill 1.4)

46. Which of the following is not a characteristic of a fable?

   A. Animals that feel and talk like humans

   B. Happy solutions to human dilemmas

   C. Teaches a moral or standard for behavior

   D. Illustrates specific people or groups without directly naming them

(Rigorous) (Skill 1.4)

47. Which poem is typified as a villanelle?

   A. "Do not go gentle into that good night"

   B. "Dover Beach"

   C. *Sir Gawain and the Green Knight*

   D. *Pilgrim's Progress*

(Rigorous) (Skill 1.4)

48. In classic tragedy, a protagonist's defeat is brought about by a tragic flaw, which is called:

   A. Hubris

   B. Hamartia

   C. Catarsis

   D. The skene

(Rigorous) (Skill 1.4)

49. Which sonnet form describes the following?

   My galley chargèd with forgetfulness,
   Through sharp seas, in winter night doth pass
   'Tween rock and rock; and eke mine enemy, alas,
   That is my lord steereth with, cruelness;
   And every oar a thought with readiness,
   As though that death were light in such a case.
   An endless wind doth tear the sail apace
   Or forc'ed sighs and trusty fearfulness.
   A rain of tears, a cloud of dark disdain,
   Hath done the wearied cords great hinderance;
   Wreathed with error and eke with ignorance.
   The stars be hid that led me to this pain;
   Drowned is reason that should me consort,
   And I remain despairing of the poet.

   A. Petrarchan or Italian sonnet

   B. Shakespearian or Elizabethan sonnet

   C. Romantic sonnet

   D. Spenserian sonnet

(Rigorous) (Skill 1.4)

50. What is the salient literary feature of this excerpt from an epic?

   Hither the heroes and the nymphs resort,
   To taste awhile the pleasures of a court;
   In various talk th'instructive hours they pass'd,
   Who gave the ball, or paid the visit last;
   One speaks the glory of the British queen,
   And another describes a charming Indian screen;
   A third interprets motion, looks, and eyes;
   At every word a reputation dies.

   A. Sprung rhythm

   B. Onomatopoeia

   C. Heroic couplets

   D. Motif

(Average) (Skill 1.5)

51. In preparing a unit on twentieth century immigration, you prepare a list of books for students to read. Which book would not be appropriate for this topic?

    A. *The Things They Carried* by Tim O'Brien

    B. *Exodus* by Leon Uris

    C. *The Joy Luck Club* by Amy Tan

    D. *Tortilla Flats* by John Steinbeck

(Average) (Skill 1.5)

52. In exploring the relationship of literature to modern life, which of these activities would not enable students to explore comparable themes?

    A. After studying various world events, such as the Palestinian-Israeli conflict, students write an updated version of *Romeo and Juliet* using modern characters and settings

    B. Before studying *Romeo and Juliet*, students watch *West Side Story*

    C. Students research the major themes of *Romeo and Juliet* by studying news stories and finding modern counter-parts for the story

    D. Students compare the romantic themes of *Romeo and Juliet* and *The Taming of the Shrew*

(Rigorous) (Skill 1.5)

53. Mr. Phillips is creating a unit to study *To Kill a Mockingbird* and wants to familiar-ize his high school freshmen with the attitudes and issues of the historical period. Which activity would familiarize students with the attitudes and issues of the Depression-era South?

    A. Create a detailed timeline of fifteen to twenty social, cultural, and political events that focus on race relations in the 1930s.

    B. Research and report on the life of author Harper Lee. Compare her background with the events in the book.

    C. Watch the movie version and note language and dress.

    D. Write a research report on the stock market crash of 1929 and its effects.

(Rigorous) (Skill 1.5)

54. Which choice below best defines naturalism?

    A. A belief that the writer or artist should apply scientific objectivity in his or her observation and treatment of life without imposing value judgments

    B. The doctrine that teaches that the existing world is the best to be hoped for

    C. The doctrine that teaches that God is not a personality, but that all laws, forces, and manifestations of the universe are God-related

    D. A philosophical doctrine that professes that the truth of all knowledge must always be in question

(Average) (Skill 1.6)

55. The students in Mrs. Cline's seventh-grade language arts class were invited to attend a performance of *Romeo and Juliet* presented by the drama class at the high school. To best prepare, they should:

    A. Read the play as a homework exercise

    B. Read a synopsis of the plot and a biographical sketch of the author

    C. Examine a few main selections from the play to become familiar with the language and style of the author

    D. Read a condensed version of the story and practice attentive listening skills

(Average) (Skill 1.6)

56. What is the best course of action when a child refuses to complete a reading/literature assignment on the grounds that it is morally objectionable?

    A. Speak with the parents and explain the necessity of studying this work

    B. Encourage the child to sample some of the text before making a judgment

    C. Place the child in another teacher's class in which the students are studying an acceptable work

    D. Provide the student with alternative selections that cover the same performance standards the rest of the class is learning

(Average) (Skill 1.6)

57. The English department is developing strategies to encourage all students to become a community of readers. From the list of suggestions below, which would be the least effective way for teachers to foster independent reading?

    A. Each teacher will set aside a weekly thirty-minute in-class reading session during which the teacher and students read a magazine or book for enjoyment

    B. Teacher and students develop a list of favorite books to share with each other

    C. The teacher assigns at least one book report each grading period to ensure that students are reading from the established class list

    D. The students gather books for a classroom library so that books may be shared with each other

(Average) (Skill 1.6)

58. Which of the following responses to literature typically gives middle school students the most problems?

    A. Interpretive

    B. Evaluative

    C. Critical

    D. Emotional

(Average) (Skill 1.6)

59. Which of the following is a formal reading-level assessment?

    A. A standardized reading test

    B. A teacher-made reading test

    C. An interview

    D. A reading diary

(Average) (Skill 1.6)

60. Which of the following would be the **most significant** factor in teaching Homer's *Iliad* and *Odyssey* to any particular group of students?

    A. Identifying a translation at the appropriate reading level

    B. Determining the students' interest level

    C. Selecting an appropriate evaluative technique

    D. Determining the scope and delivery methods of background study

(Average) (Skill 1.6)

61. Which of the following definitions best describes a parable?

    A. A short, entertaining account of some happening, usually using talking animals as characters

    B. A slow, sad poem or a prose work expressing lamentation

    C. An extensive narrative work expressing universal truths concerning domestic life

    D. A short, simple story of an occurrence of a familiar kind, from which a moral or religious lesson may be drawn

(Average) (Skill 1.6)

62. Which teaching method would best engage underachievers in the required senior English class?

    A. Assign glossary work and extensively footnoted excerpts of great works

    B. Have students take turns reading aloud from the anthology selection

    C. Let students choose which readings they'll study and write about

    D. Use a chronologically arranged, traditional text, but assign group work, panel presentations, and portfolio management

(Rigorous) (Skill 1.6)

63. How will literature help students in a science class understand the following passage?

Just as was the case more than three decades ago, we are still sailing between the Scylla of deferring surgery for too long and risking irreversible left ventricular damage and sudden death, and the Charibdas of operating too early and subjecting the patient to the early risks of operation and the later risks resulting from prosthetic valves.

—E. Braunwald, *European Heart Journal,* July 2000

A. They will recognize the allusions to Scylla and Charibdas from Greek mythology and understand that the medical community has to select one of two unfavorable choices.

B. They will recognize the allusion to sailing and understand its analogy to doctors as sailors navigating unknown waters.

C. They will recognize that the allusions to Scylla and Charibdas refer to the two islands in Norse mythology where sailors would find themselves shipwrecked, and understand how the doctors feel isolated by their choices.

D. They will recognize the metaphor of the heart and relate it to Eros, the character in Greek mythology who represents love. Eros was the love child of Scylla and Charibdas.

(Rigorous) (Skill 1.6)

64. Which is not a Biblical allusion?

A. The patience of Job

B. Thirty pieces of silver

C. "Man proposes; God disposes"

D. "Suffer not yourself to be betrayed by a kiss"

(Rigorous) (Skill 1.6)

65. Before reading a passage, a teacher gives her students an anticipation guide with a list of statements related to the topic they are about to cover in the reading material. She asks the students to indicate their agreement or disagreement with each statement on the guide. This activity is intended to:

A. Elicit students' prior knowledge of the topic and set a purpose for reading

B. Help students identify the main ideas and supporting details in the text

C. Help students synthesize information from the text

D. Help students visualize the concepts and terms in the text

(Rigorous) (Skill 1.6)

66. Recognizing empathy in literature is mostly a(n):

A. Emotional response

B. Interpretive response

C. Critical response

D. Evaluative response

LANGUAGE

(Average) (Skill 2.1)

67. **If a student has a poor vocabulary, the teacher should recommend first that:**

    A. The student read newspapers, magazines, and books on a regular basis

    B. The student enroll in a Latin class

    C. The student write the words repetitively after looking them up in the dictionary

    D. The student use a thesaurus to locate synonyms and incorporate them into his/her vocabulary

(Average) (Skill 2.1)

68. **Which of the following sentences contains a subject-verb agreement error?**

    A. Both mother and her two sisters were married in a triple ceremony.

    B. Neither the hen nor the rooster is likely to be served for dinner.

    C. My boss, as well as the company's two personnel directors, have been to Spain.

    D. Amanda and the twins are late again.

(Average) (Skill 2.1)

69. **The synonyms *gyro, hero,* and *submarine* reflect which influence on language usage?**

    A. Social

    B. Geographical

    C. Historical

    D. Personal

(Rigorous) (Skill 2.1)

70. **Which aspect of language is innate?**

    A. Biological capability to articulate sounds understood by other humans

    B. Cognitive ability to create syntactical structures

    C. Capacity for using semantics to convey meaning in a social environment

    D. Ability to vary inflections and accents

(Easy) (Skill 2.2)

71. **To understand the origins of a word, one must study the:**

    A. Synonyms

    B. Inflections

    C. Phonetics

    D. Etymology

(Easy) (Skill 2.2)

72. **The Elizabethans wrote in:**

    A. Celtic

    B. Old English

    C. Middle English

    D. Modern English

(Average) (Skill 2.2)

73. **Which event triggered the beginning of Modern English?**

    A. Conquest of England by the Normans in 1066

    B. Introduction of the printing press to the British Isles

    C. Publication of Samuel Johnson's lexicon

    D. American Revolution

(Average) (Skill 2.2)

74. **Which of the following is not true about the English language?**

    A. English is the easiest language to learn

    B. English is the least inflected language

    C. English has the most extensive vocabulary of any language

    D. English originated as a Germanic tongue

(Rigorous) (Skill 2.2)

75. **Which word in the following sentence contains a bound morpheme: "The quick brown fox jumped over the lazy dog"?**

    A. The

    B. fox

    C. lazy

    D. jumped

(Rigorous) (Skill 2.2)

76. **Which event was responsible for the standardizing of dialects across America in the twentieth century?**

    A. With the immigrant influx, American became a melting pot of languages and cultures

    B. Trains enabled people to meet other people of different languages and cultures

    C. Radio, and later television, used actors and announcers who spoke without pronounced dialects

    D. Newspapers and libraries developed programs to teach people to speak English with an agreed-upon common dialect

(Rigorous) (Skill 2.2)

77. **Latin words that entered the English language during the Elizabethan age include:**

    A. *Allusion, education*, and *esteem*

    B. *Vogue* and *mustache*

    C. *Canoe* and *cannibal*

    D. *Alligator, cocoa*, and *armadillo*

(Easy) (Skill 2.3)

78. **Which of the following sentences is properly punctuated?**

    A. The more you eat; the more you want.

    B. The authors—John Steinbeck, Ernest Hemingway, and William Faulkner—are staples of modern writing in American literature textbooks.

    C. Handling a wild horse, takes a great deal of skill and patience.

    D. The man who replaced our teacher, is a comedian.

(Rigorous) (Skill 2.3)

79. **Which sentence below best minimizes the impact of bad news?**

    A. We have denied you permission to attend the event.

    B. Although permission to attend the event cannot be given, you are encouraged to buy the video.

    C. Although you cannot attend the event, we encourage you to buy the video.

    D. Although attending the event is not possible, watching the video is an option.

(Rigorous) (Skill 2.3)

80. The arrangement and relationship of words in sentences or sentence structures best describes:

    A. Style

    B. Discourse

    C. Thesis

    D. Syntax

(Average) (Skill 2.3)

81. Which of the following sentences contains capitalization error?

    A. The commander of the English navy was Admiral Nelson.

    B. Napoleon was the president of the French First Republic.

    C. Qeen Elizabeth II is the Monarch of the British Empire.

    D. William the Conqueror led the Normans to victory over the British.

(Easy) (Skill 2.4)

82. The substitution of *went to his rest for died* is an example of a(n):

    A. Bowdlerism

    B. Jargon

    C. Euphemism

    D. Malapropism

(Average) (Skill 2.4)

83. If students use slang and expletives, what is the best course of action to take in order to improve their formal communication skills?

    A. Ask the students to paraphrase their writing, that is, translate it into language appropriate for the school principal to read

    B. Refuse to read the students' papers until they conform to a more literate style

    C. Ask the students to read their work aloud to the class for peer evaluation

    D. Rewrite the flagrant passages to show the students the right form of expression

(Rigorous) (Skill 2.4)

84. Which level of meaning is the hardest aspect of a language to master?

    A. Denotation

    B. Jargon

    C. Connotation

    D. Slang

COMPOSITION

(Easy) (Skill 3.1)

85. Reading a piece of student writing to assess the overall impression of the product is:

    A. Holistic evaluation

    B. Portfolio assessment

    C. Analytical evaluation

    D. Using a performance system

(Easy) (Skill 3.1)

86. What is not one of the advantages of collaborative or cooperative learning?

    A. Students who work together in groups or teams develop their skills in organization, leadership, research, communication, and problem solving

    B. Working in teams can help students overcome anxiety in distance-learning courses and contribute to the students' sense of community and belonging

    C. Students tend to learn more material and retain the information longer than when the same information is taught using different methods

    D. Teachers reduce their workload and the time spent on assignments and grading

(Easy) (Skill 3.1)

87. Writing ideas quickly without interruption of the flow of thoughts or attention to conventions is called:

    A. Brainstorming

    B. Mapping

    C. Listing

    D. Free writing

(Easy) (Skill 3.1)

88. Which of the following should not be included in the opening paragraph of an informative essay?

    A. Thesis sentence

    B. Details and examples supporting the main idea

    C. Broad general introduction to the topic

    D. A style and tone that grabs the reader's attention

(Easy) (Skill 3.1)

89. In the paragraph below, which sentence does not contribute to the overall task of supporting the main idea?

    1) The Springfield City Council met Friday to discuss new zoning restrictions for the land to be developed south of the city. 2) Residents who opposed the new restrictions were granted fifteen minutes to present their case. 3) Their argument focused on the dangers that increased traffic would bring to the area. 4) It seemed to me that the Mayor Simpson listened intently. 5) The council agreed to table the new zoning until studies would be performed.

    A. Sentence 2

    B. Sentence 3

    C. Sentence 4

    D. Sentence 5

(Average) (Skill 3.1)

90. **In preparing your high school freshmen to write a research paper about a social problem, what recommendation can you make so that they can determine the credibility of their information?**

    A. Assure them that information on the Internet has been peer-reviewed and verified for accuracy

    B. Tell them to find one solid source and use that exclusively

    C. Suggest they use only primary sources

    D. Suggest they cross check their information with another credible source

(Average) (Skill 3.1)

91. **Modeling is a practice that requires students to:**

    A. create a style unique to their own language capabilities

    B. emulate the writing of professionals

    C. paraphrase passages from good literature

    D. peer evaluate the writings of other students

(Average) (Skill 3.1)

92. **Which of the following are secondary research materials?**

    A. The conclusions and inferences of other historians

    B. Literature and nonverbal materials, novels, stories, poetry, and essays from the period, as well as coins, archaeological artifacts, and art produced during the period

    C. Interviews and surveys conducted by the researcher

    D. Statistics gathered as the result of the researcher's experiments

(Average) (Skill 3.1)

93. **Which of the following is the least effective procedure for promoting consciousness of audience?**

    A. Pairing students during the writing process

    B. Reading all rough drafts before the students write their final copies

    C. Having students compose stories or articles for publication in school literary magazines or newspapers

    D. Writing letters to friends or relatives

(Average) (Skill 3.1)

94. **In general, the most serious drawback of using a computer in writing is that:**

    A. The copy looks so good that students tend to overlook major mistakes

    B. The spell check and grammar programs discourage students from learning proper spelling and mechanics

    C. The speed with which corrections can be made detracts from the exploration and contemplation of composing

    D. The writer loses focus by concentrating on the final product rather than the details

(Average) (Skill 3.1)

95. The new teaching intern is developing a unit on creative writing and is trying to encourage her freshman high school students to write poetry. Which of the following would not be an effective technique?

    A. In groups, students will draw pictures to illustrate "The Love Song of J. Alfred Prufrock" by T.S. Eliot

    B. Either individually or in groups, students will compose a song, writing lyrics that use poetic devices

    C. Students will bring to class the lyrics of a popular song and discuss the imagery and figurative language

    D. Students will read aloud their favorite poems and share their opinions of and responses to the poems

(Rigorous) (Skill 3.1)

96. In this paragraph from a student essay, identify the sentence that provides a detail.

    (1) The poem concerns two different personality types and the human relation between them. (2) Their approach to life is totally different. (3) The neighbor is a very conservative person who follows routines. (4) He follows the traditional wisdom of his father and his father's father. (5) The purpose in fixing the wall and keeping their relationship separate is only because it is all he knows.

    A. Sentence 1

    B. Sentence 3

    C. Sentence 4

    D. Sentence 5

(Rigorous) (Skill 3.1)

97. To determine the credibility of information, researchers should do all of the following except:

    A. Establish the authority of the document

    B. Disregard documents with bias

    C. Evaluate the currency and reputation of the source

    D. Use a variety of research sources and methods

(Rigorous) (Skill 3.1)

98. Which of the following situations is not an ethical violation of intellectual property?

    A. A student visits ten different websites and writes a report to compare the costs of downloading music. He uses the names of the websites without their permission.

    B. A student copies and pastes a chart verbatim from the Internet but does not document it because it is available on a public site.

    C. From an online article found in a subscription database, a student paraphrases a section on the problems of music piracy. She includes the source in her Works Cited but does not provide an in-text citation.

    D. A student uses a comment from M. Night Shyamalan without attribution, claiming the information is common knowledge.

(Rigorous) (Skill 3.1)

99. Students have been asked to write a research paper on automobiles and have brainstormed a number of questions they will answer based on their research findings. Which of the following is not an interpretive question to guide research?

A. Who were the first ten automotive manufacturers in the United States?

B. What types of vehicles will be used fifty years from now?

C. How do automobiles manufactured in the United States compare and contrast with each other?

D. What do you think is the best solution for the fuel shortage?

(Rigorous) (Skill 3.1)

100. In preparing a speech for a contest, a student has encountered problems with gender-specific language. Not wishing to offend either women or men, she seeks your guidance. Which of the following is not an effective strategy?

A. Use the generic "he" and explain that people will understand and accept the male pronoun as all-inclusive

B. Switch to plural nouns and use "they" as the gender-neutral pronoun

C. Use passive voice so that the subject is not required

D. Use male pronouns for one part of the speech and then use female pronouns for the other part of the speech

(Rigorous) (Skill 3.1)

101. For their research paper on the effects of the Civil War on American literature, students have brainstormed a list of potential online sources and are seeking your authorization. Which of the following represents the strongest source?

A. *http://www.wikipedia.org*

B. *http://www.google.com*

C. *http://www.nytimes.com*

D. *http://docsouth.unc.edu/southlit/civil-war.html*

(Rigorous) (Skill 3.1)

102. A formative evaluation of student writing:

A. Requires thorough markings of mechanical errors with a pencil or pen

B. Requires making comments on the appropriateness of the student's interpretation of the prompt and the degree to which the objective was met

C. Should require that the student hand in all the materials produced during the writing process

D. Requires several careful readings of the text for content, mechanics, spelling, and usage

(Rigorous) (Skill 3.1)

103. In preparing a report about William Shakespeare, students are asked to develop a set of interpretive questions to guide their research. Which of the following would not be classified as an interpretive question?

    A. What would be different today if Shakespeare had not written his plays?

    B. How will the plays of Shakespeare affect future generations?

    C. How does Shakespeare view nature in *A Midsummer Night's Dream* and *Much Ado About Nothing*?

    D. During the Elizabethan age, what roles did young boys take in dramatizing Shakespeare's plays?

(Easy) (Skill 3.2)

104. In writing a report, Hector has to explain where acid rain comes from and what it has done to the environment. What is the most likely form of organizational structure?

    A. Cause and effect

    B. Problem and solution

    C. Exposition

    D. Definition

(Easy) (Skill 3.2)

105. Explanatory or informative discourse is:

    A. Exposition

    B. Narration

    C. Persuasion

    D. Description

(Easy) (Skill 3.2)

106. Which of the following is not a technique of prewriting?

    A. Clustering

    B. Listing

    C. Brainstorming

    D. Proofreading

(Easy) (Skill 3.2)

107. The following passage is written from which point of view?

    As she mused the pitiful vision of her mother's life laid its spell on the very quick of her being—that life of commonplace sacrifices closing in final craziness. She trembled as she heard again her mother's voice saying constantly with foolish insistence: *Dearevaun Seraun! Dearevaun Seraun!**

    * "The end of pleasure is pain!" (Gaelic)

    A. First person, narrator

    B. Second person, direct address

    C. Third person, omniscient

    D. First person, omniscient

(Easy) (Skill 3.2)

108. Which of the following is most true of expository writing?

    A. It is mutually exclusive of other forms of discourse

    B. It can incorporate other forms of discourse in the process of providing supporting details

    C. It should never employ informal expression

    D. It should only be scored with a summative evaluation

(Easy) (Skill 3.2)

109. **Which of the following is <u>not correct?</u>**

    A. Because most students have wide access to media, teachers should refrain from using it in their classrooms to diminish media overload

    B. Students can use CDs and DVDs to explore information using a virtual reality experience

    C. Teachers can make their instruction more powerful by using educational media

    D. The Internet enables students to connect with people across cultures and to share interests

(Easy) (Skill 3.2)

110. **Which of the following should students use to improve coherence of ideas within an argument?**

    A. Transitional words or phrases to show relationships between ideas

    B. Conjunctions like "and" to join ideas together

    C. Direct quotes to improve credibility

    D. Adjectives and adverbs to provide stronger detail

(Average) (Skill 3.2)

111. **Which transition word would show contrast between the following two ideas?**

    We are confident in our ability to teach English. We welcome new ideas on the subject.

    A. We are confident in our ability to teach English, and we welcome new ideas on the subject.

    B. Because we are confident in our ability to teach English, we welcome new ideas on the subject.

    C. When we are confident in our ability to teach English, we welcome new ideas on the subject.

    D. We are confident in our ability to teach English; however, we welcome new ideas on the subject.

(Average) (Skill 3.2)

112. **In preparing students for their oral presentations, the instructor provided all of the following guidelines except one. Which is not an effective guideline?**

    A. Even if you are using a lectern, feel free to move about. This will connect you to the audience.

    B. Your posture should be natural, not stiff. Keep your shoulders toward the audience.

    C. Gestures can help you communicate as long as you don't overuse them or make them distracting.

    D. You can avoid eye contact if you focus on your notes. This will make you appear more knowledgeable.

(Average) (Skill 3.2)

113. Which of the following statements indicates an instructional goal for using multimedia in the classroom?

    A. Audio messages invite the listener to form mental images consistent with the topic of the audio

    B. Print messages appeal almost exclusively to the mind and push students to read with more thought

    C. Listening to an audio message is more passive than reading a print message

    D. Teachers who develop activities that foster a critical perspective on audiovisual presentation will decrease passivity

(Average) (Skill 3.2)

114. What is the main form of discourse in this passage?

    It would have been hard to find a passer-by more wretched in appearance. He was a man of middle height, stout and hardy, in the strength of maturity; he might have been forty-six or -seven. A slouched leather cap hid half his face, bronzed by the sun and wind, and dripping with sweat.

    A. Description

    B. Narration

    C. Exposition

    D. Persuasion

(Average) (Skill 3.2)

115. In literature, to evoke feelings of pity or compassion is to create:

    A. Colloquy

    B. Irony

    C. Pathos

    D. Paradox

(Average) (Skill 3.2)

116. Which of the following would not be a major concern in an oral presentation?

    A. Establishing the purpose of the presentation

    B. Evaluating the audience's demographics and psychographics

    C. Creating a PowerPoint slide for each point

    D. Developing the content to fit the occasion

(Rigorous) (Skill 3.2)

117. Mr. Ledbetter has instructed his students to prepare a slide presentation that illustrates an event in history. Students are to include pictures, graphics, media clips, and links to resources. What competencies will students exhibit at the completion of this project?

    A. Analyze the impact of society on media

    B. Recognize the media's strategies to inform and persuade

    C. Demonstrate strategies and creative techniques used to prepare presentations using a variety of media

    D. Identify the aesthetic effects of a media presentation

(Rigorous) (Skill 3.2)

118. In the following excerpt from "Civil Disobedience," what type of reasoning does Henry David Thoreau use?

Unjust laws exist; shall we be content to obey them, or shall we endeavor to amend them, and obey them until we have succeeded, or shall we transgress them at once? Men generally, under such a government as this, think that they ought to wait until they have persuaded the majority to alter them. They think that, if they should resist, the remedy would be worse than the evil. But it is the fault of the government itself that the remedy *is* worse than the evil. … Why does it always crucify Christ, and excommunicate Copernicus and Luther, and pronounce Washington and Franklin rebels?

A. Ethical reasoning

B. Inductive reasoning

C. Deductive reasoning

D. Intellectual reasoning

(Rigorous) (Skill 3.2)

119. Which of the following is not a fallacy in logic?

A. All students in Ms. Suarez's fourth-period class are bilingual.
Beth is in Ms. Suarez's fourth-period class.
Beth is bilingual.

B. All bilingual students are in Ms. Suarez's class.
Beth is in Ms. Suarez's fourth-period class.
Beth is bilingual.

C. Beth is bilingual.
Beth is in Ms. Suarez's fourth-period class.
All students in Ms. Suarez's fourth-period class are bilingual.

D. If Beth is bilingual, then she speaks Spanish.
Beth speaks French.
Beth is not bilingual.

(Rigorous) (Skill 3.2)

120. Which of the following is an example of the post hoc fallacy?

A. When the new principal was hired, student reading scores improved; therefore, the principal caused the increase in scores.

B. Why are we spending money on the space program when our students don't have current textbooks?

C. You can't give your class a ten-minute break. Once you do that, we'll all have to give our students a ten-minute break.

D. You can never believe anything he says because he's not from the same country as we are.

(Rigorous) (Skill 3.2)

121. Identify the type of rhetorical appeal used by Molly Ivins in this excerpt from her essay "Get a Knife, Get a Dog, But Get Rid of Guns."

As a civil libertarian, I, of course, support the Second Amendment. And I believe it means exactly what it says:

A well regulated militia being necessary to the security of a free state, the right of the people to keep and bear arms shall not be infringed.

A. Ethos

B. Pathos

C. Logos

D. Literary

(Rigorous) (Skill 3.2)

122. What is the common advertising technique used by the following advertising slogans?

"It's everywhere you want to be."
　　　　　　　　　　　—Visa

"Have it your way."
　　　—Burger King

"When you care enough to send the very best."　　　　—Hallmark

"Be all you can be."
　　　　—U.S. Army

A. Peer approval

B. Rebel

C. Individuality

D. Escape

(Rigorous) (Skill 3.2)

123. In presenting a report to peers about the effects of Hurricane Katrina on New Orleans, the students wanted to use various media in their argument to persuade their peers that more needed to be done. Which of these would be the most effective?

A. A PowerPoint presentation showing the blueprints of the levees before the flood and new designs for reconstruction

B. A collection of music clips made by street performers in the French Quarter before and after the flood

C. A video showing the areas devastated by the flood and the current state of rebuilding

D. A collection of recordings of interviews made by various government officials and local citizens affected by the flooding

(Rigorous) (Skill 3.2)

124. Based on the excerpt below from Kate Chopin's short story "The Story of an Hour," what can students infer about the main character?

She did not stop to ask if it were or were not a monstrous joy that held her. A clear and exalted perception enabled her to dismiss the suggestion as trivial. She knew that she would weep again when she saw the kind, tender hands folded in death; the face that had never looked save with love upon her, fixed and gray and dead. But she saw beyond that bitter moment a long procession of years to come that would belong to her absolutely. And she opened and spread her arms out to them in welcome.

A. She dreaded her life as a widow

B. Although she loved her husband, she was glad that he was dead for he had never loved her

C. She worried that she was too indifferent to her husband's death

D. Although they had loved each other, she was beginning to appreciate that opportunities had opened because of her husband's death

(Rigorous) (Skill 3.2)

125. Which part of a classical argument is illustrated in this excerpt from the essay "What Should Be Done About Rock Lyrics?"

But violence against women is greeted by silence. It shouldn't be.

This does not mean censorship, or book (or record) burning. In a society that protects free expression, we understand a lot of stuff will float up out of the sewer. Usually, we recognize the ugly stuff that advocates violence against any group as the garbage it is, and we consider its purveyors as moral lepers. We hold our nose and tolerate it, but we speak out against the values it proffers.

A. Narration

B. Confirmation

C. Refutation and concession

D. Summation